ETHICS OF INDIA

ETHICS OF INDIA

BY

E. WASHBURN HOPKINS, Ph.D., LL.D.

Professor of Sanskrit and Comparative Philology
Yale University

KENNIKAT PRESS, INC./PORT WASHINGTON, N. Y.

TO M. C. H.

WHO, COMBINING IN HER OWN PERSON THE
MOST EXCELLENT INTELLECTUAL, ETHICAL AND
SPIRITUAL QUALITIES, HAS FOR MANY YEARS
HELPED AND ENCOURAGED HIM IN HIS WORK
THIS LITTLE BOOK IS NOW
WITH THE GRATITUDE OF A LIFETIME
AFFECTIONATELY DEDICATED
BY THE AUTHOR

CONTENTS

PREFACE

Although the West discovered mental India years ago and now talks quite glibly about that fabled land with its imagined "millions of Buddhists," yet apart from some erroneous familiarity with India's religions there is little known in this country of what the Hindus have thought and said; as for the field of Hindu ethics, it is *terra incognita* to Europe and America. The author would be loath to state how often, across the water and here at home, he has dejectedly listened to sermons in which well-meaning pastors have soothed their sheep with the comforting assurance that no other religion than Christianity ever inculcated purity of heart and sympathy for the sorrowing. At last, some years since, he concluded that it would not be amiss to collect, as an appendix to his *Religions of India*, the ethical data found in Hindu literature, and in 1920, by way of a beginning, he read before the Oriental Society an essay entitled *The Ethical Element in the Rig Veda*. After further investigation, as President of the same Society, the author in April, 1923, gave, as his formal address, a condensed account of the matter contained in the present volume, under the title *Development of Hindu Ethics*, prefacing his discourse with the remark that this was a first attempt to make such a study. He soon discovered that in this regard he was mistaken, for a book on the same subject, *Hindu Ethics*, by Professor McKenzie of

Bombay, was already on its way to him, having been published a few months earlier. It covers a good part of the ground traversed in the present volume. On the other hand, much material, which to the present writer seems valuable, has been ignored by his predecessor and the points of view revealed in the two studies are, if not irreconcilable, at least quite different.

Professor McKenzie finds the ethics of India defective, illogical, and anti-social, lacking any philosophical foundation, nullified by abhorrent ideas of asceticism and ritual, and altogether inferior to the "higher spirituality" of Europe. He will not deny that the Hindus favor some virtues, such as liberality and hospitality, and he is careful to point out that an altruistic motive in exercising these virtues may not be entirely absent; but he reminds his readers that they are of savage origin; when properly interpreted they reveal themselves as based on selfishness and magical superstition, so that, historically considered, they would appear to be surviving vices rather than honest virtues, at least among the Hindus. But what troubles Professor McKenzie most is that Hindu ethics is anti-social—though he admits that "the most attractive features in Hindu social life are to be found in the family affections . . . and in the sense of the identity of the interests of the individual with those of the community, which are so common in Hindu society"—and that, though anti-social in its asceticism and not spiritual enough, this ethics is in fact better than it ought to be, because Hindu philosophy has predicated a God without attributes and such a God is unmoral and hence by implication should be incapable of inspiring anybody with a logical desire to practice ethical behavior. Professor McKenzie devotes most of his book to upholding this thesis and comes to what seems to be the triumphant conclusion that Hindu philosophical ideas, "when logically applied, leave no room for ethics"; furthermore, they prevent "the development of a strenuous moral life." Incidentally, Professor McKenzie explains that a morality which is not strenuous is not a true morality. One is not really moral unless engaged in active social service. This is perhaps the keynote of his inspiring work.

The present author has, as will be seen, offered here and there a mild protest against a too logical interpretation of historical facts. He has also been more inclined to establish the fact that through the Hindu codes runs always the pleasing admonition, "A seat for a guest, water, and a welcoming word should never be lacking in the house of a good man," than to show that Hindu hospitality was based on egoism. In a word, he has been more eager to exploit the value of Hindu ethics than to depreciate it, though he trusts that he has not been blind to its deficiencies. But he doubts whether logic and philosophy are so vital as Professor McKenzie thinks in evaluating ethics, especially as ethics was practiced long before either logic or philosophy was taught. And even if the Hindus followed no safe ratiocinative processes in being virtuous, the fact that they were schooled to be so, and the means by which they were persuaded that ethical behavior was incumbent upon them, seem to the author more important than proving that philosophically the Hindus ought not to have been ethical.

For this purpose, though with no polemical intent, the author has here gathered together a large number of passages, from which the moral injunctions and ethical appeals made by those who were often neither logicians nor philosophers may be conveniently studied. He has written his little book not to sustain any logical, philosophical, or religious dogma, but to exhibit the ethical teachings of the ancient Hindus, feeling confident that it will be a pleasure to many and a grief to none to know that truthfulness, generosity, kindness of heart, purity of soul, forgiveness, and compassion were taught in India as everyday precepts long before the Christian era.

Throughout this book the word Hindu has been used, *faute de mieux,* for Indian, which, especially in America, is ambiguous. Properly speaking, one confines Hindu to the later stages of Indian history, when the Aryan element, in more or less diluted condition, began to be more largely intermingled with that of native tribes, India was overrun by foreign invaders, and Brahmanism had to contend not only with Buddhism but with peoples and faiths only half brahmanized, or even half civilized, but powerful and ever encroaching, a period that began formally with Alexander's brief invasion of India in the fourth century B.C. This in itself was an event of the slightest importance, for Alexander did not even get into the real India of that day, but it heralded a succession of further invasions and marked more deeply a change which had commenced centuries before with the entrance into Brahmanic life of alien factors. In colloquial Western speech, a Hindu is any native-born inhabitant of India, whatever his ancestry or faith; but in this book such "Hindus" as Mohammedans and Parsis have been excluded and ethics has been treated accordingly, except that one or two later writers have been mentioned, such as Kabîr, a Hindu who was brought up as a Mohammedan (died in 1518 A.D.), and Tulasîdâs, who lived a century later. But Hindu ethics after the Mohammedan invasion loses individuality and becomes the first amalgam of various ethical systems, which have continued to coalesce under different reformatory movements to the present day. These movements and their ethical content are sufficiently treated elsewhere. They represent only an ethical and religious union of West and East, or religious and political antagonism to that union, and while of the highest interest to the student of modern Hindu thought are too modern and mixed to be regarded as of native Hindu origin.

As for the transcription employed in this book,

it ignores *visargas* and diacritical signs, but it will be intelligible to the few who care to see the original texts, when, as is rarely the case, the author has found it preferable to cite the Sanskrit words.

CHAPTER I

ETHICS IN THE RIG VEDA

THAT the foundation of Hindu ethics was laid before the Aryan race reached India may easily be demonstrated. For a moral element lies in the very recognition of bright, beneficent, and holy gods as opposed to dark demoniac powers. Avestan and Slavic parallels reveal that these conceptions were pre-Indic. Less important is the fact that the Sky-god is called Father, but there is latent in this term something more ethical than the usual savage distinction between father sky and mother earth. It connotes an attitude of faith[1] in a benevolent Power. So much may be learned from a broad survey of Indo-European mythology. Within narrower bounds, the pre-Indic Aryans shared with the disciples of Zoroaster the conception of a dominant Pure and Wise Spirit, who rules the world as a moral Power. It is even probable that the idea of ceremonial expiation for sin belonged to the common ancestors of both these peoples.

It is thus clear that the Indic tribes, when first

[1] See below on Father as Our Father with its implication of affection. Latin *credo* is Sanskrit *çraddhâ.* The Russian *bogu,* god, is the Vedic *bhaga,* generous. Greek *hagios,* holy, is the Sanskrit *yajata,* worshipful, holy (Av. Yazata). The idea of bright as fair, and so good, appears in Sanskrit *vasu* which, like Sanskrit *deva* (deus), means shining, fair, good, and so god (compare Greek καλός, originally bright, then fair, good).

domiciled between the Indus and Ganges rivers, had passed beyond the stage of undiluted fear in the presence of unnamed demons and had already invested with a moral quality the "kind bright" *devas* or spirits of light, which quality differentiated these powers from the *rakshas* or "injurers that go about by night" and "rejoice in darkness." That the *devas* also injure man is recognized, but they do not harm men wantonly; hurt from them is in the nature of a punishment for wrongdoing. Very rare in the Rig Veda is the later confusion of concept which regards a *deva* as a demon who is by nature maleficent. That gods are good and demons evil is the general Vedic view.

But when it is declared that gods are good, the meaning is not only that the gods are good to man but that they are morally good; they uphold righteousness. This takes us to the consideration of what is meant by good and bad. Our English word good meant originally fit and so proper, appropriate (old German *guoti*, fit, suitable; Russian *godno*, suitably). Similarly the Vedic word *rita* (connected with Greek ἀρετή and Latin *ratus*) means fit, orderly, good, and as a noun *ritam* is the right order of the universe, of the sacrifice, and of ethical conduct, the true way as opposed to its negative, *anritam*, that is, false or untrue. It connotes a certain "harmony" (which is etymologically from the same root) between ideal and practice. In a cosmic sense, it designates the harmony of the world, the regularity of nature, as evinced by the orderly procession of celestial bodies, of seasons, and of their earthly representatives in the seasonal sacrifices and the regular conduct of men, as opposed to irregular conduct. It is not, like the Chinese Tao, a cosmic power, but it is the order instituted by the Wise Spirit as regulator of the world.

But back even of this early Vedic belief lies a distinction between right and wrong which is more fundamental because older and more general. It is one which, as it were, leads to the notion of regular and righteous conduct but is still without the connotation of "fitting" or harmonious action. And this distinction is of peculiar interest because the very words used in the Rig Veda are the exact linguistic equivalents of our English words right, Vedic *riju,* and wrong, Vedic *vrijina,* literally straight and crooked (wrong is *wrung,* twisted, crooked). This pair of words gives therefore a long look back to what is probably the very earliest Aryan conception of an ethical distinction in conduct. So simple and yet so enduring is this conception that it survives today in ordinary speech not only in these particular words but in their general meaning (a "straight" man as contrasted with a "crook"). The Rig Veda contains a large number of passages illustrating this distinction of right and wrong as straight and crooked, but one in particular may be cited here because of its poetic beauty. It describes in rapid succession the phenomena of sunrise, the sudden change from darkness to brightness, the rush of dawnlight (not slow but swift in India), and the ascent of the Sun-god, who from above looks down upon the straight and crooked ways (good and bad activities) of men:

> The turbid darkness vanished, bright the sky shone,
> Upward the light of Dawn, the heavenly, hastened,
> Unto his fields on high the Sun ascended,
> The ways of mortals, straight and crooked, seeing.[2]

In other hymns the sun is described as the eye of the Heaven-god, who watches man with unwinking eye, the Heaven-god being the Wise Spirit or his counterpart Mitra (Mithra). The conception varies between that of the Sun-god as a personal observer and as the all-seeing agent or "eye" of some higher divine Power,[3] but the thought is the same in all these instances. Some divine heavenly power has its eye on man's conduct. This tie between ethics and religion was never much relaxed in India even in philosophical speculation, except in the rarefied religious atmosphere of Buddhism, and even there the fear of offending a deity above was merely modified

[2] RV. 4, 1, 17. Another common word for "good," *sâdhu,* has the same original meaning of straight, right, and is used like *riju* antithetically to *vrijina, e.g., ibid.* 2, 27, 2-3: "The pure gods, the holy ones, without wrong, without blame, the many-eyed, discern (human) right and wrong, *vrijinota sâdhu;* all is near to them, even that which is afar off." Later texts keep the same figure with new words, *vañc,* vacillate, *jihma,* athwart, crooked: "May we not fall into hell by going crooked," etc., from AV. and subsequent literature.

[3] RV. 1, 50 and 3, 59; also *ibid.* 1, 115, 1, *seq.*

into the fear of grieving the saints above and angering the lord of hell below, as they too watch men.

Vedic religion has been somewhat superficially blamed because of its lack of "deep faith," argued from the fact that the hymns contain constant calls for help from the gods. On the contrary, while the native blacks[4] are unbelieving pagans and have no faith or fire-sacrifice, the Aryan population never expresses doubt in the existence and power of its moral rulers. Even in the war-god, belief in whom would be apt to vary with success in battle, the Vedic poet shows no lack of faith when he cries "Have faith in him," whom some have doubted, and the worshipper of the Fire-god, when he says that some do not revere him, may well have in mind those "fireless" tribes that are without the Aryan pale.[5] In many cases the poets of the Rig Veda substantiate their faith by enumerating the kind acts of the gods in the past. Thus one hymn gives a list of cures performed by the Heavenly Twins and ends with the prayer that the poet may also enjoy the favor of these gods.[6] The deeds of the gods are described as "worthy of praise," which implies gratitude as well as belief. But the statement of a firm faith is by no means lacking in categorical form. "The man who serves Mitra and Varuna (Heaven-god), him do

[4] The "black clans" (RV. 7, 5, 3) are the native un-Aryan tribes.

[5] *Ibid.* 1, 147, 2; 189, 3; and 2, 12.

[6] *Ibid.* 1, 116.

they guard on every side in security. They, the gods, guard him, the mortal, from distress. Aryaman (the clan-god) protects the man who is righteous according to the law (of the gods) . . . I will declare my reverence for high Heaven . . . for Varuna, the generous and very kind god."[7] Again, a priest prays:[8] "O Mitra and Varuna, if a priest serves you, toiling with sacrifice and prayer, you come to him, you accept his sacrifice. So, loving us, come now to our laudation, to our prayer." Of the Fire-god Agni, *ignis,* it is said: "Prayers never deceive the man who offers them (to Agni); Agni is my shield; he loves me as I am," as of the pious man is uttered the general statement: "The gods further him that loves them and like suitors rejoice in him who loves the *brahma.*"[9]

Varuna, Mitra, and Aryaman are the chief of the Âdityas or ancient gods, a group of pure benevolent spirits who protect the pious: "Never is he injured whom the Âdityas protect; easy and thornless is their path to the pious man."[10] A more formal pronouncement as to the Âdityas is as follows: "The married pair who worship religiously never deny the good will of the gods . . . rich in sons and daughters they reach old age, both of them, adorned with jewels. They serve the gods, showing honor by offering obla-

[7] RV. 1, 136, 5, *seq.*
[8] *Ibid.* 1, 151, 7.
[9] *Ibid.* 1, 83, 2 and 148, 2 (*mama tasya câkan*).
[10] *Ibid.* 1, 41 and 2, 27.

6

tions and worldly goods to the immortals. In that our protectors are Mitra, Aryaman, and Varuna, the path of right is easy to follow. He who by worship seeks to win the mind of the gods soon overcomes those who fail to worship."[11] Prosaic as are the words, materialistic as is the outlook, the faith is here sure and even in the impassioned cry of one in distress who exclaims "O ye gods, what to you are truth and untruth?" there is only a lyric despair quickly followed by the deep expression of faith in the immutable character of ethical verities: "Cares consume me although I have often made hymns to the gods . . . and though I am related by birth to the (celestials) where yonder shine the seven (stars). . . . But even the rivers stream forth right, the sun shines forth truth, . . . and the path of the ancient gods in heaven is not to be transgressed."[12]

The Indic tribes had not yet arrived at the conception of an omnipresent deity and if a god failed to answer prayer the devout worshipper regarded it as proof either that the suppliant had sinned and was out of favor with the god or, in humility, that the god was on a visit to some other worshipper whose call he preferred to honor. So the poet of one hymn cries, "What lover of the god is now enjoying his

[11] RV. 8, 31, 5, *seq.*

[12] *Ibid.* 1, 105, 5, *seq.* Varuna here makes the prayer successful and "finds the way" for the sufferer's salvation, possibly by inspiring the prayer itself, for prayer is said to be *devattam*, god-given, *ibid.* 1, 37, 4.

friendship?"[13] This expression of love for the god is almost a commonplace in Vedic phraseology, as, conversely, the gods are represented as intimate with and fond of the worshipper. The high gods "extend their wings like birds" to cover and protect him. The god of battle appears and guards his suppliant "as friend to friend" and "him who loves him and sacrifices to him, the Lord blesses with prosperity."[14] The *bhakti* or loving devotion, which some scholars imagine to be only a late development of Hindu religion, is already evident in the Rig Veda, even in its dangerous trend toward eroticism: "All my thoughts, seeking happiness, extol Indra, longing for him; they embrace him as wives embrace a fair young bridegroom, him the divine giver of gifts, that he may help me! My mind is directed to thee, Indra, and does not turn from thee; on thee I rest my desire, O much-invoked one."[15]

The mutual relations between god and devotee are of the highest importance from an ethical point of view, for they determine the whole attitude of the moral man, whether his life is directed by fear or by affection. The Indic attitude is undoubtedly in part

[13] RV. 4, 25, 1.

[14] *Ibid.* 8, 47, 2; 10, 42, 9.

[15] *Ibid.* 10, 43, 1, *seq.* Our word "god" is etymologically "the invoked." The god grants material desires, yet he is invoked as a dear friend or even as a lover; but sometimes more as a "comforter." Compare *ibid.* 10, 64, 2, "There is no comforter save the gods"; 1, 84, 19, "There is no comforter save thee, O Indra" (so 8, 66, 13; 80, 1). Rare is the cry of despair: "I found no one to comfort me among the gods" (4, 18, 13).

that of one whose gods inspire fear, for, as the Vedic poet says, "all the world is full of fear" when Indra's bolt (lightning) falls. Also one must fear disease, which is sent by the gods as punishment for sin; *ergo,* one fears the disease-sender. Nevertheless, the approach to the gods is generally through something much higher than fear. They are admired and loved. Particular gods are naturally more loved than groups of gods, who are apt to receive proper but not fervent thanks, like those addressed to a charity-board. The Maruts, or Rudriyas, for example, as individuals are not known to the worshipper by name, so that they have to be invited to the sacrifice by the Fire-god, who alone knows them "personally."[16]

Conversely, the gods love man. They are not only by nature "generous and kind"; they are fond of men. Though they punish disobedience and crookedness, they seek to keep the "simple and foolish" from sin; they surround him with watchful guardians as well as spy upon him, and above all they are of one family with man. Individual gods are directly addressed as "our relation" and, more intimately, as father or brother. Erotic expression, in which the *devayu,* god-seeker, and *devakâma,* god-lover,[17] is thus early (as above) tempted to dwell on his spiritual experience with a somewhat sensuous delight, is

[16] RV. 5, 43, 10, *nâmabhir rûpebhis,* "by name and form," *i.e.,* as individuals. Name and form constitute personality; the name is real.

[17] Not "loved by gods," as some scholars interpret it. Compare *yajñakâma,* sacrifice-loving.

9

toned down by the consciousness that his relation with the god is rather one of family affection. The spirit called Energizer (expressed chiefly in the form of the Sun-god) is besought to come to the worshipper "as husband to wife," but only as "a very gentle spirit" and as friend of the house.[18] So it is said: "Ye, the immortals, guard him whom ye love . . . this of old being your relationship that ye favor him that worships you."[19] It is probable that this sense of relationship began with the cult of the Fire-god. Various Vedic clans bear names which originally are epithets of Agni, such as Angiras, Atri, Viçvâmitra, Bharadvâja, Jamadagni, and this god was believed to be the ancestor of the clan to whom he is "as a father to the son." He is the "much loved god," the "most dear"; to whom are addressed the words "thou art our father and we are thy relations."[20]

About Agni revolves constantly a reverent, tender, but almost playful devotion, which expresses itself by calling him by all these terms of relationship. He is not only the "most kindly friend," but he is "father, brother, and son"; or again he is the "visible savior, father and mother of men," as he is the "dear guest, to be guarded as the ancestor and as son," the "kindest of the gods," nearest and dearest of divinities: "Agni I regard as my father, my relation, my brother, my friend; his light will I adore; it shines in

[18] RV. 1, 35, 10; 10, 149, 4.
[19] *Ibid.* 1, 166, 8, 13.
[20] *Ibid.* 1, 31, 10; *cf.* 1, 67, 1; 3, 3, 4; 5, 1, 9.

heaven, as holy as the sun."[21] But Indra the battle-god is also invoked as "father and mother" and his alliance, too, is one of friendship and brotherhood, while as protector of the clan he is "the most fatherly god." The Vedic poet says of him, "sweet (*svâdu*, ἡδύ) is his friendship"; his "brotherhood" is felt to be so real and intimate that he is addressed, with astonishing familiarity, "Come hither, brother Indra."[22] In his cult is already expressed the idea, familiar through the later conception of the Buddhist Avalokiteçvara, of a god "looking down with pity." Thus the Vedic poet cries to Indra, "Be our savior, thou who art recognized as our relation, who looks upon us and pities us, as a friend, a father, most fatherly of fathers," and again, "Look upon us who need thy help."[23] He is "better than father, like a mother"; he "alone among the gods sympathizes with man."[24]

This attitude of the worshipper, passing far beyond the formal acknowledgment of Dyaus (Zeus) as "father" of men, is intimate and familiar to a degree unknown in any other ancient religion. It reminds one of the respectful but affectionate manner in which Italians speak of the saints and even of

[21] RV. 1, 94, 14; 2, 1, 9; 3, 22, 5; 6, 1, 5; 2, 7; 10, 7, 3, *seq.*

[22] *Ibid.* 3, 53, 5; 4, 23, 6; 25, 2; 8, 68, 11; 98, 11.

[23] *Ibid.* 4, 17, 17; 10, 112, 10. Compare the expression used of Agni as protector "looking (down) with pity upon man," *ibid.* 5, 3, 9.

[24] *Ibid.* 7, 23, 5; 8, 1, 6. Literally, "shares with man," *dayate*, first of material things, then of feelings (compare δαίεται ἦτορ).

divinity. Indra, the "smashing god of terror," is a "near friend" on whom the suppliant "leans like an old man on a staff," while entreating the god "not to smite because of one, two, three, or many sins"; for "as brother he is easily invoked, very kind, a helper, a savior." So by degrees other gods are embraced in a similar relationship: "Look on us as your relations," the poet cries to Indra, Vishnu, the Maruts, and Twins; and to another group of gods another poet prays thus: "Ye gods are all of you connections of mine; as such be kind to me when I beseech you. . . . I have committed many a sin against you, as you have punished me, even as a father punishes his son who gambles; but afar be your bonds (forgive me) today, O holy ones; trembling in heart may I approach near to you. . . . Save me, O ye gods, save me from the wolf's devouring, from the fall into the pit." The relationship here and elsewhere insisted upon ("born of the same womb," "having a common navel") is not a poetic fancy of the Vedic priests, and Bergaigne was quite right in saying that these terms indicate a real, family relationship between men and gods, even with such high gods as Varuna (Ouranos) and Mitra (Mithra).[25]

Yet, for all this familiarity, the gods are a race ethically apart, since they are all "regarded as sin-

[25] Bergaigne, *Religion védique,* vol. 1, p. 35. The quotations above will be found in the Rig Veda order, 1, 105, 9; 2, 29, 4, *seq.;* 6, 47, 10, *seq.;* 8, 45, 18, 20, 34; 83, 8; 10, 64, 13. Mitra shares with Agni (with whom he is identified) the epithet "dearest to man," *ibid.* 7, 62, 4.

less," even Indra, to whom from a human point of view many "sins" are imputed. Such sins worried the later theologians, as similar sins on the part of the gods worried the Greeks, and they interpreted them either allegorically or philosophically. Indra was said to be a name for storm or for life. Or again, more simply and dogmatically, the later teachers of the law said bluntly that, though man ought to imitate the seers and gods, yet man may not imitate their misdemeanors, because those divine beings had more luster than men today and being so glorious they might do what ordinary men may not do.[26]

But the early Vedic priest did not attempt any such sophisticated arguments. He related Indra's deeds as the acts of a stormy god, yet declared that Indra as god was "sinless."[27] Indra was one of the "holy ones" and man looked to him not for ethical example but for help in battle, while most of the moral ordering of the world was attributed to the Heaven-god, Varuna, the type and model of ethical purity. Man relies upon the help of all these gods for the furtherance of his desires and for forgiveness when he has done wrong. He bases his claim partly on family affection and partly on the plea that he wishes to do right and act in conformity with the "law of the gods." In the end, if his petition is not

[26] Kaush. Up. 3, 1; Âpast. Dh. S. 2, 13, 8, *seq.* Indra is "regarded as sinless," RV. 1, 129, 5 (*anenâs*).

[27] The Atharva Veda hints that Indra was once a doer of evil but has now reformed: "(As) Çakra (Indra) has turned from the doing of evil; (so) have I turned away from sin" (AV. 3, 31, 2).

granted, he sometimes adds the pious expression, "so be it as thou wilt," *tathed asad yathâ vaças*, as in the following petition: "O Indra, thou eternally true and mighty lord, may we through thy favor speedily obtain sustenance; but so may it be even as thou wilt."[28]

The Rig Veda is not entirely free from the attempt to compel spiritual powers rather than entreat them. Sin, like disease, may be cast upon a scapegoat (literally, a bird) and may be wiped or washed away by purificatory means, plants or water. Even perjury is made good by water, and healing herbs are said to free one from every offence against the gods.[29] Sympathetic magic, however, is applied not to sin but to disease,[30] and even in the application of water and fire as purificatory of sin, especially untruth, it must be remembered that these, like plants, were divine Powers speaking through ordeals. So the drum averts evil not as a mere noise-machine but as being symbolically the "fist of Indra"; the stone that by its "speaking" (noise) drives away evil spirits is the sanctified stone of the moon-plant.[31]

The priests of the Rig Veda, while they admit some of this religiously modified magic, relegated

[28] RV. 8, 61, 4. In longer form, "As the gods will, so may it be," *yathâ vaçanti devâs tathed asat* (*ibid.* 28, 4).

[29] *Ibid.* 1, 23, 22; 10, 97, 16.

[30] Compare *ibid.* 10, 60, 11: "Down blows the wind, down shines the sun, down goes the cow's milk, and down with thy complaint" (*rapas*, physical injury).

[31] *Ibid.* 6, 47, 30; 10, 36, 4.

most magical practices to votaries of the lower cult
and clothed their own utterances in petitions. No
magic is used against the demon of ill-birth, but
Agni is besought to ban the evil one. So the magical
rain-formula is set aside in favor of this appeal: "O
Agni, rend apart our enemies, drive from us weakness and evil spirits, and from the sea of high heaven
pour down upon us here on earth a plenitude of
water."[32]

The Vedic Aryans describe themselves not without
reason as a "god-seeking folk," *âdevo janas,* and im-
partially they turned to all their gods to help them.
As ministrant of these gods, the Fire-god, by his
report to other gods, might influence their judgment
and even "avert the hurt of Varuna" or, as another
poet expresses it, "find gentleness for us with Varuna" and turn aside his just anger, "deprecate his
wrath."[33] But the gods concerned are more often
addressed directly without mediation and Agni himself receives the report of men's sins from another
god. Other gods also avert divine wrath. There is
thus no general mediator between gods and men. Owing to its resemblance to *advocatus* the word *adhi-
vaktar* has sometimes been mistaken as a pleader or
advocate; but this word is not used of Agni and in
itself does not mean advocate but helper or blesser,
who "declares for" one man when several men are

[32] RV. 10, 162 and 98.
[33] *Ibid.* 2, 4, 2; 1, 128, 7; 4, 1, 2, *seq.* Compare *ibid.* 6, 48, 10,
"Keep off the anger of the gods."

contending for his favor; it never means "speak for" a man to other gods. Thus Indra declares for the pious in their incessant strife against the pagans who are "lawless and heterodox."[34]

It is the more necessary to emphasize this point because a popular translation of the Rig Veda and another of a second Veda, in which the same verse occurs, give quite a wrong impression of a prayer to Rudra, the god of healing, treating him as a mediator, thus: "May the heavenly physician plead for us as our intercessor," or, as the rival translator has it, "the Advocate, the first divine physician." But with whom should Rudra "plead"? The verse means only "may the god of healing bless us."[35] Parenthetically, it may be observed also that the translators have injected into the Rig Veda more consciousness of sin than really attaches to it, through rendering the con-

[34] The idea of a divine intercessor is excluded anyway by the fact that all the gods are invoked together with this word or its verbal equivalent. Compare, for example, RV. 10, 63, 11, *seq.:* "O all ye holy gods, favor us and bless us, *adhi vocata;* save us from falling into evil ways . . . remove from us sickness, remove your wrath, give us protection (and lead us) to happiness." So in 8, 30, 1, *seq.,* the gods as a body are besought to bless, *adhi vocata,* the suppliant: "bless us, protect our cow and horse, lead us not far from the (right) path." Compare *ibid.* 8, 47, 8: "O ye gods, keep us far from (every) sin, small and great." The "divine wrath" of the god is averted by Rudra himself, also by Soma, *ibid.* 1, 114, 4; 8, 48, 2. But a direct appeal to the gods (as in 1, 171, 1; 6, 62, 8) to "lay down hate" is more usual.

[35] The phrase *adhi vocat* is exactly like *adhi brûhi,* "bless." The mistranslated verse, VS. 16, 5, is rendered as above by Eggeling and Griffith.

stant expression "be kind to us" by "have mercy upon us." Where sin is really confessed, the expression may by implication be taken in the sense of "have mercy" (forgive us); but such cases are rare compared with the great number where the suppliant merely prays the god to be good to him. The word *mrila,* like its Latin cognate *mollis,* means gentle and kind, and is used repeatedly as in these petitions: "show us good-will, bless us, be kind to us"; "O Indra, when wilt thou be kind to us?" Often the "kindness" is to be shown in giving rain; it is even used of being kind to cows, *i.e.,* not injuring them. On the other hand, in this prayer, "If in my folly I have violated thy laws, then do thou be kind," the implication of forgiveness is obvious; but such instances should not convert the whole Rig Veda into a book of penitential psalms.[36]

There is no very consistent view in the Rig Veda concerning the way in which the sins of men become manifest to the gods. The older view, as shown above, conceives of the sun as an eye watching man. Crossing this view, however, is the conception of Agni in two characters, one as the "divine priest of sacrifice," who either on his own initiative pardons sins or refers the matter to the god especially concerned in the breaking of divine law, and one as the ordeal-god, who tests truth (by fire). As priest of sacrifice, Agni himself judges any "break" or omission in the

[36] RV. I, 114, 10; 8, 6, 25; 10, 25, 3.

ritual. Thus a suppliant begs Agni to pardon any break caused by absence from home and consequent lack of ritualistic propriety. Again, the ritual may be changed through forgetfulness and in that case the suppliant begs Agni to "make him sinless." Such also may be the meaning of the prayer, "Whatever offence we have committed, forgive it, O Agni," though the offence here may be moral rather than ritualistic. Thus Agni alone may forgive sin, though he sometimes is asked to forgive in conjunction with other gods: "O Agni, call thou hither (to our sacrifice) Mitra, Varuna, and Indra, and if we have committed any sin, do thou be kind (forgive it) and may Aditi and Aryaman loosen (remove) it."[37]

But while it must be admitted that Agni is a meticulous divinity and "sin" in his eyes is often merely a liturgical neglect or error, as, on the other hand, the merely ritualistic prayer "destroys crookedness"; while, too, sin can be transferred and removed by more or less magical means, yet it does not follow that the Vedic Aryan was without a keen perception of sin in terms of ethical value. Such sin is the conscious or unconscious violation of the divine moral

[37] RV. 1, 31, 16; 4, 12, 4, *seq.*; 3, 7, 10; 7, 93, 7. The words *âgas* and *enas* are used synonymously for "sin" (offence). The latter is the later word. In RV. 5, 3, Agni is apparently the god of judgment at an ordeal. He is begged to "keep from us the sin that makes crooked" (leads astray), *ibid.* 1, 189, 1. Agni makes good the deficiencies of the worshippers who have neglected the sacrifice and thus broken the laws of the gods through weakness of mind, *ibid.* 10, 2, 3, *seq.*

law; freedom from sin is a free gift of the gods. Aditi, the divine Mother, or "Sun and Dawn," are besought to grant "sinlessness,"[38] as well as Varuṇa and Agni.

It is not only the "stern ruler" Varuna who judges men. "Mayst thou, O Savitar, as sender send us forth sinless, if we have done anything to the race of gods through lack of knowledge and intelligence, or acted insolently before men." The same god is begged as house-friend to "proclaim us free of sin to Sûrya," as Sûrya (the sun) proclaims men sinless to Agni as well as to Mitra and Varuna.[39] Agni may indeed blame a man before the gods unjustly or through error impute to one man the sin, *repas,* of another, and it is a common prayer that one "should not suffer for another's sinning," a prayer addressed to the highest gods, and sometimes explicitly explained as sins inherited from the father: "Release from us the sins of my fathers and what sins we ourselves have committed."[40]

[38] RV. 1, 162, 22; 4, 23, 8 (*ritasya dhîtir vrijinâni hanti*); 10, 35, 2. The prayer to be made sinless is very common. "O Agni, make us sinless, remove our offences," *ibid.* 4, 12, 4; "May Agni as messenger of the gods declare us sinless in entirety," *ibid.* 3, 54, 19. Agni is described, as is the Sun, as "the gods' law-guardian," *vratapâ, ibid.* 5, 2, 8, etc.

[39] *Ibid.* 4, 54, 3; 1, 123, 3; 7, 60, 1.

[40] *Ibid.* 4, 3, 5, *seq.;* 6, 51, 7; 7, 86, 4, *seq., drugdha* as *enas* and *âgas.*

CHAPTER II

THE VEDIC IDEA OF SIN AND LAW

IN the later period of the Rig Veda, the gods are represented as holding a secret council where the other gods proclaim to Varuna the name of the sinless man: "In the secret council, to which the gods come together and we (men) know not of it, may Mitra there and Aditi, and Savitar the god proclaim us sinless unto Varuna."[1] As Savitar, the impeller or sender, is usually the Sun-god, it is probably the sun (he, as we have seen, watches men and serves as "the eye of Varuna") who is here the proclaimer of innocence, though Varuna himself is supposed to see what goes on among men: "May Varuna, the sinless worker of wonders, free us from whatever untruth he looks upon."[2] But not unusual is the grandiose conception of the whole body of high gods acting as an observant host of mortal affairs and especially interested in their moral behavior: "The many-eyed guardians of the world, pure and blameless gods, not crooked; to whom even what is far off is near; they see into wrong and right (the crooked and the straight) and being holy they punish sin."[3] Of these gods, some of whom appear to be hypostases of

[1] RV. 10, 12, 8. "Secret thinking" to which "the gods come together" seems to imply such a council.

[2] *Ibid.* 7, 28, 4; compare 1, 50, 6; 4, 1, 17; 7, 49, 3; 60, 2; 10, 35, 8 (the sun as spy). Varuna knows too "by thought" alone.

[3] Literally "exact the debt" (see below), RV. 2, 27, 2, *seq.*

Varuna himself, Varuna and Mitra are the chief pair. They are thus described: "These two, observant of Right Order (as Righteousness), look down from high heaven as shepherds upon their flocks, supreme kings, ready for man's reverence, seated for supreme kingship, the very wise, whose laws are firm, lords of power who have obtained the ruling power, *kshatram*, who with unveiled eyes see the way better than any eye; and, even with closed eyes, watchful they perceive all."[4]

The idea that the high gods never close their eyes is repeated in another fine passage: "Watching men and never closing their eyes, the gods through their worth have obtained immortality. They have chariots of light, forms as of dragons, and sinless they live in the height of heaven. . . . As such, O ye ancient gods, give us protection, make easy for us the path to happiness, ye who rule the world in wisdom and have knowledge of all that stands and moves." Of Varuna alone it is said that "his two eyes embrace the three earths and three heavens" and in the later Atharva Veda it is declared that he sees him who goes crooked (vacillates), and that he is the third whenever two men plot in secret; also, "even if one should fly to the ends of the heaven" he could not escape from Varuna, "for the gods know all that is

[4] RV. 8, 25, 7, *seq.* As shepherds (cowherds) the gods seem here also to be looking down with merciful kindness. The expression "better than any eye" may hint at the older idea of the sun as one divine eye.

going on in secret" and "Varuna sees all that is in the universe; numbered of him are the winkings of the people . . . his spies go from the sky; thousand-eyed they look over the earth."[5]

The spies of the gods, or, more particularly, those of Varuna, are spirits who "never rest or sleep but go about here on earth," watching those who violate the laws of the gods. As such they can scarcely be the stars, especially as elsewhere they are said to be sent from earth and heaven and to go everywhere, being "in plants" as well as on earth and "among the people." Poison-ordeals may explain the spies in plants.[6]

As in Zoroaster's teaching, it is particularly the "lies of men" that Varuna's harassing spirits, called *druhas,* hunt down and punish: *druhas sacante anritâ janânâm.* The *druhas* here are not evil spirits but "injurers" under command of the high god. So the man who tries to injure the pious shall be slain by the Maruts after being caught in the noose of the *druh.* "May I be sinless before Mitra Varuna in the protection of Agni,"[7] is the almost universal prayer of the Vedic poet. It is a prayer full of moral significance yet not wholly without material implication,

[5] RV. 8, 41, 7, *seq.;* 10, 63, 4 and 8; Atharva Veda, 4, 16, 1, *seq.*

[6] RV. 7, 61, 3; 87, 3; 10, 10, 2 and 8; *cf.* 9, 73, 4. Indra as a spy, RV. 8, 61, 15, detects and slays evil demons and men who "break troth and go crooked" (*ibid.* 10, 27, 1). He "slays with his arrow all those that commit great crimes ere they know" of their danger (*ibid.* 2, 12, 10).

[7] *Ibid.* 7, 59, 8; 61, 5; 10, 36, 12 (*cf.* 7, 86, 7, "sinless before the god").

for it is often conjoined with the entreaty that the
speaker may also be "free," that is, free of the outward effect of sin in the shape of sickness or misery:
"In sinlessness and in freedom" may the sacrifice be
established, is a common prayer explained more fully
in the remarkable petition: "May we with good mind
and eye, being without sickness and sin, O Savitar,
see the sun rise every day. . . . O yellow-haired Sun,
rise for us with daily better sinlessness. . . . If with
the tongue or by reason of carelessness of mind we
have committed any heavy cause of anger against
you gods, do ye put that offence, *enas,* on the niggard
who tries to harm us."[8] This means that the sin causing divine anger has its outward manifestation in
sickness or some other "lack of freedom" called a
bond, which can by divine good-will be transferred
to some other sinner, just as it can be transferred to
the water-god or to water itself: "O ancient gods,
send away to Trita Âptya whatever I have done ill";
or again: "In water is healing. . . . O water, bear
forth now whatever in me is unlucky or that wherein
I have offended or sworn falsely."[9]

8 RV. 7, 51, 1; 10, 37, 7-12.

9 *Ibid.* 1, 23, 19, *seq.;* 8, 47, 13. On the waters as "medicinal,"
compare *ibid.* 10, 9, 6, etc. The "good eye" of the prayer above is
connected with the sun as eye and giver of sight. Compare *ibid.*
10, 158, 3, *seq.:* "May the Sun send us the eye to see and understand." The prayer "better and better day by day" is not un-
common. It anticipates Coué. Compare the Atharvan prayer:
"Grant us what is better and better, morrow by morrow" (AV.
10, 6, 5). Later this becomes a phrase, *Çvas-çreyasa,* continual
improvement, literally "morrow-betterment."

Allusion has been made above to the notion of inherited sin. Just what this means may be illustrated by a few examples. When the prayer is raised, "Sinless before Aditi, on the impulse of Savitar, may we obtain all good things," it must be remembered that the rising sun drives away "all distress and shame" and that, on the rising of the sun, Mitra, Varuna, Earth, and Sky drive them away.[10] Compare the implications of the following petition: "With the light wherewith thou drivest away darkness and arousest the whole world, therewith drive from us all weakness, lack of oblation, sickness, bad dreams, weak offspring and death . . . without sickness and without sin may we live long." Sun and Dawn and Heaven and Earth are invoked thus to keep one from sin. Bad dreams bring sins and these, like bad luck, are driven away by the rising sun, which disperses all evil spirits.[11] Consequently, these two prayers express almost the same thing, though only one is on the surface ethically phrased: "O Savitar, drive away what is bad, drive hither what is good" and "drive away the sins (debts, see below) I have committed; may I not suffer for another's doing."[12] The suffering is so much the result of sin that it is itself a sin. Ill-health is immoral in that it is a sign of divine wrath; sickness is punishment for sin and is even the objec-

[10] RV. 5, 82, 6; 1, 115, 6; *cf.* 4, 53, 6.

[11] *Ibid.* 1, 35, 3; 7, 86, 6; 10, 35, 2; 37, 4, *seq.*

[12] *Ibid.* 5, 82, 5, and 2, 28, 9. The sin of another includes the sin of parents.

tified form of sin. If a man has gone crooked morally, he will not appear straight physically. "Not in secret have we done you wrong; not openly have we committed anything to anger the gods; so, O gods, may none of us be of untrue form; we desire for ourselves wholeness and freedom; may Savitar drive away sickness."[13] And what is implied here is openly expressed in this prayer: "O Soma-Rudra, give us all curative things; loosen and release from us the *offence committed and now bound upon our bodies* . . . be merciful to us." The disease "bound on the body" is here identified with the "offence committed against the gods."[14] Therefore the inherited sin is in the nature of inherited bodily evil and the prayer (above) that one may not be punished for another's sin means that one should not suffer bodily through sin committed by another member of the family, either in the same generation or, more usually, by one's ancestor. So one prays: "I ask what was the offence, *enas*, and the sages say, 'Varuna is angry.' What was my sin, *âgas?* Release the wrongs (sins, *drugdhâni*) of my fathers, O Varuna, and what I have in person committed. It was not (in conse-

[13] RV. 10, 100, 7, *seq.*

[14] *Ibid.* 6, 74, 3. AV. 6, 115 and 116 repeat this idea: "Free us from sins committed consciously or unconsciously . . . as one that has sweated out filth on bathing." Disease is driven out of the body, as if it were a sinner condemned by a judge, through the imprecations of a witch-doctor (RV. 10, 97, 12). Compare the use of the same expression in these petitions: "loosen the sin I have committed," "loosen my distress," in RV. 1, 24, 9, and 2, 28, 6.

quence of) my own will; it was (because of) deception, drink, anger, dice, lack of thought."[15]

Other punishments than material and bodily harm, generally in the shape of hunger, disease, and want, are seldom implied. A theological or religious sinner is metaphorically condemned to suffer through his own "burning" falsehoods in the following vivid imprecation: "May the lies of the man who blames priest and prayer become hot brands wherewith Dyaus (Zeus) shall burn him"; apparently this sinner is to suffer sunstroke. He has gone the "crooked way"[16] in speaking ill of divine things. But occasionally it is implied that the sinner suffers less in material happiness than in losing spiritual rewards. "Those who speak wrong (lies) to the righteous, fool themselves" and "through deceit man is bereft of divine benefits"; also "he who betrays a trustful friend has no share in the (divine) Word; what he hears he hears in vain, for he has no knowledge of the paths of right-doing."[17] By far the greater number of sins inveighed against in the Rig Veda are those of verbal and moral "crookedness," which are sins not only because all crookedness is opposed to the straight course of nature as a divine ordinance

[15] RV. 7, 86, 3, *seq.* Compare AV. 6, 116, 2, *seq.:* (May we be forgiven) "for the sins our parents have committed, or our brother or son." The "sin unknowingly committed" is identical with the "sin against Varuna's laws," committed "through lack of thought" RV. 7, 89, 5, and often (*e.g.* 4, 12, 4; 54, 3).

[16] *Ibid.* 6, 52, 2; 9, 97, 18.

[17] *Ibid.* 5, 12, 5; 8, 47, 6; 10, 71, 6.

but also because the vice of crookedness or duplicity is opposed to the divine model of the gods: "O ye gods, ye are simple (without duplicity); in your hearts ye distinguish the mortal who is and who is not double (false)."[18]

But there is one form of punishment which approaches near to the idea of hell. It is often alluded to in the form of this short prayer: "Aditi, Mitra, Varuna, be kind (forgive) if we have sinned against you, wide safety and light may I obtain, Indra, may the long darkness not attain to us."[19] This darkness, as opposed to the "wide light" of the upper world, ·where the pious expect to go as an asylum (safety), is described as a pit or sheol from which one cannot escape. Thus Indra and Soma are besought to "smite with lightning all sinners" and to "cast them into the pit, darkness without a hold, from which none shall ever come up again." In that pit are not only sinning mortals but also evil spirits.[20] It lies apparently "deep under the three earths" and may be identical with that "lap of destruction" which is the abode of the Earth Dragon. It is also referred to as the "endless pits of liars and slanderers," to judge from other clauses in the same denunciatory hymn.

This hymn is rather a late product and shows an advance on the earlier Vedic conception of the fate of sinners. This first notion is that of "endless dark-

[18] RV. 8, 18, 15.
[19] *Ibid.* 2, 27, 14.
[20] *Ibid.* 7, 104, 3 and 17.

ness" or "lower darkness," as opposed to the light of heaven above. Probably it meant at first nothing more than the endless darkness of death, but coupled with the idea of the body buried underground it led to a vague belief in an eternal subterranean abode of evil ghosts, not clearly differentiated from the abode of the Dragon of the underworld.[21] Those whose fate is desired to be of this sort are generally foes of the pious speaker and foes of the gods (because they are foes of the pious). The gods are begged to burn their hearts and send them to the blind darkness below earth. But the sinner also fears this as his own fate, if not forgiven by the offended gods, as in the prayer cited above.

The "bonds" with which a sinner is tied are fastened upon him not only by Varuna but also by Dyaus, Rudra, and Agni, while the punishment of instant death, by lightning, is inflicted by Indra and Parjanya, the rain-god, as well as by the lesser followers of Indra, the Maruts, storm-spirits whom some have interpreted as ghosts. At any rate the human spirits called the Manes also punish men for sin: "If after the manner of men we have committed any sin, O our Fathers, do not injure us on account of that."[22]

[21] RV. 10, 103, 12 and 152, 4.

[22] *Ibid.* 10, 15, 6. The Maruts slay "niggards" and destroy the harmful, as they guard the pious from hurt and evil, *ibid.* 1, 64, 3, *seq.;* 166, 8. Even Aryaman punishes those "who are not worthy of praise" (1, 167, 8). But often Agni or Indra punishes for violations of the laws of the higher gods.

There is no need to expatiate in detail upon the kinds of sin recognized by the Rig Veda, but it may be said that they comprise sins of faith as well as sins of omission (in the liturgy) and ethical faults. Religious unbelief on the part of pagans or Aryans, expressed either as mere mental doubt or, more practically, in the refusal to support true religion and its representatives, the priests, calls forth the severest denunciation. These "godless" men are naturally included under the head of evildoers, though an ethical quality attaches to the rebuke of those who express their unbelief openly by phallic worship and possibly of those who "eat raw flesh." But a list of Vedic sins might well begin with heterodoxy. They may be briefly enumerated as (religious) unbelief, liturgical errors or omissions, stinginess, lying, trickery, cheating at dice (perhaps gambling in any form), unfilial behavior, inhospitality, betrayal, robbery, theft, drunkenness, murder, incest, the use of harmful magic including cursing, false swearing, and all forms of "crookedness," whether directed against a member of the clan or against a stranger. "O Varuna, loosen (pardon) whatever sin we have committed against a relation or friendly companion or brother, against a member of our own clan or against a stranger. If we have cheated at play or committed any sin, whether we realize it or not, O god Varuna, do thou loosen from us all such sin and remove it and may we be dear to thee."[23] Some sins are only casu-

[23] RV. 5, 85, 7, *seq.* The phrase *yad vâ ghâ satyam* (repeated

ally alluded to: "Agni shall burn those who infringe the laws of Varuna and Mitra, those who err like brotherless girls, evil as women who deceive their husbands, wicked, lying, untruthful." Mockers of the gods are wicked, as is one who commits incest with a sister.[24] The general word for sinner or bad man is *pâpa*, which also means bad without ethical connotation ("work badly like unskilful weavers").[25]

Sin is called *enas*, offence, *abhidroha*, *drugdha*, treacherous, malicious, assault, and *repas* and *kilbisha*, stain; but this last conception is more common in later literature, as are those of sin as "transgression" and "failure," though all these ideas are expressed in the Rig Veda interpretation of sin.[26] The

in 10, 139, 5) shows that *satya* is "apparent." Even *sat* is not absolute being, but visible, as opposed to invisible, existence (10, 129, 1). In 6, 24, 5, Indra makes visible the invisible; he makes real what has not yet become apparent.

[24] RV. 4, 5, 4, *seq.;* 1, 190, 5; 10, 10, 12. The "brotherless girl" is undefended, apt to go astray. The prostitute is an object of pity rather than of moral detestation.

[25] *Ibid.* 10, 71, 9. Compare also the "bad road" of death entered by a saint and the bad noise of the ass; but this may be ominous (10, 135, 2; 1, 29, 5). The change from physical to ethical is, however, in line with that taken by compounds in *dus, dur-vidvas,* (δυρ-ειδως), *duritam*, ill-going, *dureva,* from the same root, ill-going, sinner, *dushkrita*, ill-done, evil act. So *agha*, originally ill, then evil. An "ill-thinker" may be merely a foe or he may be a sinner (10, 185, 2). So of the *dureva:* "Men who impair divine laws are ill-goers, *durevâs;* O Indra, sharpen thy weapon against them" (10, 89, 9). The cognate word *anhas* (*cf. angor*) is physical distress, but later becomes "sin" rather than distress and in some early texts interchanges with *enas*, sin (*cf.* AV. 4, 27, 1 and 7, with the varied readings).

[26] The later Sanskrit rather emphasizes sin as stain, *kalmasha,*

sense of debt is usually given to still another word for sin, *rina,* in the common expression "forgive us our debts" and in the epithet "debt-exacting" used of angry gods. The word may originally have meant injury, as in the royal proper name Rinamcaya, perhaps "avenger of injuries." In most passages either meaning would apply, for example: "Long thoughts have the gods; they guard their spiritual power, loving the right order, and punishing wrong" (or "exacting the debt"). So Indra "goes for the wrong," attacks it, rather than "goes for the debt." He is not yet a commercial god: "Thou, as a wise *rinayâ,* O Indra, cuttest wrong to pieces as a sword cuts joints."[27]

kalusha, dosha, and as failure, *delictum, aparâdha.* Transgression, literally "going over," *atyaya,* is recognized before the word is used as fault or sin; but a commoner Vedic notion is that of *upâra* and its cognates as "assault." The "fall-making" idea becomes later the word for sin as causing a fall from caste, *pâtaka,* not yet Vedic. The old word for sin, *âgas,* is perhaps one with Greek ἄγος and later texts have *âgas devânâm* = ἄγος θεῶν (*cf. enas turânâm,* 7, 58, 5). The etymology of the word is doubtful and so is that of *enas,* for the root *in,* from which it is supposed to be derived, is not used of sinful assault but rather in a good sense, *ina,* energetic.

[27] RV. 2, 27, 4; 4, 23, 7; 10, 89, 8. A later theory is that man is born in debt to gods, Manes, seers, and men, paid respectively by sacrifice, progeny, study, and hospitality (ÇB. 1, 7, 2, 1, etc.). The early Vedic text says apparently that when a god "smashes the demons," he arranges wrong (puts it to rights), as in the case of demons there is no thought of paying a debt of sacrifice (9, 47, 2). The word *rina* is connected with Latin *reus* and as an adjective applied to a thief (6, 12, 5) it may still mean injurious (*cf. upâra,* above, from the same root). The verb *ci* with which it is associated means arrange; *apaciti* is ἀπότισις.

The image of the straight road or true path is expanded in the verse cited above, which says that one who betrays his friend loses his hold of the Word, "because he has no understanding of the paths of well-doing." This is the path to which one returns when one becomes "sinless before Aditi" or in particular before Varuna, whose laws determine the straight course of the stars, which is in heaven the Path of the Âdityas.[28] Only when one has "returned" can one be forgiven: "Ye make to live, O ancient gods, everyone who *returns from his sin*."[29] This return is implied in petitions where the suffering sinner begs for relief, such as this: "May we who have sins upon us, O Varuna, not suffer for the sin we have committed against thee."[30] The prayer itself is, as it is termed, a "pacifier" (remover): "May this my prayer be their pacifier, *avayânam*, if I have committed sin against the gods or against a friend or against the lord of the clan." When pacified, the wrath of the god is *avayâta*, removed. "Lay aside

[28] RV. 1, 24, 9, 15 (*enas as âgas*); *ibid.* 10; 8, 18, 2.

[29] *Ibid.* 8, 67, 17, *pratiyantam cid enasas*, "returning from sin" (repenting).

[30] *Ibid.* 7, 88, 6, *enasvantas* and *âgas*. Repentance may be indicated by simple homage, as in 6, 51, 8: "By obeisance I seek to overcome the sin I have committed." Literally, overcome is "get," "get into my power," a desiderative of the root appearing in English as "win," usually applied to winning a god or a god's good-will. The native explanation is that it means here "destroy my sin," but that is only by implication. Varuna, it may be observed, punishes not only by sickness, but, as a Sky-god, by lightning, with "weapons that burn the sinner," 2, 28, 7.

33

your wrath" is a common petition.[31] No one knows
whom the god of storm and lightning may strike:
"Even the sinless man is afraid when the storm-god
(Parjanya) thundering smites evil-doers"; but the
sinless man rests secure in the thought that evildoers
alone are slain by the just gods.[32] Hence the prayer,
"May we be sinless before Aditi," is always accom-
panied, either implicitly or explicitly, by the addi-
tional expression "by following the divine law."
There is no sure hope in sacrifice and obeisance,
though these are the means employed to express the
worshipper's submission and faith: "With obeisance,
sacrifice, and oblation, O Varuna, we deprecate thy
wrath. . . . Loose from us the sins we have committed (remove thy 'fetters') and (by abiding) *in
thy law* may we be sinless before Aditi."[33]

The Vedic poet feels that there is an indissoluble
connection between human and divine laws, nor is he
at a loss in regard to the origin of those "laws of the
gods." It is a modern mistake of interpretation to
suppose that the immutable laws, *vrata,* of the gods
are imposed by the autocratic will of one divine
heavenly Power. The word *vrata* means way, course,
procedure, action and sphere of action, realm (compare *Gebiet* and *gebieten*), and, after the Rig Veda

[31] Usually of sky and storm-gods, RV. 1, 171, 1 and 6; 185, 8.
The wrath of storm-gods is implied by their very activity and
when in action they become supreme, *ibid.* 2, 33, 7; 7, 46, 1
(Rudra).

[32] *Ibid.* 5, 83, 2.

[33] *Ibid.* 1, 24, 14.

period, obligation and vow. It derives from *vart* (Latin *verto;* compare *vritti,* way and rule) and is usually associated with a verb of motion, in the sense "follow the way," or rule, set by the gods, while the other meaning of rule, in the sense of realm, is preserved in the magnificent prophecy of the Rig Veda: "(The gods) spread abroad over the earth the Aryan realm" or rule (*âryâ vratâ*). Later this word becomes synonymous with moral order: "The king and the scholarly priest are the sustainers of the moral order."[34]

But to understand the "laws of the gods" it must be remembered that each Vedic god is supreme in his own sphere. The Vedic pantheon is not, like that of Greece and Rome, under one head, a host forcibly made obedient by a sovereign god. Indra, for example, is acknowledged not only by men but by gods as supreme in his own sphere; he is the battle-leader and there is no conflict between him and Varuna, who is lord of the highest sphere, for Indra rules the lower atmosphere. As battle-god, Indra leads all the gods to battle and they either follow him as subordinates or they evade battle altogether in person but "put their strength in Indra"; that is, as a substitute for fighting they endow him with their powers. On the other hand, Varuna, supreme lord of the upper sphere, directs the order of the universe and controls the harmony of nature in its regular course, though as controller of the "heavenly flood" he may also

[34] RV. 10, 65, 11; Gaut. Dh. 8, 1.

pour out rain and use the thunderbolt, just as, conversely, Indra, in clearing the atmosphere after the
storm of battle, may be said to bring forth again the
sun. Hence on the one hand it is rightly said that "the
gods follow the laws of Varuna" and on the other
that they "follow the laws of Indra." When it is said
that the gods yielded their powers to Indra, this does
not mean that he became supreme god of all, but
that he assumed their powers freely bestowed upon
him by the other gods in their general fight against
the powers of evil, darkness, and drought; they
"yield their strength to his lordship as warrior," just
as of the sun it is said, "the gods yield to thy vigor."
So it is said again: "In Indra the gods deposited
their own manly strength, intelligent power, and
might." Indra by protecting the gods protects their
laws. It is thus that the so-called henotheism of the
Rig Veda is largely to be explained. Thus Dyaus,
the Sky-father, and Earth "bowed themselves before
Indra *for the winning of glory* and all the gods with
one accord made Indra their leader."[35] The worshipper of the Vedic gods does not forget all other
gods while worshipping one, but he realizes that all
the gods work together for righteousness and that
each in his own sphere of activity is master. What
he finally perceives is that all become blended into
one spiritual power, called in their various concrete
manifestations by various names; as Fire, whether
on the hearth or altar or in the sun or lightning, or

[35] RV. 1, 80, 13-16; 131, 1; 163, 8; 7, 21, 7.

as heat, is one divine Power. There are many ways in which the divine presence makes itself manifest to man, or, as the Vedic poet phrases it: "The cars are many but the road is one."[36]

This brief theological discussion has been rendered necessary on account of its ethical significance. The "laws of the gods" are expressed in the regular rotation of seasons and their corresponding sacrifices, for the sacrifice is ordered according to days and seasons. Each day illustrates the "laws divine" incorporate in the sacrifice, and pious men are like gods in "not diminishing the laws," which give security and peace. Very likely there was the feeling that the sacrifice even helped preserve the order of the universe, as later it was seriously believed that the sun would not rise unless the morning rite was performed. But what is more important is the recognition that the laws of the gods effect peace and security on earth as in heaven. Even in heaven it was not always thus, for Indra once fought against the gods. But he is represented as now reconciled with them and acting in agreement with them. So that now Indra follows Varuna's laws, while Varuna in turn follows the laws of Indra or of Vishnu.[37] Now, although many

[36] *ekam niyânam bahavo rathâsas,* RV. 10, 142, 5.

[37] The same words are used of each. Thus Varuna and the Maruts and Twins "follow the will" of Vishnu, and all the gods "follow the will of Varuna," RV. 1, 156, 4; 4, 42, 1. Compare also for the statements above, *ibid.* 1, 123, 8; 124, 2; 5, 69, 1; 7, 75, 3; 8, 35, 13; and, for Indra's older attitude, *ibid.* 4, 19 (2, 12). Law as *dhâma,* themis, belongs to all the gods as something "set-

of these laws are what we should call the laws of
nature and unethical,[38] they yet include the great
idea of a divine harmony, not a harmony imposed
upon the gods by cosmic law or by Fate, but a harmony induced by laws which the gods themselves
made and which results in the gods living at peace
with each other, so that, as human laws only reflect
these laws of the gods, the first effect of law is that
it "binds men together." Indra himself says, "Being
a god I do not impair the commands of (other) gods,
Âdityas, Vasus, and Rudriyas; it is these gods that
have made me invincible." There is a feeling of
noblesse oblige among the divine hosts, and men "follow the law" by conforming to this mutual respect.
Violation of the law is seen in insolence and in trans-
gressing the bounds of others' rights; obedience to
the law is shown by lack of transgression and by
avoidance of arrogance, for "by that sin fell the
angels," as the next age, almost in these words,
loudly proclaimed.[39]

tled," *ibid.* 10, 48, 11; as *dharma* it "supports." The "will" of the
gods is *kratu,* sometimes the same as plan ("all the gods follow
one plan," 6, 9, 5). Mitra and Varuna and Savitar have one law,
respected by all the gods (10, 36, 13). Varuna and the Sun-god
follow Indra's special laws (1, 101, 3), as all nature (including
animals) conforms to the Sun's laws and to those of Parjanya (2,
38, 7; 5, 83, 5).

[38] Such as "all the gods feared fire" and "rivers go according to
the law of Indra and Agni," or, again, "rivers flow according to
the law of Varuna," *ibid.* 6, 9, 7; 7, 47, 3; 8, 40, 8.

[39] *Ibid.* 3, 59, 1; 10, 48, 11. See especially 1, 36, 5, *vratâ dhruvâ
yâni devâ akrinvata,* "the strict laws which the gods made for
themselves." Almost identical language is used of the stars and

38

Furthermore, it is assumed that the gods will gladly help man to keep the law of the gods and that they have done so in the past, so that the true ethical way is the path of the Fathers as well as of the gods. "Help us, all ye gods; may I not get into any sin" and "May the gods grant that our law-abiding lords do not get into ill-fortune or into sin" are concrete cases expressing the same idea as that uttered in the general formula "May we not do what (as we know by the Fathers' teaching) the good gods punish,"[40] but expressing also hope of divine assistance; to which is added the assurance of divine forgiveness in case one should fail to do right, "for Varuna pardons the sinner."[41]

The Rig Veda, as just observed, is not lacking in

moon going according to the law of Varuna and of men following the moral law of Varuna, *ibid.* 1, 24, 10; 7, 87, 7; 89, 5. The sacrifice, as the connecting link between gods and men, is not infringed by the pious; it is established as firmly as earth and sky by the divine laws of Soma and Varuna, which in this instance are one (6, 70, 1; 10, 167, 3; *cf.* 1, 91, 3).

[40] RV. 1, 125, 7 and 10, 128, 4 (sin, *enas*, here cannot mean misfortune). Savitar not only advises the gambler to stop gambling but adds the divine advice to go to work (*ibid.* 10, 34, 13; "The god Savitar declares this to me: Gamble not with the dice, plough your ploughing and rest content with what you have got").

[41] Indra also pardons sin, as he helps to guard from sin. One poet cries: "O Indra, we have faith in thy power; give us a share in the sun, in water, in sinlessness" (*ibid.* 1, 104, 6; *cf.* 10, 92, 7, "With Indra they found joy in the light of the sun"). The common formula "far be thy bonds" as in 2, 29, 5: "Many a sin have I committed, but far be thy bonds" implies a petition for forgiveness like that addressed to Soma: "May Soma be merciful whatever my sin, for man is full of desires" (1, 179, 5).

hints that of old the war-god Indra battled against
the gods. He also performed various acts at variance
with ethical behavior. These acts are, however, in
part at least the operation of natural phenomena, as
when Indra's matricide is explainable as lightning
bursting from a cloud as mother, and, apart from
the statement that Indra is "sinless" because divine,
it is probable that the Vedic poets under their im-
agery really recognized that Indra's crimes were fig-
ures of speech, as they also imply that, whatever the
old contests may have been, the gods are now a peaceful union of benevolent powers, all of whom uphold
morality and punish crookedness. The laws of other
gods have their origin in the Right Order of Varuna
and in so far as they are individual they merely uphold the general principles of that Right Order.
Higher than Varuna at a later stage, or perhaps one
with him, is "the Overseer in highest heaven" and
the Asura or (Supreme) Spirit.[42] The Vedic beginning of pantheism tends to reduce the personal god
as but a form of the All-god; yet, as we shall see, the
ethical constituents of the Vedic pantheon persist
even beyond its apparent dissolution. In fact it never
dissolved, but the bright gods, like the parts of a
kaleidoscope, rearranged themselves and became
united into one whole. At the very end of the Rig
Veda the personification of Right Order as a divine

[42] RV. 10, 129, 7, and 177, 1; cf. 5, 63, 3, where Asura is used
in the same way of Varuna.

personal Power, preceded by such parallel statements as that the regular succession of days is in accordance with the statutes "of Varuna" and "of Rita" (Order), leads to Great Order being invoked as a god along with other deities.[43]

Yet in no passage is Varuna subject to Rita as a superior Power, but rather Rita (Right Order) has its very source in the Wise Spirit (Varuna) and all the laws of Varuna and of the lesser gods are expressions in concrete detail of the divine Order which emanates from heaven, born, as a later theologian puts it, of the religious fervor of the Creator.[44]

The pious soul that has passed through life without incurring the deadly anger of the gods does not "go into darkness" like the impious, but passes upward to the celestial abode of the high gods and, "leaving behind all that is blamable," enjoys the satisfaction of his desires as he carries with him the merit of his good deeds. This speeding to heaven of the passing soul is called "going home," so that the inner thought appears to be that man, related to the gods, naturally rejoins at death the heavenly family of gods and Manes. His sins forgiven, "pure and sin-

---

[43] RV. 1, 123, 8, *sacante dhâma,* and 9; *cf.* 124, 3, "follows the path of Rita." The "spring of Right Order" (or righteousness) in 2, 28, is Varuna's, as is the "law" and "order" according to which flow the rivers (a Zoroastrian belief).

[44] *Ibid.* 10, 66, 4; *cf.* 1, 75, 5, *ritam brihat,* and 10, 190, 1. Religious fervor becomes asceticism, a later Vedic note. Right Order is eternal Truth, as opposed to untruth, and Varuna is by nature a hater of untruth, the sustainer of Rita, *ibid.* 7, 66, 13.

less" he rejoices "under a fair tree" with other sin-less beings. During life he had no wish to die. The later superficial pessimism of philosophy was far from his thoughts and his prayer to the god was always: "Sight and life and joy do thou give us; long may we see the sun as it rises,"[45] but, having died, he still expects life and joy as the last reward of virtue. On the other hand, the thought is ever present that sin is an offence against the divine order of the world and that these gods do not punish arbitrarily, but, as is said in the case of the Father of Gods, a late divine abstraction, he "punishes wrong and slays deceit in the maintenance of the Holy Order."[46]

Men are children of Dyaus, the Sky-father, by nature, but they are also the "children of Varuna" as the Holy Father, *pitâ yajatras,* or spiritual father. As such he not only guards men but guides them in their acts and in their prayers, so that the inspiration of the poet-priest and his aspiration to "ever daily betterment" is implicitly a divine guidance. Compare the prayer: "Do thou, O Varuna, strengthen the prayer, the will, and the mind (ability) of him who would serve thee." A simple prayer of the earlier Rig Veda gives expression to this belief in its invocation to all the holy gods to guide aright the wor-shipper:

[45] RV. 9, 113; 10, 14, 8, *punar astam ehi;* 59, 6. The philoso-phers were pessimistic only as to the value of earthly life; they believed in ultimate bliss as attainable by all.

[46] *Ibid.* 2, 26, 3, and 23, 17, *ritasya dhartari.*

THE IDEA OF SIN AND LAW

O Father Sky and faithful Mother Earth,
And Brother Fire, good gods, be kind to us!
May all ye gods of old with Aditi
Stretch wide for us your manifold protection.
Neither to wolf nor she-wolf, nor to any
Who worketh harm, O Holy Ones, deliver us;
For ye the guiders of our bodies are,
As in our mind and word ye also guide us.
May we not suffer for another's sinning,
Nor do ourselves what ye, the good gods, punish,
And may our foes, since all things ye control,
Injure not us but only hurt themselves.

The view that the gods direct men's thought and action was not worked out into any system of determinism but rested on the oft-repeated thought "may we not do what ye punish," which is scarcely more than a Vedic "lead us not into temptation," and on the thought of the prayer: "Blessed shall be the mortal, O Mitra, who serves thee according to thy law." The question as to what is good for man was answered by the simple solution: "All that is good which the gods approve."[47]

In concluding this sketch of ethics in the Rig Veda it may be remarked that, though the Karma doctrine is not yet formulated, its ethical principles are

[47] RV. 2, 23, 19; 3, 59, 2. On Varuna as Our Father (*pitâ nas*), see *ibid.* 5, 65, 5 and 7, 52, 3. The same expression is used of Agni perhaps as a form of Varuna, as of the abstract All-maker. The prayer to Varuna to "strengthen the prayer" is found *ibid.* 8, 42, 3. The hymn above is from *ibid.* 6, 51, 5-7. ("Mind," as opposed to word, is *daksha,* mental ability, connected with *dexter,* etc.).

43

already in evidence. Thus suffering is recognized as the fruit of previous sin and when a good man dies he goes to the next world carrying his merit with him.[48] Further, as to magic, there is no sin in magic as such, only in sinful magic. It is a blameless matter to employ magic in love-affairs, to effect cures, or to harm enemies; it is "crooked" to use it against a friend. The Vedic "sorcerer" was deemed a sinner because he was crooked, not because he employed magic. He illustrates the Vedic belief that deceit is immoral.

To sum up the ethical content of the Rig Veda: Morality is an expression of divine law; sin is opposition to that law. The sinner is one who is out of harmony with the higher spiritual environment, which encompasses and controls the world.

[48] McKenzie, *Hindu Ethics,* p. 15. In the developed Karma doctrine, this view was united with the belief in metempsychosis, which is also known in a vague form to the Rig Veda.

CHAPTER III

ETHICS OF EARLY PANTHEISM

WE have just seen that the tendency to unite all
spiritual powers into one universal spirit-power led
to the merging of divine identities and a consequent
vagueness of appeal on the part of the religiously-
minded. This worked together with the inherited
tendency to turn to magical practices, where the
appeal was to a mystical natural power. The result
was that a mass of the old Rig Veda verses began to
be used as charms and spells and the sacrificial ritual
soon became a mechanical panacea for disease,
death, and sin, controlled by the priests, who in turn
controlled the gods. Something similar is perceptible
here and there in the Rig Veda itself, which represents an accumulated number of hymns composed
during a long period; but the general tone of the Rig
Veda is, as has been shown, quite different. The gods
are not generally coerced but entreated and magic
itself is religiously modified. Now this religious modification of magic lasts much longer than has usually
been recognized. The Veda of magical usages and
crude philosophical speculation known as the Atharva Veda is by no means a purely magical collection of formulas. Its ritual is deeply interwoven with
religious and (through religion) with ethical ideas.
The healing herbs, magically potent, are divine and
still act "at the command of Heaven" and "with the

45

help of the Fire-god"; misfortune is repelled by a prayer to Dyaus Pitar (Jupiter); Varuna is still "the best among the gods"; Agni is still "the righteous god of right and light" and is entreated to "put from us our evil deeds"; Varuna "favors the truthful" and is begged "not to harm us if we have violated thy ordinances"; the sin wiped off on the scapegoat Trita by the gods is to be removed, if it comes upon a man, by the prayer or spell, but only through the help of the gods; the Maruts release men from the fetters of sin; those who live evilly "fall under the wrath of the gods"; for the sin of inhospitality, "the gods cut off" the sinner. All these and more, in part echo of the old hymns but in part new matter, yet couched in the same vein, show that, despite the prevailing magic of genuine sort, as where herbs free from sin without mention of the gods, the ancient connection between ethics and religion is almost intact. Moreover, there is still preserved the old ethical vocabulary; the same words for offence, sin, and for forgiveness as an act of grace on the part of the gods.[1] The notion of sin as a pollution or miasma, however, is the prevailing conception; it is a stain wiped away or washed off by holy water or herbs or ointment (unction guards one from "evil deeds and

[1] The word *çamala*, pollution, is an exception, not appearing in the earlier Veda. It applies, for example, to the pollution "wiped off" on a man who offends another by cutting off his sunlight, and takes the place of a preceding curse intended to rob a man of his shadow if he passes between another and the fire or urinates against the sun, all breaches of religious ethics. AV. 13, 1, 56, *seq.*

46

evil eye"); it emphasizes the sin of sickness, as in the unique passage: "Waters and heavenly herbs have made thy *sinful sickness* disappear." Yet the element of divine assistance is never far off: "The god Agni has ascended into heaven; himself free from sin, *enas,* he has freed us from the curse; on him we wipe off our stains, *ripra;* we have become holy and pure."[2]

There is, however, a theological advance in this Veda which is of ethical importance. Instead of the "long darkness" and "pit" into which sinners fall, they go to a hell where "one with a noose," later epithet of Yama, may plague them. Again, the passing soul may reach heaven only to be thrust out, if sinful, and "burned down" by the sun (the sun in this Veda is definitely identified with Vishnu) to "evil worlds afar," withal, while "Yama's seat" still represents paradise. Later popular theology also has the soul conveyed to heaven, to be judged, where it appears before the three divine witnesses whom man always carries with him on earth, namely, Fire, Sun, and Wind (residing in the body as heat, sight, and breath).[3] The hitherto indefinite locality of hell as

[2] AV. 12, 2, 12, *seq.* Stain is here sin, as *ibid.* 40, "what stain, pollution, we have committed, and what ill-doing, from that, water shall purify us." The unique expression "sinful sickness" (above), *ibid.* 8, 7, 3, is the embodiment of the notion that sickness is the objectified form of doing wrong, but it makes sin a form of more general evil, anything abhorrent, showing the deep intrusion of the savage taboo-idea upon the idea of moral wrong.

[3] Mbh. 12, 322, 55. On Yama and his seat, compare AV. 6, 118, 2; 12, 5, 64.

lower darkness was soon established as in the south-eastern district and the various hells under Yama's management were multiplied into seven or thrice seven or more, each representing some form of torture, in part imagined from the kinds of punishment inflicted by royal officials on criminals, in part drawn from the vivid realism which in India delights in disgusting details, a very mild instance of which occurs in the Atharvan, where a man wicked enough to spit on a priest is condemned (in priestly imagination) to die and going to the next world to sit in a stream of blood, devouring hair (in hell).[4]

Other ethical and religious advance appears in this later Veda. The sin of gambling is in part religiously justified by being put under the authorization and support of heavenly nymphs, who "love the dice" and give luck in gambling; they too are begged like gods to forgive the sin of one who takes up the dice. Sin, again, is the evil (ill) done by women wailing for the dead (tears injure the departed). Sin is a stain or an encompassing environment like the egg-shell round a bird unhatched. It leads to (something) being born deformed since "the sin cannot be

[4] AV. 5, 18, 13 and 19, 3. Those that die "pure" go to the "bright world," where they have *bahu strainam*, 'plenty of women' (in heaven, *svarge loke*), *ibid.* 4, 34, 2. Despite the emphasis on sensual pleasures in heaven, the Veda as a whole recognizes as normal on earth the union of one wedded pair, married under religious sanction. "Mutual fidelity till death" is demanded of the married pair; who in heaven remain at the age they were when they were married, AV. 12, 3, 1, just as, according to later belief, the gods always appear to be twenty-five years old.

escaped," a clear indication in unclear words that the Karma doctrine of retributive birth is in the speaker's mind. Another and very important ethical doctrine from the religious point of view is the statement that a man who knows a certain mystic doctrine becomes "dear to the gods," *priyo devânâm bhavati ya evam veda,* the very formula of philosophic mysticism. Further later thought is here anticipated by the utterance that, by being hospitable, the host "has his sins eaten up" and has purified himself of all evil.

But, in its bearings on the development of religious ethics, no factor is more significant than that of the rise of a god scarcely recognized in the Rig Veda, who now and from now on becomes the arbiter of law. Out of the mass of abstract deities that belong even to pre-Vedic times and embrace, in the Rig Veda and the literature following, such forms as Amity, Concord, Mercy, Faith, All-maker, Creator, Time, and Love, there emerges one known as Lord of Creation, who was first imagined as the physical father of the world of gods and men, who are his children. With one of these, later tradition declared that the Lord of Creation had an incestuous connection; but this was merely a misinterpretation of natural phenomena to satisfy the myth-makers, and the view taken by religious philosophers was that the Lord of Creation produced the world not by propagation but by his own religious fervor or by his mental fiat. For us at present the most significant fact in regard to this Lord of Creation is that at a very early period he became a religious and ethical authority. Certain judgments and decisions were referred to him; he was cited as having said certain weighty things. In not too long a time, when the somewhat indefinite name 'Lord of Creation' began to be recognized as one with that of the Father-god, Brahmâ, this Lord still retained his old title as the ethical ruler and expounder of morality and law. He became the arbiter of ethics and giver of divine laws in a degree to which the mythless Varuna or Creator never attained. The myth helped to humanize him, made him in a way more authoritative. For a thousand years or more it sufficed, if a rule of conduct or law was enunciated, to make the statement "thus said Prajâpati" (Lord of Creation) and it was as if a Mohammedan said "so spoke the Prophet"; it was no longer a disputable point. He is the Father-god; "we are his children," as the sacred texts proclaim over and over, and his word is law.

What a tremendous influence the *ipse dixits* of earthly teachers has had is evident from the works of Zoroaster and Buddha. It was one of the mightiest weapons of early Christianity as compared with the vagueness of appeal made even by the Stoics. The appeal to reason as pitted against the appeal to a strong personality has no chance with the mass. It is of course somewhat different when the authority is not a man, divine or semi-divine, but a mere god; yet even a god who gives oracles has a great power and these aptly manufactured laws and sayings of

Prajâpati as "our Father" were until Buddha's day almost the only general legal-moral precepts which could be quoted as coming from a divine personal source. One has to say legal-moral because, in the early period, law was a moral jumble and ethics was more or less a legal matter. Prajâpati may be said to have attained to his high place and to his charac- teristic rôle even as early as the Vedic period, for in the Atharvan his *obiter dictum* is accepted, albeit merely in a matter of physical interest, in just the way the later moralists were to cite him, with a "thus said Prajâpati" (equivalent to 'that settles the mat- ter'). Incidentally, either he or Death (the readings vary) is called the "overlord of creation," but, more important, Prajâpati is described as the "first-born of Right Order," that is, he is the personal divine representative of that Righteousness or Right Order which rules the world for ethical betterment.[5]

The Brâhmanas or ritual texts which, ending in philosophical speculations, eventually evolved the Upanishads, wherein for the first time pantheism is formally inculcated, bear witness to the popularity of Prajâpati and incidentally throw a strong light upon the ethics of their time, which may be about 800 B.C. In the Rig Veda itself, the Word as a divine Power strikes the note of predestination and reli- gious favoritism in the utterance, "Whom I love, I exalt" (make powerful). In the next stage, this Di- vine Word is conceived as the first-born of the Lord

[5] AV. 5, 24, 13; 6, 11, 2; 12, 1, 61.

of Creation, who, again, as we have just seen, is born of Rita and as such represents ethical order. As Father of all, the Lord sends forth his first-born, the Divine Word, who appears in the world as the Divine Light, a sort of mediating principle: "I will send forth the Word and the Word will become the world," for now "through the mind alone the Lord of Creation created the world."[6] The idea of a cosmic sacrifice on the part of One God, *deva ekas,* is known as early as the Rig Veda. This god also is not only the Creator and Maker of all; he is "our Father." Now, in the succeeding period, the Creator and Father becomes also the great moral controller and in the earliest law books, after the Vedic age, his word is decisive in every point of ceremony, penance, moral, and social rule.[7]

But other important changes were taking place during this period. The geographical and social environment had changed. The people represented by the literature were no longer in the Punjâb but had moved as far southeast as the Keys of Florida are from the mountains of Georgia. Castes in the Brahmanic state had become fixed orders, theoretically distinguished as Aryans and slaves, the former natu-

[6] PB. 20, 14. Or (ÇB. 11, 1, 6, 7), "By his mouth (breath) he created gods, then there was light; demons, and then was darkness; and he said, 'I have created evil' and with their evil he destroyed the demons; so the battles of gods and demons are an illusion."

[7] Thus in Vas. Dh. 14, 16; Âp. 1, 19, 14; and often. For the cosmic sacrifice, see RV. 10, 81 and 90.

rally falling into divisions represented by priests, warriors, and Aryan farmers or merchants; but practically the mass of the people were submerged with the slaves under the two aristocratic orders of priests and warriors. The king was not now exhorted to be honest, but was directed to find in favor of any priest who had been accused by a man of low caste. The rise of a caste system and of a theory of "repeated births" and of a hell of punishment, led to sins being punished by a "fall" into a lower caste on rebirth, and the conversion of the sacrifice into a mystical machine led to abuse of power on the part of the priests and to quite a different conception of the remedy for sin. A new ethics was imported into human consciousness by the conviction that to eat flesh was wicked, like lying, which resulted ethically in a general aversion from injurious acts done to any living creature, probably strengthened by the teaching that "If a man devours flesh in this world, that (animal) will eat him in the next world."

The sacrifice was no longer a gift or bribe but became a cure for sin so easily administered that it "purified" through its mechanical performance. Impure gains (our "tainted money") might thus at a trifling expense be made "pure" by a *pro formâ* sacrifice. Sin might be transferred by a sacrificer to anyone who criticised his sacrificial work; a few mumbled words on the part of an officiating priest shifted the sin. A priest, if dishonest, might even turn a sacrifice paid for by one man against the giver and direct the power of the magical rite to the destruction of the righteous man who had piously paid for it to be performed in his own behalf. But this betrayal was recognized as sinful; as it was also sinful to bargain for a fee. Again, the theory of mystical sacrifice conceives of a man as identified with his sacrifice and thereby with the divine nature. Man thus "redeems himself" through his own divine nature; the sacrifice becomes a mystical sacrament of redemption,[8] as the Supreme Being becomes a spiritual and ethical power.

But the old ethical rules and models were still vital and potent: "The gods are truth and man is untruth"; the reason why men should speak the truth is that they should follow the law of the gods: "Men should speak the truth because the gods speak the truth." Traditional usage, ever a strong argument, now becomes almost as potent as a god-given decree. In connection with this it is interesting to see that, when the old story of the Lord of Creation committing incest is brought to the attention of the gods, they express their horror with the simple words *akritam akar*, "he has done what is (hitherto) not

[8] Redemption is first from Death and then from sin: "By sacrifice one redeems oneself from one's debt to Death." Thus one who sacrifices, fasts and redeems himself as one given to the gods; his sacrifice becomes his spiritual body in the next world. With the thought, 'my new body is formed by the sacrifice,' he frees himself from his mortal body and from sin. This sacrifice of self is better than the sacrifice to the gods, which is merely tribute, like that of a farmer to a king. ÇB. 3, 6, 2, 15; 11, 1, 8 and 2, 6.

done"; *non factum* had become *non faciendum*. "It has not been done before" is a stigma. Conversely, but in more guarded fashion, what was done of old becomes a precedent. Tradition determines all that may be done, from "dividing property among sons" to "washing the hands" before a sacrifice. Yet here, as has been said, advancing ethical sense restrained the application of this rule: "When improper acts on the part of the gods are cited as a precedent for man's behavior," says an old epic poet, "neither practice such acts nor blame the gods," that is, do not be irreverent, but do not follow their example; as another epic sage says, "Cease to cite these famous transgressions . . . do thyself what is suitable and proper."[9] Thus the usage of man, as he ethically developed, bettered the example of the ancient gods, as it has always done. And, despite much that is unethical, this second period marked a distinct moral advance. For one thing, it localized unethical custom, permitting it perforce where it was grounded in inexpugnable tradition, but prohibiting it elsewhere, so that we get the formal statement in one of the later legal codes that such and such caste-conduct is permissible in the North but immoral in the South, where it had no tradition to support it. The growing weight of public opinion also attempted to restrict the use of intoxicants; reprobated usury; lauded hospitality and respect for parents; and emphasized spiritual purity in antithesis to ritual purity. When

[9] Mbh. 12, 292, 17, *na caret tâni na kutsayet;* and *ibid.* 323, 20.

55

an obscene old rite had to be performed, it was duly performed; but then the participants had to purify themselves from the use of the obscene language used in the ceremony.

In outward form, the most striking feature of the new ethics as compared with the old is the prevalent penance of fasting as expiation for trifling lapses. One must fast at certain seasons (*e.g.*, at new and full moon) in any circumstances; but the purification induced by fasting now becomes the rule in cases where any offence against Right Order has been committed. The gods are more rarely besought to forgive; man purifies himself. A more spiritual tone prevails in eschatological speculation. In olden days even cattle went to heaven to provide food for the pious dead, who demanded all earthly pleasures enhanced in heaven, and though the Rig Veda declares that the dead body is dispersed, yet the bones were carefully collected that hereafter one might have a complete earthly body. But now "man conquers heaven by faith and truth" and imagines hereafter a spiritual body. Immortality is no longer a favor of the gods, but "everyone who partakes of the divine body of the god (drinks of the moon-plant) becomes immortal"; and, through knowledge alone of religious truth, "one thereby becomes composed of truth and immortality." But also there is a salvation through ethical behavior: "Heaven is the world of those who have done good." The soul of the dead man, it is said now (but perhaps this is an ancient

belief first chronicled here), goes on the path of the
gods between fires, which scorch the sinful but let
the sinless pass unharmed. According to another
view, it is weighed in a balance on reaching the next
world and its fate is decided by its moral value.[10]

Brahmanic theories of immortality differ from
the earlier view, according to which man won immortality by pleasing the gods, and the gods themselves, at first mortal, won immortality through their
acts or by other means. One story is that only Fire
was immortal and, based on this, arose the theory
that the gods became immortal by placing that immortal element in themselves. As for man, the real
self or soul is a form of divine breath or of fire,[11]
which is the guardian of vows and laws: "The breath
is fire, is the immortal" (part). Hence, when a child
is born, it is the Fire-god that puts breath into its
body and before the navel is cut the priest must
"breathe over" it, to give it full measure of life. The
cult of Fire becomes a spiritual, ethical act, symbolic
of truth-speaking; by sacrifice one increases one's
spiritual vigor, and as one redeems oneself (pays his
debt to Death) so one frees oneself from sin by

[10] AB. 7, 10; KB. 2, 8; 5, 10; ÇB. 1, 9, 3, 2; 11, 2, 7, 33; the
"knife-path" to heaven, ÇB. 13, 2, 10, 1, may indicate the existence
of a belief in a bridge of judgment.

[11] Fire is identified with breath (wind) and also with the sun,
ÇB. 10, 4, 5, 1. The (neuter) Brahma appears manifested in various gods as illusive spirits, really powers of Brahma; the mortal
gods become immortal by becoming possessed of Brahma (the
spiritual Power), *ibid.* 11, 2, 3, 6.

the same cult of Fire as truth. At this time rebirth on earth was by no means a punishment in itself. In fact, it was only a form of living after death and is sometimes interpreted, like life in heaven, as a reward. Only when rebirth was in animal guise was it to be feared; in human form, it was not undesirable. But ordinarily the preference was for life with the gods, and the human soul might even anticipate becoming some sort of a divinity. All divinities are "beings of joy," for here for the first time we find emphasized the truth that "gods are bliss" and that "the soul of a god is always joyful," a truth retained in the later interpretation of the All-soul as pure Being, Intelligence, and Joy, which had a real influence upon ethics in popular religion.

Besides the ethical results already summarized, attention may be drawn here to certain minor points brought out by the theological and mystic speculations of the Brâhmanas as they affect moral behavior. It is repeatedly admitted that the special evil of the demons or devils, who, as compared with the gods, were the "older children of the Creator," was arrogance. They spoke untruth and the gods spoke truth and in the contest between them the gods at first lost ground, and became poor and contemptible, "just as a man does who always speaks the truth"; but in the end it was the gods who overcame the demons (powers of darkness and evil). They were defeated because of their arrogance.[12] Again, anger

[12] ÇB. 5, 1, 1, 1, and 9, 5, 1, 13, *seq.;* 11, 1, 8, 1.

is unmoral in that it breaks the sacrificial vow and so "if a man is consecrated, suppression of anger behooves him," and from this as a starting point arises the feeling that wrath is not conducive to the spiritual state; it becomes one of the marks of "badness" as opposed to goodness. On the other hand, energy, constant activity, to perfect the world, is extolled, because it imitates the divinity, which is always at work: "Ever moving (active) are waters, sun, moon, and stars; so let the student be ever active"; his daily study is a sacrifice.[13] The identity of man as spirit with the Supreme God, which is now pure spirit, has a strong ethical effect. In God is no evil and man must strive for his own perfection and for the world's perfection, for man is one with God.[14]

The element adverse to a natural growth of morality was above all else, besides the magical interpretation of sacrifice, that caste-feeling which not only deprived the slave of "god and sacrifice" and made the mere "people" (that is, the agricultural and mercantile classes) the "food of kings," but exalted the priest to the position of a god on earth. Gifts to

[13] ÇB. 11, 5, 7, 1 and 10. He redeems himself from his debt to Death in part by his service of the Fire-god, *ibid.* 11, 3, 3, 2, *seq.*

[14] "Brahma is freed from darkness, separated from all evil; in him are the three lights of Prajâpati; the immortal soul (of the world) is wise and free from (evil) desires," AV. 10, 7, 40 and 8, 44, which anticipates the *apahatapâpmâ,* "the soul, deathless, free from evil," of the Upanishad (Ch. 8, 1, 5). The unity of man with God as Father is carried on to the epic: "I am the Father, the Mother and the Son; I am in the heart of every man and I am the soul of all." Mbh. 5, 46, 27-28.

priests were like gifts to the gods: "There are two kinds of divinities, gods and priests"; to get to heaven both kinds must be placated. Murder is only "real murder" when it is committed on the person of a priest. The priest is exempt from capital punishment and from oppression.[15] None may insult or hurt him.

In such hands it is not strange that the sacrifice, despite the tendency to interpret the Fire-service allegorically and spiritually, became a mere mill mechanically worked to grind out future rewards as well as present blessings. The rare and expensive sacrifice performed by a king who wished to claim suzerainty of the land was so efficacious that "a single oblation at this sacrifice of the horse atones for all sins, even that of slaying a priest," a dictum startling to the priest but one that he does not hesitate to record. Even the later lawgivers agree in part with this theory of atonement of all sins through the Vedic sacrifice.[16]

Liberality to these priests is excessively lauded; but it must not be forgotten that hospitality and family life (described as a harmonious unit, in which mutual affection and respect are to be found) are also praised, as well as peace and good-will and honesty. It is recognized that there is a heaven for the good, as for the bad there is "a house below"

[15] ÇB. 2, 2, 2, 6; 3, 3, 2, 8; 11, 5, 7, 1; 13, 3, 5, 3. "The slave has no god and no sacrifice." PB. 6, 1, 11.

[16] ÇB. 13, 3, 1, 1; 5, 4, 1.

(hell), where live sinners and sorcerers and where those injured by others in this world repay their debt on the bodies of their former injurers, a primitive hell of accomplished revenge, probably older than the dawning notion of a divine tormenter.[17]

It is not to be expected that a Veda expressly directed toward expounding magical practices and a liturgical literature devoted to ritualistic details will prove fruitful in the exposition of spiritual ideas. But it would be a mistake to deduce from a contemplation of these religious extravagances that they represent a world of spiritual and ethical anarchy. These books show us but one side of religion presented by but one class, which utilizes its mighty power and grand spiritual inheritance for its own selfish advantage, and prostitutes much that was pure. But the idea of the gods as ethical upholders of the world still remains and morality itself, if feebly represented, is not debauched, only overshadowed by the meretricious attractiveness of magical power. The priest may be a deluded or even a sinful teacher; but he has not been able to withhold his tribute to the qualities still recognized as virtues. Ethical and ritual sins are not clearly distinguished as such, but ethical lapses are regarded as sinful. Sin may be conceived as pollution instead of being an

[17] AV. 2, 14, 3; ÇB. 11, 6, 1, 4. The notion lingers long, strengthened by a pun in the *mâmsa* (flesh) doctrine, this word being interpreted as me, *mâm*, he, *sa:* "me he will eat whose flesh, *mâmsa*, I eat" or, as cleverly adapted by Professor Lanman, "*me eat* will he whose *meat* I eat."

act opposed to a divine will; but the old interpretation still lingers and the consciousness of the gods' anger against the "crooked" man is still alive. Hence it is not quite justifiable to say with Professor Sylvain Lévi that "this system has no place for morality."[18] Theoretically it has not, logically it has not; for the sacrifice is not only mechanical but it governs and controls the gods. But the moral sense is not dead and a clear distinction is made between right and wrong. A lower order of magic submerged the loftier thought of the Rig Veda (which was itself later than magic but in its higher expression had risen above it), yet it could not do away with the ethical consciousness already awakened, nor did it entirely suppress the idea that morality was an expression of spiritual worth divinely implanted in man.

[18] Lévi, *Doctrine du sacrifice,* p. 9.

CHAPTER IV

ETHICS IN THE UPANISHADS

WE have been considering hitherto the ethical
notions and theories that arose among and were
taught by the priestly caste, whose early interest
was centered upon the sacrifice and its ritual. Out
of that caste, but not given over to the rather servile
attendance on the royal families who supported the
sacrificial priests, came the thinkers whose lives were
devoted to the study of philosophy. There is current
a rather ill-considered modern theory to the effect
that the philosophers were not of the priestly caste
but of the warrior caste, perhaps of non-indigenous
origin; that even Buddha may have been of a foreign
race. But there is little to support this theory and
much that goes to disprove it. The germs of the philosophy of the Upanishads lie buried in the (priestly)
Atharva Veda and Brâhmanas and it is from them
that we have to derive the unsystematic philosophic
utterances of the later sages, in whose debates, however, the Râjas of the day probably took the condescending interest customary to cultured royalty
and in which, when they took part, they were
credited with victory.[1]

[1] The "warrior-knowledge" credited (Ch. Up. 5, 10, 7) to one
of these was already well known to the old priests, BAU. 3, 2,
13. Debates at court on theological and metaphysical subjects were
always popular in India and survived to the time of Akbar.

These sages have not much to say in regard to ethics. As one is rather surprised in the literature concerning ritual (above) to find so much of ethical import, so in discussions regarding the relation of human soul to All-soul, it is not the paucity of moral teaching that is striking but the fact that ethical instruction is found at all. For in this philosophy ethics is taken for granted; the real questions are concerning metaphysics, so that we may be thankful for such hints as are given in regard to the sages' opinions on morality.

Perhaps the most definite and positive utterance in the Upanishads as to ethical behavior in its relation to religion is this: "He who has not ceased from immoral conduct cannot obtain God through the intelligence." Nor, it is added, can one get to God if one is not "self-restrained," an expression of wide ethical import, as we shall see later. For the present it is enough to emphasize the clear moral teaching in this avoidance, as a necessary preliminary to religion, of *dush-carita*, immoral conduct. We may set it beside the description of godhead, already cited, "free of all evil," *apahatapâpmâ*, in the same body of scripture. A verse following the former description declares that he who is always impure is born again and again, that is, he fails to reach the highest goal.[2] God is ethically pure; the very word for right and law and virtue, *dharma*, is employed to characterize the nature of God, who "brings right and re-

[2] Kath. Up. 1, 2, 24 and 3, 7.

moves evil" from the world. The man who is wise is the morally good man whose nature approximates to the divine model: "The good and the pleasant approach a man and the wise man discriminates between them, choosing the better, not the more pleasant; the fool, through greed and avarice, chooses the more pleasant, but well for him who chooses the better; whoso forsakes the better and chooses the more pleasant fails of his aim."[3]

The teacher of ethics is here the same Lord of Creation whose word was decisive in the previous age. He enjoins upon all the practice of "self-restraint, generosity, and compassion" as the three cardinal virtues. Every man must "give gifts at the sacrifice" in the old ritualistic religion, but now this has a fine interpretation: "A man's religious gifts are austerity, generosity, rectitude, non-injury (not harming living creatures), and truthfulness."[4] Reverting to the idea of the balance, one of these sages cites with approval an old verse which declares that great sinners cause the balance to sink and names as such the thief of gold, the drinker of intoxicants, the

[3] Çvet. Up. 6, 6; Kath. 1, 2, 2. Compare Ch. 8, 4, 1 and 3: "The Brahma-world is free from evil . . . only those who have lived as chaste students can enter the world of Brahma," and Kath. 2, 5, 8 and 11: "God (as the pure Brahma, *çukram*) is not sullied by the world's evil" (God is pure both as Brahma and as the Lord of Creation, Çvet. Up. 4, 2).

[4] BAU. 5, 2, 3, and Ch. 3, 17, 4 (*ibid.* 3, 16: "man's life is one long sacrifice"). Austerity or the practice of self-inflicted hardships may be given up in favor of faith, for "faith is austerity," *ibid.* 5, 10, 1.

violator of his spiritual teacher's home, the slayer of a priest, and the man who associates with such sinners, a list taken up in the legal aphorisms, which still exalt the priest and make crimes against spiritual teachers especially heinous. Yet, even with such caste-limitation, it is evident that the Upanishad teachers did not countenance in any way the antinomian practices which found expression in the heretical pre-Buddhistic teachers. One reason for the utter collapse of those heretical teachers was precisely because they taught immorality. Received Brahmanic and Buddhistic philosophy never taught or countenanced unethical behavior. Much that is quoted as to popular belief and practice is the result of misunderstanding rather than of intelligent interpretation. For example, both Upanishad and epic say that "sin does not cling to a wise man any more than water clings to a lotus-leaf," but this is not to declare that the sage may sin and be free, but that one free from worldly attachments sheds sin, is not attached to it; though it is true that popular belief endorsed the wrong meaning. The real meaning is seen in another epic passage bearing on the same point: "The man who has wisdom does not sin; he ceases to do evil and through his wisdom annuls the evil of his former life"; and still more strongly: "If a man be intemperate and lustful, penances and sacrifices will avail him naught."[5] So the oldest Upanishad says that the

5 Mbh. 12, 270, 20, *seq.;* 286, 46; 299, 7 (copied from Ch. Up.

perfect sage is a saint who "burns evil away, is free from evil."

That this is in reality the attitude of the older sages of the Upanishads may be further illustrated by some of the few ethical teachings found in their metaphysical treatises. It is chiefly in the priestly codes of law, where philosophy has little to say, that the priest is represented as still guiltless even when he sins, because he is illuminated by the Veda. But such formal pronouncements are apt to be essentially modified even there. For example, after such a statement one jurist cautiously adds that if the priest really relies on the power of the Veda he can find no pleasure in sin, which virtually annuls the reluctant admission that a learned priest is not tainted by guilt even if he commits sinful acts. Moreover, it is possible that the whole theory is a later addition to the jurist's work, for in an earlier part of his manual he says emphatically, "The Vedas do not purify him who is deficient in good conduct," which is in sum the general opinion of even the priestly code-makers.[6]

How then shall we understand such startling statements as are sometimes cited to prove that a man may commit any crimes and still be immune? First we must understand the text and then its place in the general theory. When, for example, Indra is intro-

4, 14, 3). The last passage is clarified by the Up. passage preceding, "he repels evil-doing," *apahate pâpakrityâm; cf.* BAU. 4, 4, 23.

[6] Vas. Dh. S., 6, 3: *âcârahînam na punanti Vedâs; ibid.* 26, 19; 27, 4.

duced as a divine personification of truth and says
that despite his lawless life as a god he was not injured thereby and draws the conclusion that one who
knows Indra may follow this example without injuring "his world," it will not do to stop here, but one
must follow the argument, which is that "Indra is
life (life in all its aspects), the intelligential self of
the world." He who "knows Indra" is one who has
attained to unity with all life; his acts are no longer
his, because he is no longer an individual. But if one
takes this secret doctrine without understanding it,
"one becomes devilish and perishes." Such is the
conclusion of the Lord of Creation, whose words are
still a caution to those who would make of this teaching an incitement to self-gratification and a sinful
life.[7] The life-soul here is life in all of its phases
and as such may be said to be "desire and non-
desire, right and wrong"; but it is only when the
human soul becomes one with the life-soul that
it becomes "neither greater nor less" through evil.[8]
Even in this disquisition the concepts good and bad
are recognized as still valid. The final word after all
is that which closes the discussion: "He who knows,
removes from himself all evil," *pâpman*. The idea of
the Absolute itself is still tinged with ethical consciousness: "Brahma is bright and pure, unpierced

[7] Ch. Up. 8, 7, *seq.*, and Kaush. Up. 3, 1, *seq.*

[8] Kaush. 3, 8. The doctrine of election is patent here: "Whom
the life-soul wishes to lead up he makes perform good action;
whom he wishes to lead downward, bad action."

by evil,"[9] though sometimes represented as raised above all ethical distinctions; but the moment the personal side of the "All-soul" is introduced (as God), all hesitation disappears. God is without evil, pure (sinless); and so should he be who would attain to God. But this is in any event not a practical question of everyday ethics. On that point all the accepted teachers are unanimous; ethical distinctions are never really transcended. Only the philosophers imagine an unmoral principle of life; but even they insist that in this world man must lead a moral life and that there is a vital distinction between ethical and unethical behavior.

It is not easy with our Western preconceptions to envisage the thoughts of those who were trying to make plain to themselves the dawning conception of Absolute Being, "without passions or parts," *virajam akalam,* and hence raised above all distinctions. As one in deep sleep sees all distinctions vanish, so here there is no duality. For while there is a sense of duality there can be no unity with the All-soul. What has the soul merged in God to do with good and evil works? There is a bank, as it were, dividing duality from unity, beyond which all "pairs" come to an end; the Supreme Soul is not increased nor diminished by good and evil works; yet "all evils turn back from it."[10] So the soul merged therein "is not followed by good nor by bad," *punya* and *pâpa,*

[9] Îçâ Up. 8.
[10] Ch. Up. 8, 4; BAU. 4, 3, 22; 4, 4, 22.

being released from "all the sorrows of the heart." But this is only to say that it is not followed by the effect of evil and good deeds, which is indeed the usual statement.[11] When the soul that is not yet emancipated passes from earth, it takes with it the good and the evil deed; for which, in heaven or hell and in high or low birth hereafter, it has reward or punishment. It is, then, this state which the Upanishad teaches is transcended. The liberated soul is freed from the idea of duality (pairs of opposites) and from effect of good and evil acts; all that is now a thing of the past. As one with the whole intelligential life of the universe the soul stands no more apart, with its ancient limitations and burdens of the heart, its sense of good and bad acts committed and entailing certain results. So long as a man is still a creature of desires (and he is so till unified with God), he will be as he wills to be, and will act in accordance with his will; "he will become pure by good acts and evil by evil acts; and whatever deed he does, of that will he reap the fruit." But he will not become one with God till the sense of divine unity causes all desires to cease. Furthermore, he who has not turned from wickedness cannot get to God, for

11 That is to say, it is the whole *dharma* which is transcended, including ritual works. Thus to "abandon *dharma* and *adharma*" is not to abandon virtue but the idea of performance and non-performance of good works, as part of the (erroneous) view, seeing duality. "Do thou abandon *dharma* and *adharma,* truth and untruth, and that also whereby thou abandonest (such pairs)," Mbh. 12, 332, 44.

the path to God is narrow and sharp "like the edge of a razor."[12] It is only God who is "not contaminated by impurity," as the sun is not contaminated by earthly impurity.[13] Until man becomes God, evil and good are the most real things in his existence.

To the priestly mind, "good works" (such as sacrifice) are not clearly differentiated from good deeds. Sacrifice and good deeds go together as a means of attaining a happy lot hereafter. They that perform such good works "have their reward"; but they are not united with God and may therefore be dismissed as fools in comparison with the higher spiritual souls that seek God only.[14] Yet the activities of a man, even for this reward, must be pure. The controlling Spirit of the world, which is one with the inner soul of all beings, is pure, çubhra. "Assuming the nature of mind, it guides the senses" in pure ways, as far as benighted man will let it do so. It is on realizing this God within that one is emancipated and becomes free from "doubts and from works," which can mean only that the effect of these works (in repeated rebirths) is now done away with.[15] God himself exists

[12] BAU. 4, 4, 5, and Kath. 1, 2, 24; 3, 14. The simile is transferred to Dharma in Mbh. 12, 261, 5, seq., meaning that duty is difficult to know.

[13] Kath. Up. 2, 5, 11.

[14] Mund. Up. 1, 2, 10.

[15] Ibid. 2, 2, 7, seq. Here too Brahma is "that pure (being)," tat çubhram, and can be apprehended only by him "whose nature is purified." Those who find God must be freed from all passions, viçuddha-sattvâ, vîtarâgâs; in finding him they overcome all evil, ibid. 3, 1, 8; 2, 9. It is only when they have found God that men

in a man's body "in his truth and in his virtue." He is both truth and virtue.[16] We must remember, what cannot be repeated too often, that God is never said to be free from good; but always He is "free from all evil." Man in seeking God must from the beginning eschew "foul acts," to avoid foul births; and, as in the beginning, so to the end, for "only when the whole nature is purified are the bonds released which keep the soul from God."[17] "Good deed and evil deed are lost when God is attained; from Him all evil persons turn back, for his world is free from all evil."[18] But this too emphasizes the effect of the deed, which is now lost; as elsewhere it is said that "one shakes off his deeds," on approaching Brahma, and becomes "free of his deeds," good and bad.[19] In God one rests, doing and suffering no more.

In one of the Upanishads, a spiritual teacher is represented as dismissing his student at the end of years of study. As he does so, he gives the young man a general rule of conduct, such as is incumbent on all good Aryans to follow: "Speak the truth; practice virtue; . . . neglect not the sacrifices due to gods and Manes; let thy mother be to thee as a

are free from the torment of thinking "Why did I not do what is good, why did I do what is bad?" In the bliss of God such thoughts no longer trouble one. Taitt. Up. 2, 9. Being that is pure (absolute) must be pure (morally); to become one or be one with God is to be free of all evil, moral and physical.

[16] BAU. 2, 5, 11, seq.
[17] Ch. Up. 5, 10, 7 (kapûya-caranâs); 7, 26, 2 (sattvaçuddhau).
[18] Ibid. 8, 4, 1.
[19] Kaush. 1, 4, visukrito vidushkritas.

divinity, also thy father, thy spiritual teacher, and thy guest; whatever actions are blameless, not others, shouldst thou perform; good deeds, not others, shouldst thou commend; whatsoever thou. givest, give with faith, with graciousness (or richly?), with modesty, with respect, with sympathy."

But how is the student to know what is right? Ordinarily, the customary rule of conduct is a sufficient guide, but in cases of doubt regarding what is best to do concerning oneself or the treatment of others, the young man is to take as authoritative model what is done in similar circumstances by Brahmans "competent to judge, apt and devoted, but not harsh lovers of virtue."[20]

Interesting as is this rule of conduct, with its admonition to be good, its weight laid upon the ancient "rule observed by the gods," to speak the truth, its commendation of modesty and sympathy as adjuncts of true generosity, it is more important because of its tacit admission that up to this time there was no code of ethics supported by authority. The Lord of Creation, as was universally admitted, had uttered certain ethical statements which were of course authoritative; but there was as yet no code or collection presenting a complete codification of morals or customs. The earliest codes are not referred to divine teachers, nor do their authors pretend to be inspired. They know of no general authority on ethics. Thus one of these code-makers, author of a

[20] Taitt. Up. 1, 11.

manual of rules, says: "Right and Wrong do not go about proclaiming 'Here we are,' nor do gods and angels and the Manes say 'This is right and that is wrong'; but right is what the Aryans praise, and wrong is what they blame."[21]

The virtues inculcated by the earlier philosophy are not all those of self-denial and negation. Good deeds are to be practiced, alms and philanthropic work are lauded: "the perfume of a good deed spreads abroad like that of a tree in flower." But it may be admitted that the thought of this period is chiefly concerned with those virtues which tend to quietism. To speak the truth ("One should guard oneself from speaking an untruth as a sword-walker guards himself from falling into the pit") and "always be hospitable" are the chief rules, but the negative virtues occupy a much larger place than do the active virtues. The great advance, however, lies in the substitution of these virtues as a religious practice for the older ideal of self-inflicted pain, *tapas*, as a means of attaining power and holiness. Thus the passage just cited is prefaced by the remark that "all virtues are a kind of austerity," *tapas*: "Uprightness, truth, study of the holy texts, serenity, self-restraint, almsgiving (or liberality), and the performance of sacrifice are all austerity."[22] From

[21] Âpastamba, Dh. S. 1, 20, 6, *seq.: yam Âryâs praçansanti sa dharmo yam garhante so'dharmas.*

[22] Mahânâr. Up. 8 and 9. Taitt. Up. 3, 10, 1. Compare Ch. Up. 3, 17 (above).

what virtues and vices spring, is a question scarcely raised as yet; but it is generally implied that man as a creature of free will[23] determines his own moral state and the aspects or qualities inherent in the various predispositions are analyzed, as follows: "Man is transformed (from what should be his perfect divine state) by qualities of darkness and of passion. Characteristic of the dark quality are delusion, fear, despondency, sleepiness, slothfulness, heedlessness, decay, sorrow, hunger, thirst, wretchedness (or, niggardliness), anger, unbelief, ignorance, jealousy, cruelty, stupidity, shamelessness, meanness, pride, unequableness. Characteristic of the passionate quality are inner thirst (desire), affection, emotion, covetousness, maliciousness, lust, hatred, deceit (or, secretiveness), envy, insatiability, unsteadfastness, fickleness, distractedness, ambitiousness, acquisitiveness, favoritism toward friends, dependence upon surroundings, hatred of the physically unpleasant, overfondness as regards pleasant objects, sour speech, and gluttony. The elemental soul being filled with these is overcome and hence has to undergo different forms (of rebirth)."[24] Out of this confused list it is still possible to see that, although all emotional excess was deprecated and philosophical serenity was the main object of the teaching, there yet remains a

[23] "According to a man's deeds and knowledge" is he reborn (as animal or man); "men of good conduct attain a good birth; those of evil conduct, an evil birth" (as a serf or beast); "the deed is the result of will" (as the will is the effect of desire), BAU. 4, 4, 5.

[24] Mait. Up. 3, 5.

rather complete ethical ideal, one that discountenances, as inimical to the soul's welfare, cowardice, sloth, wrath, jealousy, cruelty, meanness, pride, envy, lust, etc.

The religious aim even at this date was not uniform. The ritualist, the ascetic, the thinker, each had his ideal. Of these, the man who renounced the world sought only freedom for his soul and the seclusion of a hermit for his body. His ethical ideal was to avoid wrongdoing because it injured himself, to attain, through doing his duty to himself, a state of passive isolation of spirit, acquiring the highest by renouncing the lower, and his belief was that the man of wisdom becomes free of all desires which hamper his progress toward complete isolation or toward that supreme flash of intuition which in itself loosens forever all ties and makes him one with Brahma. Yet even this man recognized that moral conduct was the first step in the right direction, that envy, pride, selfishness, and lust were incompatible with virtue. Even in the case of the Yogi, who ventures to make the extreme statement that "sin is destroyed by control of breath,"[25] it must be remembered that what is really meant is that one must begin spiritual training by control of the organs of sense and from an ethical point of view this control starts with suppression of immoral desires, including what is called "love," that is, passion. Thus the ten injunctions of Prajâpati, the Lord of Creation, are, in the case of a

[25] Amritabindu Up. 8.

Yogi, to renounce first of all (love) passion, wrath, greed, confusion, deceit, pride, envy, selfishness, egotism, and untruthfulness; his four cardinal rules are to practice chastity, non-injury, truthfulness, and to be without worldly possessions.[26] It is worth noticing that here and in other Upanishads, from the Chândogya, one of the earliest, to the Kanthaçruti, one of the latest, the moral and religious teacher is this Lord of Creation who is even said at the close of the former treatise to have taught Manu, as Manu in turn taught man; thus paving the way for that divine authority of the code as a whole which is recognized in subsequent literature, when Manu himself becomes a form of Prajâpati.

The early religious seekers after truth taught only after they themselves had purified their souls by the strict observance of all moral rules, which they never thought of abrogating in practice. They denounce license and freedom from ethical restraint. To them good conduct was the first step to salvation. It is no impairment of this fact that as mystic philosophers they held that salvation was more important than anything else and that those who never rose above the conception of performing sacrifice and doing other religious works were spiritually of an inferior class, because they did these works for the inferior reward of attaining not to the highest state but to a lower sphere of delight, in a future "high birth" on

[26] Âruneya Up. 3, *seq.* Other vices are enumerated in the subsequent section, blame of others, hatred, etc., sixteen in all.

earth or in the sensuous heaven of the lower gods. They, the deluded, enjoy their reward, but they are none the less deluded, for they miss the highest. Faith and intuition of truth are better than sacrificial ceremonies; but the ceremonies are good for those who cannot rise to a higher ideal. But in both cases ethical behavior is imperative and the enforcement of moral laws is what gives a king his glory, as is summed up in the description of the king who could say: "In my realm there is neither thief, nor miser, nor drunkard, nor one who is altarless, nor any ignoramus, nor any unchaste (adulterous) man or woman."[27]

It would be arrogant to upbraid these thinkers because they did not reach out to a scheme of social service as part of their ethics and to blame them for not teaching that man's will should be directed in accordance with modern social ideals. They taught that man should harness the restless steeds of the senses and subdue his passions, his evil impulses, all that took him away from God as they conceived Him. The religious and even the practical goal may be decried, as one decries monasticism, but it cannot

[27] Ch. Up. 5, 11, 5. In all these discussions it must be remembered that the Hindu heaven and its rewards are temporary and offer to the spiritual-minded only sensuous pleasures, from which the good but still unenlightened soul is doomed, when its merit is exhausted, to return to earth. The only fate which corresponds to the Christian idea of infinite pure felicity is not "heaven and its rewards," but eternal oneness with God, the goal of the philosophers.

be denied that the spirit inspiring this teaching was pure and essentially ethical. We must admit also that, as in the periods immediately preceding and following, to the strictly orthodox Brahman any sins might be expiated by penance and sacrifice and gifts to the priests. But that was to be expected half a millennium before Christ in any civilization. The great wonder is not that the Hindu knew a magical (sacrificial) means of removing sin, but that he recognized the presence of sin as an impairment of spiritual power and growth and insisted, as he did, that the basis of religion must be morality.

A passage cited above shows that to the early philosophers the root of evil is desire, which determines will, as will in turn determines the act and its "fruit," that is, its consequence in a future life. But as desire may also determine the will in another direction, it is not evil in itself; since good prompted by desire is also possible. The act is caused by the will and the will is caused by desire, or, as the Buddhists were to call it, thirst. As popularly expressed by Manu, "whatsoever one does is an activity of desire," though in another passage the same law-giver derives all vices from greed, both vices of anger and vices of desire, and in still a third passage he regards greed as the manifestation of error (confusion of mind).[28] Much the same explanation of the origin of evil is found in the epic philosophic writers, who speak in terms of religion rather than in those

[28] Manu, 2, 4; 7, 45, 49, and 12, 29, 33.

of philosophy and prefer allegory and mythology to logic. As one of them explains the matter: "The tree of desire in the heart is born of mental confusion, *moha;* ignorance is its root; wrath and pride are its trunk; its vigor of growth comes from acts done in past lives."[29] Here ignorance becomes desire, but what is meant is probably that ignorance or error (confusion) leads to desire, as is said elsewhere that what leads to destruction is error, while truth gives immortality. But a mythological explanation (perhaps only allegorical) relates that "Men were at first virtuous, but the devils, who were opposed to virtue, entered into them and became arrogance (pride), from which sprang wrath and error."[30]

The possibility of error or confusion of mind causing desire (emotion based on mentality) is admitted, because in all these discussions (and the same remark applies to those found in the formal systems of philosophy) the individual is not viewed as a product of one birth but of countless precedent rebirths, and the confusion of mind is the result of these preceding minds, which the individual inherits from his former self. In general, however, while error is predicated as the root of evil, desire is recognized as the origin of all volitional activity. The interrelation of desire and ignorance is discussed several times in the great

29 *Purâdushkritasâravân* . . . *kâmadrumas,* Mbh. 12, 255, 1, *seq.*

30 *Ibid.* 277, 30; 295, 19, *seq.,* and 29. The lesson taught in the last case is that only human beings are conversant with right and wrong, a view incompatible with the developed Karma doctrine.

epic, but the doubtful conclusion seems to be that "desire comes from ignorance and ignorance from desire," though all action is instigated by desire.[31]

The Upanishad philosophers did not admit the influence of fate, except as every man makes his own fate. But, beginning with Manu, who distinguishes between fate and human effort, as deciding factors, the idea of such an overruling power became prominent and had somewhat the same effect that it had on Greek philosophy and religion, weakening the sense of personal responsibility, relaxing morale and morals. The more energetic minds, however, scorned the fatalists as "cowards." But fate was interpreted in several ways, either as something appointed by the gods, or as the inevitable effect of preceding lives, or as personified Time, or as blind Necessity. It was a doctrine which impaired the validity of the Karma theory, except where it was carefully pointed out that the word *daivam* or *dishtam* (divine, appointed fate) really meant the fruit of former acts.[32]

[31] Desire and greed are synonymous terms in these discussions (12, 158, 2, *seq.*, 12; also 167, 30). The tenets of the schools have been explained in an able essay by Mr. Susîl Kumar Maitra, *The Springs of Action in Hindu Ethics* (Poona, 1919). The Vaiçseshikas trace will to desire and aversion, which are referred by the Naiyâyikas to error; while the Sânkhyas maintain that error, greed, and wrath are the three origins of impulse. Experience in former births determines, in the view of the Vedânta, the dispositions, as inclined toward good and evil.

[32] Manu, 7, 205; R. 2, 22-23; Mbh. 12, 239, 4: "Some praise fate and some praise one's own nature." Compare also *ibid.* 32, 16, *seq.:* "Either there is a Lord, who is then responsible, or man has free will, or a man's past lives in the guise of fate determine

But the Karma doctrine suffered also from the conviction that the individual might inherit his disposition not from himself, in a former birth, but from his parents, a survival of the Vedic doctrine of sins inherited "from father and mother." However, these were probably not very important variations as affecting the general belief that man was responsible for his fate,[33] and as the belief in Karma has remained a fixed dogma to this day, it was probably accepted as a whole, with its ethical implications, but without too curious an examination into the logical results, when Karma was confronted with opposing beliefs.

The most important of these was the belief that the World-soul may prompt a man to perform either good or bad actions (above) and that God, as personal divinity, exercises a choice in saving the individual, since salvation depends on "obtaining

man's lot and actions." Fate as mere chance, *yad abhâvi na tad bhâvi,* "what's not-to-be that will not be," is also called *daivam,* and this again is opposed to rigid Necessity, although the last is really personified Luck (*ibid.* 3, 32, 12, *seq.*). The curious discrepancies have been discussed in full in the author's *Epic Mythology,* p. 73, *seq.*

[33] Though Âpastamba says that a son becomes sinful if his parents have sinned, *doshavân putras,* 2, 6, 13, 5, yet it is a startling statement when an epic sage lays down the dogma that "a vicious child is born from vicious parents," *lubdhebhyo jâyate lubdhas* (Mbh. 12, 264, 9). The speaker opposed has the laudable intent to prevent a king from executing a whole family because the father has deserved death for his crimes, and argues that a child is not responsible for its parents' sins and, though born of sinners, may yet be good (*ibid.* 268, 11).

God" and[34] "He is not to be obtained by instruction, nor by intelligence, nor by much learning. He is to be obtained only by the one whom He chooses; to such a one He reveals his own person." The revelation implies knowledge of God, which brings salvation. But although this statement is made more than once in the Upanishads and in fact but echoes the more primitive expression of the Rig Veda, "whom I will I exalt," it is opposed to the general thought of these early philosophers, whose watchword was salvation through knowledge, by which, however, they meant the illuminating knowledge which comes as the reward of a life spent in earnest contemplation and devoted to the highest ethical and spiritual ideals. They had already developed the two lines of procedure which were afterwards to be known as the schools named Pravritti and Nivritti, the "carry-on" way and the "retreat" way. The "retreat" philosopher spent his life more or less as a hermit; but he meant by retreat the withdrawal from active religious life, devotion to one spiritual object, the attainment of the highest goal, by retreat from life and from any hope of rewards in heaven (a sensuous paradise) or in rebirth in a high caste. All these were renounced in favor of a rapt sense of unity with God. The other school accepted the religious life, the duties and obligations of religion and of the world. This philosopher lived in the world, but was not of it. He knew life to be a duty entailed upon him, but

[34] Katha Up. 1, 2, 20, 23, and Mund. 3, 2, 3.

he was not bound by its ties; he was a free soul in an encompassing but not enchaining world. As such he could enjoy pleasures as well as endure pains, but he could take no pleasure in wrongdoing; for to him also, as well as to the advocate of retreat, the spiritual life was based upon a life lived ethically.[35] Enforced restraint of the senses implied that there was virtue in restraint, which tended to the maintenance of righteousness, and it was still felt that this righteousness was based on the Holy Order, as the Vedas say, only now that righteousness was synonymous with God, who is "free from all evil." His existence, as represented by that with which the perfected soul feels itself united, is that Sat which means at once Being and Goodness. Aristotle says in his *Ethics* (Ch. X): "Whatever relates to moral action is petty and unworthy of the gods." Something of this sort is what the philosophers who taught in India three hundred years before Aristotle were trying to ex-

[35] The distinction of aims, if not of schools, was already known in the Upanishads. On the one side is the philosopher who renounces life in the world, BAU. 3, 5, as contaminating, and on the other, Îçâ, 1-2, the one who lives in the world but, while willing to "live long and enjoy the world," does so only while virtually renouncing it; since he understands what is the true relation between soul and the world, and is also "free from desires," really indifferent, knowing that *not action but being bound by action* sullies the soul, *na karma lipyate nare,* which actually means that living an active life in the world is no real impediment to virtue. Dhû Nûn, the Mohammedan mystic, expresses the same idea when he says that the truly religious man looks alike upon praise and blame from the multitude and "forgets the result of work in work; forgets the reward for good conduct in the world to come."

84

press. Our human duties are not to be transferred to God; it is meaningless to speak of Him as doing right and wrong. All life and activity come from Him, if only illusively. Of course, when a man identifies himself with God, he is liable to express himself with what we regard as immoral extravagance or madness, such as the statement that, as one with God, he cannot sin. But, as already explained, this means only that, being one with the universal spirit, the individual spirit exists only in God and whatever God does is sinless. But it means also that the passionate physical and mental individual is not the real man; for this individual of body and (earthly) ratiocination is but the envelope encompassing the person's true, divine self, the soul, as life is but an outward phase of God.

Finally, in our study of Upanishad philosophy we must remember that by no means all the philosophers of this period rested content with an Absolute It, Brahma. All of them, and this is most significant, taught that this neuter Power (for such was always the real meaning of *brahma,* underlying the later meanings of spell and spirit) was synonymous with the (masculine) Soul of the World, and many of them, before the rise of Krishnaism (see below), regarded this All-soul or Âtman as a personal God, of grace and mercy as well as of power. Now this Supreme Spirit, for such we may call the Âtman, is identified with Righteousness (virtue, law, the later equivalent morally of the old Right Order) and whenever described is said to be morally pure, so that there was really a philosophical basis for morality in the moral nature of God. But even the monism based on an impersonal Brahma or un-moral Power, which appealed most to the most philosophic minds of that day and later, conceived of this Power as not immoral and showed that man must be moral (according to earthly tenets) in order to attain divinity. For immoral acts and thoughts were recognized as bonds confining him in his own prison-house. Not only must there be the outward morality of form, but the man's spirit must be purified, "clarified from evil." Austerity no longer trained one solely for physical and psychical command over nature but for the acquisition of godhead, and its base was now ethical behavior. Practically, as everyone admits, the ethics of early Hindu philosophy was the basis of training in education; but logically also this ethics rested on a firm foundation. There was no such superficial distinction as is made with us between "education" and "character" as the goal of learning and life. Education implied character; there was no "knowledge" without its ethical counterpart.[36]

[36] See on this point below, Ch. VII.

CHAPTER V

ETHICS IN THE LEGAL LITERATURE

WE have already seen that the early jurists take as authoritative the practice of good Aryans in matters of doubtful morality and that they dissent from the opinion that unethical conduct can be condoned on the ground of superior sanctity. Rather they hold that the saint must set a good moral example and one of the lawmakers even says that the higher the caste the greater the offence, when a moral rule is broken.[1] But in general the jurists, whose law-manuals were gradually evolved out of books on liturgical and social rules, are too much under the influence of the caste system to ignore the greater turpitude of a low-caste man as compared with that of a high-caste man in the case of the same offence. If a slave violates a high-caste woman, it is a much more serious matter than if her husband violates his wife; if a man of lower caste steals from or slays a man of similar caste, it is much less of a crime than if he robs or slays a priest. Such conditions must be granted; they belong to the ethics of an aristocracy consisting of a small number of whites surrounded by a huge circle

[1] G. 12, 17. Manu, 8, 336, says that a king should be fined a thousand times as much as a common man for the same offence. The epic dictum is even stronger: "Even priests should be punished; the weightier (greater) the men, *gariyânsas,* the weightier should be their punishment," Mbh. 12, 268, 15.

of blacks of inferior mental and moral status, more
or less intermixed with a large class of "poor white
trash," Aryans who, through long association with
the blacks as laborers and toilers at various sorts
of handiwork, were far removed from the wealthy
classes and the real aristocrats, the noblemen and
priests.

The early lawmakers were as far from intending
to set out a code of ethics as were the early philosophers. They were of the priestly caste and their purpose was to codify the rules of domestic and social
customs involving the use of the sacred texts, such
as the services at a wedding or funeral, and to give
a conspectus of life as it should be passed under
priestly direction. From that point they gradually
branched out into the compilation of rules of life and
so came to compose what we call "law books," more
correctly books in regard to Right Usage or Good
Form, which included, as an inconspicuous part, what
a king should do; under which head was later included a body of rules more properly called laws.

It is then only in the occasional remarks of the
lawmakers (to retain this term as a convenience)
that one finds or could expect to find ethical material. The study of ethics for itself appealed neither to
jurist nor to philosopher; like history, it is a subject
incidentally broached but never systematically pursued by the Hindus. Morality, its origin and its expression in various commands and interdictions, was
too much taken for granted to be discussed. The

source of legal power was the king, and in regard to
the origin of kingship there was room for divergent
opinions, which are duly given. According to one, he
expressed the wish of the people, by whom he was
(originally) elected, to avoid confusion and lawless-
ness; according to another, he was appointed by
Brahmâ, invented by divine prescience to keep order
in the State. But in both assumptions the order to be
kept is an expression of ancient divine rules, of the
Right Order of the world, which in the social world
is seen in the due observance of hereditary custom,[2]
in obedience to those promptings of a good nature
which lead to avoidance of strife, of infringement
upon every man's right to happiness undisturbed by
the violence of others, and for one's own sake to the
avoidance of evil thoughts and acts, since such
thoughts and acts cloud with darkness the brightness
of the soul and lead to unhappiness after death.

Custom as received from the venerable fathers and
countenanced by "good Aryan" practice determined
most cases of social procedure. But the lawmakers
are fully aware that the spirit is more vital than the
overt act and not a few of their admonitions are
directed to this point. Assuming that everyone wishes
after death to go to heaven, Baudhâyana takes pains
to say that "to deserve heaven, one must avoid mean-

[2] Usage, *proyoga*, is said to be the expression of sacred rules
the text of which has been lost; it therefore stands next to scripture in authority (Âp. 1, 12, 11). The real lawmaker is not the
king but good usage, voiced by the priest and enforced by the
king.

ness, hardheartedness, and crookedness," and in the same tone Vasishtha gives the admonition: "Neither Veda nor sacrifice nor liberality can save him whose conduct is base, who has departed from the right path. . . . A man of bad conduct is blamed by men; evils constantly befall him; he is afflicted with disease and short is his life."[3] Passing over for the moment the question of retribution raised here, we may consider another exhortation to ethical betterment remarkable for its flat denial of the value of ceremonial purity and formal observance of the law as compared with ethical excellence. It is found in the law-manual of Gautama, perhaps a contemporary of Gautama Buddha, at any rate one of the oldest of the makers of works on Dharma (Right Usage, law). As introduction he has just finished the description of the forty sacred ritual observances which a good man ought to perform; then he adds this warning: "These are the forty sacred observances. And now (I will explain) the eight good qualities of the soul. They are, compassion for all creatures, patience, freedom from discontent, purity, earnest endeavor, auspicious (thought), freedom from avarice (or from a whining disposition), freedom from envy.[4]

[3] Baudh. Dh. S. 2, 2, 4, 25; Vas. 6, 2 and 6.

[4] "Not being wearied," *anâyâsa*, G. 8, 24, is taken by Bühler to mean quietism, but it is rather not being wearied in good endeavor. The epic commentator, 5, 34, 72, a parallel passage, defines it as *acâñcalyam*, steadfastness. "Good work" also cannot be the meaning of *mangalam* (auspiciousness) in this passage, since it is

He that has performed all the sacred observances and has not these good qualities comes not into union with Brahmâ, comes not to his world; but he who has performed only one of these sacred observances and has the good qualities, enters into union with Brahmâ, comes into his world." This is a double-edged attack; it hits at the ritualist on the one hand and at the mystic philosopher on the other. It proclaims very definitely that salvation is a matter of spiritual excellence as exhibited by ethical, not by ritualistic, observances, and it eliminates the mystic intuition of God in favor of compassion, contentment, purity, and a generous, earnest disposition.

There are of course more stringent rules for an ascetic than for an ordinary man, but the lawmakers take account of this. For example, in the passage cited above from Vasishtha, the author goes on to explain that the ascetic should not yield to desires of the flesh, but be indifferent to the world, the flesh, and to other men, "doing neither injury nor favors"; but the path of duty for all the orders, that is, for a man in other than the ascetic stage of life, is as follows: "Avoid jealousy, backbiting, pride, self-consciousness, unbelief, dishonesty, self-praise, blame of others, deceit, covetousness, delusion, anger, and envy." This priestly jurist makes also the following fine ethical appeal: "Practice righteousness, not unrighteousness; speak the truth, not untruth; look far,

a "soul quality." The connection between "whining" and "avarice" is that between miserable and miserly.

not near; look toward the highest, not toward that which is less than the highest."[5]

The meaning of the word righteousness, or ethical Good Usage, Dharma, is supposed to be well understood. It implies in itself a whole code of conduct, to avoid all crimes, murder, adultery, theft, etc., to avoid no less spiritual sins, arrogance, envy, jealousy, for example, and to avoid all injury of other beings. It implies all recognized virtuous conduct, which includes on the social side approved usage in the matter of family customs, caste distinctions, the stages of life to be passed through by all Aryans, in short, the maintenance of the established order. The student, the householder, the hermit, the ascetic, have their own special rules. So when the ascetic is told to be "indifferent to other men" it means that this is the proper attitude for a man who has devoted his remaining years to ascetic observances, living remote from human habitation, devoted to the cult of his own soul. We may not approve of the ascetic's life, but, granted that his is a received mode of living for those spiritually inclined, it is inevitable that such should be his rule; he must not injure others and he must not leave his devotions to perform the acts usually incumbent on the good citizen, such as giving alms and helping others in their mundane affairs.[6]

[5] Vas. Dh. S. 10, 30, and 30, 1.

[6] This is the meaning of *anugraha* in the precept of Vasishtha (above); it is the showing of favors or going out of one's way to help, not (as Bühler renders it) simple "kindness." The same lawmaker says in general, comparing outward and inner forms of

LAW AND ETHICS

On the other hand, to turn to the further extreme of life, that of the young student, he is told that he does wrong if he "looks at dances or goes to assemblies and festivals, or gambles." If he transgresses this rule, "his life is shortened and he goes to hell." He is restricted, as is a Buddhist friar in such matters; though after he has become a householder, when he has finished his years of study and has married, there is no objection to his taking part in innocent amusements. The rules for student life were rather slowly evolved. In the Brâhmana period he was permitted a little more indulgence than later. Some ancient authorities even allowed him to eat honey, but by the time of the lawmakers he was circumscribed in every way and permitted only the luxury of bathing, though some authorities object even to this unless the student has reached adult age. Gambling, stealing, and injury to inanimate objects (plants and trees) are listed as similar moral offences on his part and one old rule seems to condense his duty into the formula: "Let him have black teeth and be dusty and speak the truth." Another bids him speak the truth, bathe, beware of women, and avoid all luxury, self-praise, and blame of others. Perhaps the best exposition of the student's moral rule of life is this: "Let him be humble, modest, upright, forgiving; not gossip or talk too much with women, but be active, self-

benevolence, "compassion is better than giving gifts," *dayâ dânâd viçishyate*, 10, 5.

restrained, free from anger and envy."[7] The student lives in the family of his spiritual teacher, Guru, to whom he acts as valet and general servant, and has to beg food for him and for himself. Whether the housewife, from whom the virtuous student begs, gives him food or not, he comes off best, for in one case he gets his dinner and in the other "he wrings from her her religious merit," transfer of merit being as possible as transfer of sin or disease, a principle paving the way for the redemption theory of later Buddhism, according to which a Savior-god redeems the world by transferring his own unlimited merit to the sinner.

But these rules for students, like those for ascetics, are not for all and it remains to be seen whether the lawmakers assume a similar moral standard for the mass of men. Fortunately they have left to us not only moral precepts for boys and ascetics but rules for all the orders and all the castes. Thus Âpastamba describes the "faults tending to destruction" in a Brahman as "wrath, exultation, grumbling, covetousness, doubt, hypocrisy, injury, *droha*, lying, gluttony, calumny, envy, lust, fury (or 'secret hatred'), lack of self-restraint and of concentration"; but to avoid

[7] Çat. Br. 11, 5, 4, 18; Âp. Dh. S. 1, 1, 3; 1, 5; 1, 7; Gaut. Dh. Çâs. 2, 8, *seq.*, and 17. Vas. 7, 17, with great liberality says, as to bathing, *tris kritvo 'bhyupeyâd apas*, "let him bathe thrice a day." Bathing in hot weather is a debatable luxury to the Buddhist also. Cleansing the teeth (above) was a sort of adornment, hence forbidden; "be dusty" interdicts bathing. For the next rule below see Âp. 1, 1, 3, 26.

these and furthermore "to be generous, self-sacrificing, upright, gentle, calm, kind to all creatures, to do as Aryans do, to be peaceful and contented, leads to salvation."[8] Thus for all the castes the lawgivers insist on virtues of the spirit as well as on outer behavior, so much so that "sins of thought" are punished hereafter as rigidly as sins of mind and body, and this tripartite division of "thought, word, deed" is manifest throughout the legal literature where one would naturally expect the emphasis to be almost entirely on the outer act. It seems, therefore, quite unfair to the Hindus to belittle the weight they laid on the spiritual side and to ignore entirely the "sins of thought." Rules expressly "for all men" are given in the law books in their proper place and include purity, restraint of the senses, generosity, sympathy, and other virtues. To put as command what is reiterated from Gautama to the epic: "Be not envious, be upright, pure, contented; speak kindly to all, be self-restrained, speak the truth; be earnest."[9]

In distinction from the student, adult Aryan citizens might attend all such gambling-halls and music-halls as were under royal supervision in the king's establishments for gaming; but for anyone to be

[8] Âp. 1, 8, 23, 3, *seq.* Âryavam is a made-up word meaning to act in an Aryan manner, that is, nobly, like a gentleman; the ethnical designation becomes ethical, as in Buddhism and in the epic the word *ârya* means noble, applied to acts or persons.

[9] Manu, 10, 63; Yâj. 1, 122, and 3, 66; Compare M. 4, 175: "delight in the truth, in virtue, in conduct worthy of an Aryan, and in purity."

"addicted to gambling" was a sin. Later moralists would permit no gambling at all. In regard to a king, it was admitted that he was prone to vices, especially hunting, drinking, women, and gambling; but they are condemned only when indulged in too freely; he might practice them "with discretion," *yuktyâ*, but "addiction to them is culpable."[10]

The king, it is said, should banish from the realm all gamblers, rumsellers, players, and infidels; but this was a counsel of perfection and, as to the infidel, Vasishtha merely remarks with the simple severity of Jowett that "an infidel shall perform a penance for twelve days and renounce his infidelity." From the legal point of view, infidelity is a "sub-sin," *upapâtaka*, though to the sub-sinner himself it is a grave matter, since "to deny the authority of the Vedas and carp at the teaching of the saints is to destroy one's soul," *nâçanam âtmanas*. Baudhâyana says, however, that "want of faith is the greatest sin," and the infidel, *nâstika*, is often paired with moral sinners[11] as a danger to the state, as in the general

[10] Âp. 2, 25, 13, *seq.;* Vi. 71, 45; Mbh. 12, 140, 26 (*prasango doshavân*). The rule as to gaming in royal establishments is abrogated at festivals. Such places are watched over by the police, to detect thieves. Yâj. 2, 201, *seq.*

[11] Vas. 1, 23; 12, 41; 21, 29; Baudh. 1, 5, 10, 6; Manu, 9, 225. Gautama says that one must not give food to an infidel, who, says Vishnu, must, as a penance for his infidelity, live upon alms for a year (G. 15, 16; Vi. 54, 15). Manu and Vishnu also rank this "crime" as a sub-sin (M. 11, 67; Vi. 37, 31) as compared with the most flagrant cases of incest or such "great sins" as killing a priest, drinking intoxicants, stealing a priest's wife or gold; or with

admonition of Manu: "Avoid unbelief, cavilling at the Vedas, reviling of gods, hatred, immodesty, pride, wrath, and cruelty," where one scholiast defines unbelief as lack of belief in Vedic authority and another as doubt in regard to the next world.[12]

Despite the absence of systematic discussion, the Hindus, having the same problems to meet as are found elsewhere, are forced now and then to evaluate the legal rules laid down as general proprositions. One of these concerns that oldest moral rule handed down from the gods to man, as to speaking the truth. Is it always sinful to tell a lie? The epic gives instances in which it is proved that to speak the truth is to do wrong; if a saint be pursued by murderers and they ask a wayfarer whether he has seen the saint, he should mislead them, should tell a lie; the greater sin would be to betray the saint, etc. At the same time the epic exalts truth-speaking in general and gives eminent cases showing that a certain extra divine power goes out of a king who does not speak the truth, whereas a royal speaker of the truth is so

similar crimes, such as killing a friend and certain specified cases of adultery, which are ranked as equal to the former class, but are put into a separate category. The word *nâstika* (above) is often mistranslated "atheist," but it means one who denies (*na-asti=non est*) either the traditional authority of the Vedas (Manu, 2, 11; Mbh. 12, 270, 67) or, according to later scholiasts (*e.g.* to Vas. 6, 23), God and immortality. A *nâstika* is in general an unbeliever, one who shows incredulity, for example, in regard to the efficaciousness of works (M. 3, 65).

[12] Manu, 4, 163 (with Medhâtithi and Nârâyana, followed by Kullûka, as interpreters).

elevated by his virtue that his chariot will glide above the earth, but when he tells a lie it sinks into the ground; or, to take another case, a king noted as "truthful in word and deed," *satyavâdin satyaçîlin,* can drive over the water without sinking in, "a miracle unlike other men," though, as a matter of fact, almost the same tale is told of a third king, for whom "when he was about to walk upon the sea the water became solid."[13]

Venial untruths, however, are permitted by the lawmakers, especially when a lie will save a man's life, an innocent example of which has just been cited. This laxity has of course a danger in inducing witnesses to swear falsely; but this in turn is guarded against by the most solemn invocation of gods as "witnesses of witnesses," while as witness a man has to imprecate injury upon himself or stand an ordeal by oath.[14] Âpastamba says plainly that every perjurer goes to hell; but Gautama and Manu permit perjury to save life, though having sworn falsely one must purify oneself by an oblation to the deity of Speech or of Truth (Sarasvatî or Agni). Untruth to save priests or (sacred) cows, at weddings and in

[13] The car of Yudhishthira and the tales of Dilîpa and Prithu Vainya (Mbh. 7, 61, 9; 69, 9). The king is divine anyway as being composed of the divine natures of gods, but that does not usually result in his skimming above, instead of on, the surface of earth and water.

[14] The oath is practically an ordeal when one "swears by his head" or "by his cattle," since the perjurer will be mulcted by the gods in that amount.

love-affairs, in jest, under duress, and in anger is declared by most authorities to be venial.[15]

The wide generalization made from this principle is that truth in the abstract is not so important as "beneficial" lying. It is one of the cases where "duty depends on circumstances,"[16] a thesis which leads first to the mild assertion of the old moralist that "one should say what is true and what is agreeable, but not say disagreeable truths nor agreeable lies" (that is, because they are, respectively, true or agreeable), or, as the epic has it: "Speak if you must, though silence is better than speech; but speak only the truth; yet speak if you can only that which is pleasant."[17] But this again leads, beyond the general recognition of venial untruths as beneficial, to the sweeping anticipation of modern thought: "Speak what is beneficial rather than what is true (if you have to choose between them); in my opinion, truth

[15] Âp. 2, 11, 29, 9; G. 13, 24; Vi. 8, 15; also G. 5, 24; 23, 29, adosham eke. A lie is virtuous if spoken virtuously (with virtuous intent); but it is not virtuous to lie to save the life of a "very wicked man" (compare G. 13, 25, and Manu, 8, 103, seq.). For the rule in Greece, see Soph. Phil. 108, seq.

[16] Mbh. 12, 36, 11: "There are occasions where theft, lying, and injury are virtuous, for virtue (duty) is according to circumstances," dharmo hy âvasthikas smritas (âdânam anritam hinsâ are mentioned exempli gratiâ). Case of venial lies, to save a woman, in jest, etc., and theft (to save a life) are noticed in Mbh. 12, 34, 23, seq.

[17] Manu, 4, 138; Mbh. 5, 36, 12 (compare ÇB. 2, 2, 2, 20, "silence is better than speech"). This is also a Buddhistic rule, to "speak what is right, what is pleasing, what is true" (Subhâsita-sutta).

means what is of the greatest benefit to (all) living beings."[18] This dictum is not made universal; it is confined to the use of language. On the other hand, the idea of the greatest good is found practically in a concrete case, where a hero in the epic war says that the *bhûyo hitam* or "more beneficial" is the only thing to be considered, meaning thereby what is likely to be of most benefit to the majority of the fighters. The two together come close to asserting that the greatest good of the greatest number determines as a general principle what ought to be done. Most moderns will agree that lying or stealing to save life is not a great sin; but a word more may be said in regard to venial lies "at weddings," etc. These are not the oaths taken by the groom and bride, for they are married most solemnly under Vedic texts and with promises of mutual fidelity, for breaking which the code-makers curtly say they will go to hell. Marriage-lies are those told in match-making and are like the innocuous "lies in jest" and "love-lies," when antics are played verbally or bodily, innuendoes and deceptive tricks making part of the sport. Marriage-lies might also include the "sale" of the daughter, which by the later code-makers is ethically tabooed (see below).

[18] Mbh. 12, 330, 13: *satyâd api hitam vadet,* "speak rather the beneficial than the true" (the old rule), but my individual opinion, *matam mama,* is that the true means *bhûtahitam atyantam,* "extremest benefit to (all) living beings." That is, one must not lie for the "benefit" of oneself, for example, but for "benefit" taken in a wide sense.

The rule as to not speaking the truth was probably first defended in cases where one saved one's own life by a lie and then sought moral grounds for it in the righteousness of self-defence. This at any rate is the historical course of the theory of killing in self-defence, another venial sin, which, by leaps and bounds, included at last legal permission to kill any man who was caught in robbery or even in injuring verbally another who might thereby become endangered in life or limb; as when one brought before a king a false accusation liable to cause the death or mutilation of the accused. The man thus endangered had then a legal right to slay the would-be accuser. The origin and growth of the theory are interesting. As we say "draw on a man," meaning draw a revolver, so the Hindu said "stretch on" (or against) a man, meaning stretch the bow, so that the word *â-tatâyin,* "on-stretcher" (the same root as appears in τείνω, tendo), or "he that has a bow stretched against another," becomes a general word for one who makes an unprovoked assault. The theory of "righteous slaying" (of others, suicide was in a separate category; see below), as against the general rule not to kill or harm others, was then elaborated as follows. In the first place, the warrior in battle was fulfilling his duty in fighting for his king, to help him protect the people; hence to kill was for him not only venial but imperative. But the lawmakers, as far as priests could, endeavored to restrict even this example of obviously righteous slaughter by prescribing the cases in which a warrior might legitimately kill his foes. All non-combatants were exempt. Even when they stood in the ranks of the enemy, if they were not actually fighting it was forbidden to kill them. The same immunity applied to those who threw away their arms and begged for mercy. To kill them was murder, not righteous warfare, and the only king who can go to Indra's heaven is the one who can truthfully say that he has "extirpated from his kingdom all thieves, adulterers, calumniators, robbers, and murderers." Hence the king himself in battle must see to it that no murder is committed during warfare. The old rule given by Gautama starts with the statement, "it is no sin to kill in battle," but there follows immediately a list of those whom even in battle one must not kill, suppliants, fugitives, unarmed men, and those who eat grass or behave like priests. Historic instances are known of kings saving their lives in battle in this Nebuchadnezzar manner, so the lawgivers' rule can scarcely be a figment. The second case where killing is not sinful is that of the *âtatâyin,* originally meaning one who assaults with intent to kill and then gradually including any "attacker," even one who raises the hand to curse, or recites a magically dangerous spell against another, or a poisoner, or one who robs another (of land or wife or goods), or an incendiary, or one who unjustly accuses another before the king. Any one of these may be "right-eously slain"[19] by the intended victim.

According to Vasishtha, even the murder of a learned priest is not so great a sin (crime) as is usury, by which he means "selling at a high price what a man has bought at a low price"; but all such declarations must be estimated according to their rhetorical value. The author is here not giving his own view but is citing an old verse, which says that the god Brahmâ once weighed in his balance these two crimes and "the slayer of a priest remained up and the usurer sank down" (was the weightier sin-ner). Baudhâyana quotes the same old verse; but neither lawgiver means more than that usury is a sinful practice, permitted only to a man of the third estate under severe restrictions. Manu even says that a "liberal usurer" was praised by the Lord of Crea-tion above a niggardly priest.[20]

The ethics of royalty, which has much to do with killing, is in a class by itself. Not that the king is exempt from the ordinary rules of morality, but he has special privileges or indulgences, which though entailing recognized faults are pardonable in him if

[19] Vi. 5, 188, *seq.*, 196. Compare Manu, 8, 349, *seq.*, *ghnan dharmena na dushyati*, "who kills in a just cause does no wrong"; also Baudh. 1, 18, 13; Âp. 1, 29, 7; Vas. 3, 15, *seq.*, *na . . . kilbisham*, and G. 10, 17, *na dosho hinsâyâm âhave* (translated above). Vishnu, *loc. cit.*, says that the name *âtatâyin* is given also to those who destroy (works of) religious merit (such as sacred pools) or property of any sort.

[20] Vas. 2, 42; Baudh. 1, 5, 10, 23; Manu, 4, 225; 10, 73.

not carried to excess, such as those named above, gaming, hunting, drinking, and "women." Probably his divine character put him in a class apart. The prime duty of the king, protection, morally forces him to wage war when necessary. There is no higher duty for a military man than to fall on the field of battle;[21] it redeems him of all sins. But at the same time the king, who is the head of the military caste, must observe certain rules, such as those just mentioned in regard to fair fighting, and both in planning a campaign and as a victor after it is over he must be careful not to exceed the laws of right behavior. For example, he must not, as a victor, destroy fine architecture built by former kings, nor extirpate the family of the defeated king, but invest a prince of that family, if not of ignoble descent, with the royal dignity; he must not, as a fighter, permit the use of poisoned arrows or of concealed weapons, nor slay a man asleep, a eunuch, a suppliant, or one already fighting with another, or a fugitive, for then "the slayer incurs the sin of the fugitive slain by him." He should employ "crooked intelligence"[22] or bad magic only as an antidote to such a weapon and not employ guile except when forced to do so by the use of deceit on the part of an opponent. In general, the king sins unless he acts in a chivalrous manner toward his foes, as he sins unless he acts in a fatherly manner toward his subjects, exempting all priests

[21] A soldier must not die in a house. Mbh. 12, 97, 25.
[22] Mbh. 12, 100, 5, *vakrâ prajñā*, that is, deceit.

and women from taxation and taking his tax of a sixth (in grain, or tenth, on merchandise) without burdening the people; but "he must not be too kind; he must not cut off his own root; he must tax (on occasion) as necessary." Sometimes it is necessary to tax heavily in order to protect his subjects; but he must not tax too heavily, "the cow must not be milked too much." On the other hand, if the king absolutely must have more money, let him get it somehow, "hiding the shame of sin under the skirt of prosperity."[23] The confiscation of property of the irreligious is permitted if the king needs wealth and this includes the wealth of priests who have taken up other than priestly occupations, *vikarmasthâs*.[24]

[23] The epic rules are in brief that "it is right to deceive a deceiver" (12, 109); that a king in need may extort money from his people, promising to pay it back later (130, 36); that he may rob heretics (136, 2); that, as he gets a tax of a sixth, so he receives moral demerit if he fails to earn his tax by not protecting his people and wins moral credit by protecting properly, both in courts of law and in battle. "In a failure of justice the sin falls on the king," is the older rule, but later this sin is divided between king, judges, witnesses, and criminal, which leaves a quarter for the king. This fraction was then applied also to the sin he receives for not protecting his people in war; but some authorities make the sin (demerit) a half or, like the tax, a sixth. G. 13, 11; Âp. 2, 28, 13; M. 8, 18, 304, 308; Vas. 1, 44, and 19, 46; Yâj. 1, 336; Mbh. 12, 24, 12; 75, 7, *seq.*

[24] Mbh. 12, 76, 10. The taxes were in general paid by the third estate, as "priests pay taxes by holy works," while soldiers were supported by the king and usually had nothing to tax, and slaves paid taxes by enforced labor. See for the rules above, Manu, 7; Vishnu, 3; and epic passages cited in the author's *Ruling Caste*. The property of the unethical, as well as of the irreligious, may be confiscated, Mbh. 12, 69, 26. Warriors must practice "good

There are separate rules "in case of need," according to which a king must be hypocritical and wait for vengeance, when he must crush his enemy in any way he can, destroying houses, spoiling roads, ruining his foe as best he may, after corrupting his foe's agents. "Peace is the best thing," but, to get peace, one must not shirk war, and engaging in war one must not ignore any means to obtain victory. Ethical rules of battle must occasionally give way to necessity. For the individual soldier, "to die of disease in a house is a sin," "not to kill his foe is a sin," and for the king in general, "his maintenance of right is dependent on his might" and "might secures right."[25] The rules of polity and the rules of government laid down by Kautilya are in agreement with the sentiments here expressed. To Kautilya, any course which saves the kingdom is righteous; but his desire is to have the king abide as far as possible by the rules of ordinary morality. Only, in the case of the king, the preservation of the State is his highest duty, which ensures him his eternal reward, as in the case of the ordinary warrior it is said: "Sweet it is to die in battle; the path to heaven lies in fighting." But even

conduct"; their pain in battle is their penance and expiates their sins; but there is no expiation for deserters, Mbh. 12, 23, 11; 97, 13, *seq.*, and 21, *seq.*

[25] "Righteousness depends on power"; but "it is wrong to say that right is the will of the strong," Mbh. 12, 134, 3, *seq.* Here the corollary that might makes right is combated; might is necessary to uphold right; but only one in despair would say that might makes right.

the so-called Machiavelli of India, Kautilya, who is no formal teacher of ethics, says that righteous conduct should always be encouraged by a king.[26]

Some ethical-religious "royal rules" in the epic, which is contemporary with the metrical law books but does not in many cases reflect so brahmanized a point of view, may be worth noticing. It is felt that the king owes a debt of gratitude to the soldiers who have helped with their lives to carry on his campaigns and he "frees himself from his debt" to them by public works erected at the royal expense, such as the building of rest-houses, *sabhâs,* or halls, public watering-places, and "tanks," *tatâkâni,* artificial pools, etc. He must also provide pensions for the widows of those slain and see that their children are provided for.[27] A religious glamour hangs over the king's person as being not only representative of the old gods but as being also a part of Vishnu (when Vishnu was a form of the All-soul). "Gods and kings, *naradevâs,* are alike" and "every king is a part of

[26] See for the epic Mbh. 2, 69, 15; 5, 34, 18; 12, 133, 7, and, for Kautilya, the essay of Dr. Kâlidâs Nâg, *Les Théories diplomatiques de l'Inde ancienne* (Paris, 1923). Moral rules are mnemonically listed for the king, so that he may easily remember them. Besides the usual "three gates to hell" (desire, wrath, greed), there are six faults to be avoided (including laziness and procrastination already reprobated in the Brâhmanas), and eighteen "royal vices" (of lust and anger), including harshness of speech and of punishment, as well as misuse of wealth. The king is admonished that "the intoxication of power is worse than the intoxication of drink." See Manu, 7, 45, *seq.;* Mbh. 5, 33, 66-91.

[27] Mbh. 12, 42, 7, *seq.,* and the items in the work referred to above, p. 105, note 24.

Vishnu" are enough to illustrate this point.[28] He, the king, is especially Dharma (as god) incarnate and his "rod of punishment" is the representative on earth of the rod of punishment carried by Dharma or by Yama (the god of hell). His merit and hope of heaven are in accordance with his personal behavior, however, and, as explained above, the royal tax is not only in kind, material, but also spiritual.[29] His obligation to punish sinners and criminals is part of his obligation to "protect his people," for "through fear of the king's rod" sinners cease to sin, as well as through "fear of hell," which, as is generally admitted, is the reason people avoid to sin.[30] Finally, in his case also, it is better to "do wrong to gain a good end" than to let the good lapse through fear of doing wrong.[31]

To return to the ordinary citizen and his morals, a good instance of the adaptation of formal ethics to usage may be seen in the gradual change regarding the propriety of selling a child. The development takes a course easy to predict. The practice of such a sale was supported by established custom. Vasishtha accordingly expressly grants to the parents the

[28] See, for example, Mbh. 12, 59, 128-144.

[29] Mbh. 12, 68, 41, seq.; 72, 25; 75, 7, seq.

[30] *Ibid.* 12, 15, 5, seq. "Only the gods who kill are revered" (*ibid.* 18).

[31] The application is to royal slaughter in battle. It is wrong to kill, but it is better to kill in war than suffer wrong to thrive. "One kills (insects) even in drinking water, but it is better to do so than die of thirst." Mbh. 12, 15, 15, and 25-49.

right to give, sell, or abandon a son.[32] But Âpastamba, citing the proverbial saying as to the fallacy
of thinking that men of this debased age may follow
the example of their illustrious ancestors, says as
distinctly in his later code that "gift of offspring and
the right to sell offspring is not admitted."[33] The
next stage is seen when Manu, in a succeeding generation, fails even to discuss the moral right of selling children, but says in regard to the father accepting a wedding gift from the son-in-law that this must
not be done, because even a trifle accepted in this
manner would result in the father becoming an "off-
spring-seller," which by this time was obviously a
term of reproach.[34] The question of the marriage-
portion is legal rather than moral and too involved
to be discussed here; but it is plain, since selling a
daughter to a suitor was well known, though more
and more deprecated, that the sale of children, male
and female, was originally considered right; then
the sale, except of a girl in marriage, was regarded
as immoral; and finally even the marriage-sale had
to be disguised as a gift, but was then looked upon
with good warrant as a "secret sale" and was hence
considered unethical. But an indignant father in the

[32] Vas. 15, 2: *pradâna-nikraya-tyâgeshu prabhavatas,* "the two
(parents) are competent to give, sell, or abandon (their offspring)."

[33] He does not refer to abandonment: *dânam krayadharmaç ca
na vidyate,* 2, 6, 13, 11.

[34] Manu, 3, 51, and 9, 98 (even a slave would not sell his
daughter). In the epic, one who sells his son or gives his daughter
in marriage for a price "goes to hell" (Mbh. 13, 45, 18, *seq.*).

epic says, when reproached for selling his daughter in this way, "It is our family-custom and therefore right for me"; so it was probably a long time before the community at large recognized the sale of a daughter as sinful. Thus general usage becomes modified in response to a developing moral sense; then the expression of this feeling appears tentatively in ethical discussions; and finally ethics triumphs and bans the old usage on the ground of "righteousness."

It would be impossible and not particularly advantageous to discuss the sundry sins listed as such in the law books. Only two points need to be noticed here. First, the old Brahmanic rule, which says that "there is no sin in a new-born babe" (PB.), is extended in the law books, which agree in general that there is no ceremonial impurity in young children, some say till the initiation (into the caste). The rule may mean that there is license of behavior till that age.[35] On the other hand, the same rule is contradicted by the assumption that a child inherits sin, that is, is born sinful, because of parental sin, a theory that is approved from the Rig Veda onward. The theory of rebirth also assumes that one is born with certain predispositions toward vice or virtue; one is naturally good or bad, but more naturally bad, because if one were especially good one would not be born as a human being but become a god or at least a god on earth (a king or priest); but not ex-

[35] G. 2, 1; Âp. 2, 15, 23.

cessively bad, or one would have been born as an animal.[36] This theory also is too involved for full discussion, but such are the main facts as regards the ethical character of the infant.

The second point is that even in the case of adults, despite the minute rules in regard to the sinfulness of this or that breach of convention, there is little scrupulosity when the matter is one of pure convention and not of inherent wrongdoing. Here, as in war, a certain sturdy common sense shows itself, from the recalcitrant saint of the Brâhmana, who declared that he would eat beef if he chose, to the epic saint who, when starving, satisfied his hunger with dog's meat received from an impure low-caste man. "A saint can eat anything," he says, "and when a man is as hungry as I am, one kind of meat is as good as another." The general sensible rule enunciated here is that "it is not a serious matter, *na tad garîyas,* if one eats unclean food, provided one does not tell a lie about it."[37]

[36] The Jains say, if a man is more good than bad he becomes a god; if good and bad are even, a man; if his evil predominates, he is reborn a beast. See Mbh. 12, 298, 27; M. 12, 20.

[37] Mbh. 12, 141, 75 and 88. In Vedic belief, "meat is the best food" (ÇB. 11, 7, 1, 3). Killing an ox for a guest and eating meat as a religious rite was Vedic law and divinely moral (*ibid.* 3, 4, 1, 2). But as eating meat implies injury and death of a living creature, it becomes gradually unethical to do so. "There is no positive sin, *dosha,* in eating meat and in drinking intoxicants; but to refrain from them is productive of future happiness." Manu, 5, 48, 56; Vas. 4, 7. Later, all "injury to living beings" becomes a heinous sin (see below).

One other question arose in legal circles which cannot be disregarded here, although on the surface it affects only the efficacy of penance, which has more to do with religion than with ethics. But it has a bearing on the moral question of punishment for sin. In ancient times punishment for crime was inflicted by divine judgment or directly by the king or through the penance imposed by the priest. Gods punished by disease, violence, or ordeals; a thief was slain by the king in person, or impaled, or thrown over a cliff,[38] or mutilated by officers; or so severe a penance was imposed by the priest as to imply death. Then came the theory of punishment after death, a man being sent to hell for his misdeeds and then reborn on earth according to his crime. This raised the question whether a man ought to be penalized (by a severe penance) if he was to be punished anyway in the next life. Now Gautama says that some legal authorities (it was a debatable point in his day) declare that a man shall perform no penance at all, "because the act does not perish," that is, because the expiation for his act will be enforced hereafter. But he himself is of the opinion that penances should

[38] These punishments are well known in the Jâtakas, 444, 472, 546. The epic also tells of a thief impaled, Mbh. 1, 107. The king in Manu's code is supposed to kill a thief with his own hand and this is implied in the epic, where it is said that, if a thief repents and promises to reform, the king should not kill him but "hit him with a very little blow," 12, 268, 12. The form must be gone through with, otherwise the king himself is implicated in the guilt of the thief (see above, p. 105, note 23).

be performed and that such penances are "redemp-
tive," *nishkrayanâni.* Manu, on the other hand,
agrees with Vasishtha, making a distinction between
intentional and unintentional sins, and asserts that
some (still a debatable point) regard penance as
only for unintentional sins, while others, "having in
mind scriptural injunctions," insist that penance
should be performed for all sins. One of the epic
writers declares that "intentional sin is punished
hereafter; only unintentional sin can be expiated by
penance," and gives this judgment as "the view of
those who know the Veda and the law books"; but
another, dissenting from this, says, "all acts, good
or bad, performed intentionally or unintentionally,
bear fruit hereafter," that is, all acts are rewarded
or punished in the next life.[39] There seems to be here
an amalgamation of earlier priestly jurisprudence
with later legal practice. Originally, the "penance"
was inflicted by the king at the priest's behest; it
often entailed death according to the codes. According to Gautama's opinion, there would be no less
than five punishments for the same offence: penance,
followed by social contempt and ostracism; heaven-
sent calamity during life; hell after death; and rebirth in some low form after hell. For Gautama and
others agree that a sinner may be punished by divine
act while still alive and then be punished again after

[39] G. 19, 3, *seq.*, and 11; Vas. 20, 1; Manu, 11, 45; Mbh. 12,
292, 6, 12-14, but *ibid.* 152, 34, unintentional sins are made good
by afterwards (intentionally) doing good works, *punyâni.*

death (which is almost Buddhistic belief). But though the priests had regulated penances so that the various codes are fairly uniform in this regard, they wavered a bit as to the eschatological result. For example, Vasishtha says that a man who does not eat flesh when he ought (to show respect to gods or Manes at a sacrifice) will "go to hell for as many years as the sacrificial victim has hairs"; while Manu says that this same sinner will "become a beast during twenty-one successive births."[40]

To the Brahman and Buddhist, but not to the Jain, the guilt of an unintentional homicide is less than that of an intentional murderer; but both must reap the fruit of their sin, and, further, not only the perpetrator of a crime but also the instigator and assistant will all share in the future punishment. After long punishment in the next world a thief or murderer is reborn in a low caste; as a virtuous man of any caste will have unlimited, *aparimitam,* bliss (in heaven) and afterwards be reborn to enjoy on earth high birth, beauty, strength, intelligence, and wealth. Only human birth is recognized here as the fate of a man reborn and this is often the case.[41] Malformed and sickly persons are supposed to be

[40] Vas. 11, 34; Manu, 5, 35.

[41] Âp. 1, 29, 2; 2, 29, 1; and 2, 2, 2; 2, 11, 10, *seq.* The punishment in kind for ordinary murder is not usually exacted by the victim's family, as they (or later the king or priests) receive compensation instead (one hundred cows and a bull). The penalty for killing a priest is a "penance" equivalent to a death-sentence by suicide. See Âp. 1, 24, 1; Baudh. 1, 10, 19, 1; M. 11, 128.

expiating slight sins of this or of a former birth. Or a great sin expiated by death leaves this trace. The fear of rebirth as an animal is not very pronounced either in early Brahmanic or Buddhistic works; it is the result of a schedule drawn up by priests. One really expects low or high birth as a man, if at all, not as a beast, and the certainty of hell as punishment is more general than that of rebirth in any form. At any rate, the early lawmakers prefer hell as a deterrent, though even in regard to hell there is a certain caution in their statements. The punishment threatened for perjury in the official proclamation of the king is "going to hell" (this has some weight as a received formula in various codes). Gautama, however, is not always certain of the punishment. He says of those who commit great crimes only that they who commit them will be ostracized on earth and "after death they will be deprived of happiness," adding, "some call this hell."[42]

One very pleasing modification of the law of punishment after death is found in the law book of Baudhâyana, the author who establishes the doc-

---

[42] G. 13, 7; 21, 6 (*asiddhis, tam eke narakam*); Vas. 16, 33, *seq.;* Manu, 8, 94; Vishnu, 8, 25. Âp. 2, 29, 9: "The king shall punish him (the perjurer) and hell shall be his portion." As examples of apropos physical punishment, Vishnu (45, 11) says that if a man has dyspepsia it shows that in a former birth he stole food, a dumb man cursed a priest, an epileptic was a usurer, a blind man stole a lamp, etc. But it is a sin to mock such unfortunates (71, 2). Such people are to be avoided as real sinners at a religious rite, Manu, 3, 159-161, not because of a "magical motive," as Dr. McKenzie suggests (*Hindu Ethics*, p. 52).

trine that sundry sins in the South are not sins in the North because they are usage in the North.[43] It is found in the statement that if a man sins in youth and lives righteously in later life he will not be punished hereafter for the sins of his youth but will be rewarded for his later good deeds; but "let him sorrow in his heart because of his old sins, practicing austerities, and be careful to sin no more." Repentance is always presupposed when one undertakes austerities to offset sins; but that it has the effect, in conjuncture with austerities, of effacing the sins of youth is taught only here. It may be added that the whole system of imposition of penances for sins implies confession of sin. As early as the Brâhmana period it is said that confession "makes right what is not right," a sort of play on the word right as truth; the wrong (untrue) is made true (right) by a truthful confession (of adultery, on the part of a woman). Vasishtha says, "A sin openly proclaimed becomes smaller," *kanîyo bhavati*.[44]

The ethical advice of the lawgivers is intended, with certain restrictions, for all good Aryans, though many of the more spiritual admonitions are meant

[43] These sins are rather doubtful practices than sins, such as a priest acting as a soldier, but they are dubbed "sins" when practiced in the South, Baudh. 1, 1, 2, 5; for the quotation above, see *ibid.* 1, 5, 10, 32. The author is one of those who insists that "gods are without sin," 1, 6, 13, 2.

[44] ÇB. 2, 5, 2, 20; Vas. 20, 29. So, according to Manu, 11, 228, "The sinner is freed from sin by confession, repentance, austerity (paying the penalty by 'penance'), reciting the Veda, or, in case this means is impossible, by liberality."

for the members of the priestly caste. That caste has been greatly blamed by the Buddhists and by some Europeans for its greed and selfishness. Doubtless no great body of priests is without representatives who are no honor to it; yet the generosity to the priests extolled by the priest must be considered in its proper setting. It is true that the Hindu priests were insatiable beggars; but, in the first place, the livelihood of the priests depended upon the liberality of royal and noble patrons and even, in the case of village priests, on the hospitable generosity of their neighbors. They did not live in monasteries like the Buddhists; they did not draw salaries like Christians. All they had to live on was what was given them; they were not permitted to earn a living by worldly means. No wonder they are always rather profuse in praising "gifts." But, as is sometimes forgotten, in the second place, generosity when lauded as a virtue applies to the priest himself, as well as to others. Here, for example, is Vasishtha's definition of a true Brahman priest: "Now the mark of a true priest is this, that he be devout, austere, self-controlled, *generous,* truthful, pure, compassionate, learned, and intelligent, and believe" (in God and immortality).[45] Similarly, Vishnu's list of "common virtues," that is, universal virtues applying to the priest as well as to others, includes generosity together with patience, veracity, purity, sympathy

[45] Vas. Dh. S. 6, 23. (See above, p. 97, end of note 11.)

with the afflicted, self-control, and other laudable qualities.[46]

The Ten Commandments of Manu enjoin upon all the orders of Aryans contentment, patience, self-control, honesty (not stealing), purity, restraint of the organs of sense, devotion, knowledge (of the sacred texts), veracity, and freedom from anger. These rules have been reduced "for all men" to a group of five, "non-injury, veracity, not stealing, purity, and restraint of the senses." Manu's later follower, Yâjñavaïkya, fills out this group, as implying universal injunctions, with the addition, "generosity, self-control, sympathy, and patience"; but the ten injunctions or commandments are also found in his work in a slightly different form: (One should practice) "veracity, honesty, freedom from anger, modesty, purity, devotion, contentment, self-control, restraint of organs, and knowledge." Finally, Manu, in a passage imitated from Buddhistic works, classifies the sins he enumerates under three heads: "Covetousness, thinking of wrong things, adherence to false doctrines are the three mental sins; abuse, lying, detraction, and idle chatter are the four vocal sins; theft, killing (injury), and adultery are the three bodily sins." Each class of sins entails its corresponding punishment in the next birth, bodily sins, being the grossest, bringing rebirth in vegetable form (plant or tree); vocal sins being productive of rebirth as bird or beast; and rebirth in a low human

[46] Vi. 2, 16.

form being the consequence of sinful mental activity. But in some individuals the fruit of acts is produced here on earth before death; in some, after death; in some, both here and in the next world; it all depends on how bad the acts are.[47] One theory is that the "fruit of an act" ripens in the next birth at an age corresponding to that in which it was performed, whether childhood, youth, or age. But these modifications of the Karma doctrine often appear as the result of a desire to systematize a general rough outline of moral teaching, without regard to similar systematic presentations of a contradictory nature. For example, also according to Manu, some bodily sinners of the worst sort go to hell for many years and are then reborn as an animal, bird, insect, or worm, etc., while other "bodily" sinners become animals or vegetables.

The ethical rules of the Brahmans as enunciated in the law books are in great part Buddhistic also. Thus the theory just explained has its Buddhistic parallel: "Some people go to a new birth on earth; sinners go to hell; the righteous go to heaven; those free of desire go to Nirvâna." Not to kill, steal, or be sensual; not to lie, nor speak harshly or maliciously, nor talk foolishly (or boast); not to covet, nor hate (or get angry), nor be heretical (with an occasional variant substituting analogous prohibitions)[48] are the

[47] Manu, 6, 92; 10, 63; 12, 5, *seq.;* Yâj. 1, 122; 3, 66, 131, *seq.*
[48] The most significant variant is the substitution in the Chinese version of (do not) "sell intoxicants" for "speak harshly" in the

Buddhist Ten Rules in inverted order corresponding
to those enumerated above from Manu; and a com-
pendium of Buddhist rules for all men says: "Do
not kill, do not steal, do not be sensual, do not lie,
do not drink intoxicants, eat as you have (usually)
eaten." The ordinary rules for ethical behavior were,
in other words, the common property of the community. One striking exception occurs in the matter
of suicide. The question of the moral right to commit
suicide was decided differently by Brahmans and
Buddhists and Jains. The Jains regularly permitted
suicide for those who had been ascetics during a
number of years. The Buddhist permitted suicide
only in exceptional cases and their general attitude
was that a man should wait, as a soldier or servant
waits for orders to depart, and bear misfortunes
without seeking to escape them. The Brahman lawgivers are usually in accord with the view that suicide
is immoral. Hârîta, an early jurist cited by Âpastamba, says that a murderer and a suicide are both
accursed.[49] Vasishtha declares that even the wish to
commit suicide entails a penance and there are no
burial rites for a suicide. The only cases where suicide is permitted are when it is inflicted upon one
legally as an extreme penalty for a great crime deserving death (since such a death is admitted to be a

Hindu version. It is a later change, since it breaks the arrangement of sins of mind, voice, and body. For the Buddhist rules
above, see *Mahâsudassana Sutta*, 1, 16, and Dh. Pada, 126.

[49] Âp. 1, 28, 17, *yo hy âtmânam param vâ 'bhimanyate 'bhi-
çasta eva sa bhavati.*

"cleanser of every sin"), and when a great ascetic chooses to end his life by fire.[50]

What we call professional ethics was not without representation in India, but for the most part the caste system disposed of all professions and it was simply the duty of one born as slave, trader, soldier,[51] or priest to keep on with his born work and do nothing else. Priests who were unable to make a living became out-castes, at times outcasts; they took up with soldiering or trade or some lower occupation of the mixed castes, but were then despised and sometimes blamed morally (a hunter-priest in the epic gets well berated for his immoral conduct), and so on. The relation of priest to king in the earlier age and that of physician to patient in the later

[50] Vas. 23, 14, *seq.;* 29, 4; M. 5, 89 (Yâj. 3, 6, *âtmatyâgin*); Mbh. 12, 35, 21, and 17, where the suicide may end his forfeited life by leaping from a mountain-height, entering fire, or taking the "great departure," that is, marching to death (into the Himâlayas). Ordinary impurity (sin) may be removed by "ceremonies and gifts," or, if slight, by "prayer and fasting." Going on a pilgrimage to sacred rivers and mountains also makes a man pure, *medhya,* in the opinion of later writers, who lay increasing weight on the sin-removing quality of sacred places, especially bathing-places. Compare Manu, 8, 92; 11, 76; and Mbh. (12, 36, 6, *seq.*), which has whole chapters devoted to the cult of sacred pools. But a protesting voice is sometimes raised against this abuse: "Why go to the Sarasvatî? All rivers are Sarasvatîs (as sacred as the Sarasvatî) and all mountains are equally holy. Let thy soul be thy place of pilgrimage," Mbh. 12, 264, 40, though in 152, 23, holy places are recommended, "after repentance."

[51] But the king, whose only legal duty was to fight and protect, might become a religious *bhikshu,* mendicant, Mbh. 12, 63, 23. The epic slave also is more esteemed, *ibid.* 297, 27, *seq.*

period partook, however, of a character that resembled ethically that of lawyer and physician to their clients and patients today. The fact has already been pointed out that the priest was held to sin in a small degree if he haggled over fees and in a large degree if he misconducted his office to the injury of his client, that is, if he twisted the divine service (really a magical hocus-pocus) so that the paying client was defrauded of the goods, material or spiritual, for which he had paid. Similarly, the physician took a solemn oath that he would not divulge the patient's secrets or in any way "go back" on the patient. The oath is late and may have been borrowed from that of Hippocrates, which it closely resembles.[52] Now in all these cases the underlying ethical principle is that which is enunciated also in regard to the soldier and his king, loyalty. As it is said in the Jâtakas, "a man should always work in the interest of the man by whom he is fed,"[53] a principle which also covers the ambassadorial profession, which was independent of caste. The ambassador had to repeat verbatim the message given him without deviation of a word and no matter how insulting his message might be, it was a grievous wrong to injure him: "That an ambassador is inviolate is immemorial law."[54] Loyalty to his king is demanded on ethical grounds from the

[52] See on this oath, as compared with that of Hippocrates, D'Alviella, *Ce que l'Inde doit à la Grèce*, p. 98.

[53] J. 546. See ÇB. 9, 5, 2, 16.

[54] J. 547. Compare Mbh. 5, 88, 18.

soldier and treachery is one of the recognized sins.
Many other "sins" in the codes are really contraven-
tions of decent custom, to disturb which is in itself
a religious fault, though some of the prohibitions of
the codes are of religious origin (like the one which
duplicates Hesiod, *Works and Days,* 727), while
others, as the oldest commentator to Manu acutely
observes, are "not ethical but practical," such as
taboos in regard to swimming, sleeping, and minor
daily practices.

It is a modern idea that one can estimate the comparative civilization of a race by its attitude toward
women. It applies in any circumstances only to modern races. Three or four thousand years ago the attitude was about the same in all civilizations. Most of
them have preserved depreciatory or ribald remarks
of about the same sort; such as the Vedic epigram,
"there is no friendship with women" and the jeer
from the Brâhmana period, "a woman, a slave, a
cur, and a crow embody untruth wherever they go,"
probably associated because of their dark color as
indicative of the dark sin of untruth. Hindu dogs
are usually black and the women, drawn largely from
the conquered races, were often darker than the men
of purer blood.[55] Women were virtually slaves, for

[55] Even in the time of the Upanishads, where "white dogs" are
spectral beings, the mother of a saint's son is a slave-woman and
all the Aryans were permitted to have slave-caste wives. A Brâhmana says that women are not killed in war but robbed and taken
alive. The castes mixed freely in old days, in marriage and occupation. See RV. 10, 95, 15; ÇB. 11, 4, 3, 2 (5, 1, 9); 14, 1, 1, 31.

they neither owned property nor owned themselves, according to one of the few legal pronouncements of the Vedic period. The husband and wife eat apart. Women, it is said, are of slight mental attainments, preferring men who sing and dance to the more worthy and intellectual complainant.[56] Probably, if literature had been in the hands of women instead of priests, there might have been another side to this story. But none of these legal saws or social flippancies is of much importance in estimating the real importance of women as a member of a family and as an ethical individual. They all reflect the eternal sex antagonism or show at most the social status of a being kept in servitude. The moral importance of woman comes out first when she is recognized as wife and mother. As a daughter she is a "dearest possession" but an object of anxiety till she be married. Manu and Confucius in almost the same words declare that a woman must be under subjection to her father or brother or husband all her life. But admitting this inferiority forced upon her we may judge her true value by the estimation in which she is held as wife and mother. The Hindus here take a much higher ground than do most Orientals. They demand of course chastity from her more than from the man, because she is his possession and he is not hers; but the ideal married life is based upon "mutual fidelity ending in death." She shares as far as possible in her husband's religious life and is a

[56] ÇB. 3, 2, 4, 6; 4, 4, 2, 13; 10, 5, 2, 9.

divinity to her son, who cannot honor her enough, as to her husband she is the "highest comfort." Her ethical rules are one with those of the man and her fate hereafter, if she violates them, is like his, according to her acts, though it is also said that she may share his lot. It will be unnecessary therefore to discuss woman's moral status; there was no double standard in India in regard to ordinary ethical rules. Women were freely seen in public and went unveiled without reproach. In the early period they shared with their husbands not only in religious rites but in philosophical discussions. Tales of wifely devotion and epigrams as to the worth of good women offset the cynical tone found in other discussions. The code that proclaims woman's dependence says of her, nevertheless: "Women are to be honored and adorned by fathers and brothers, by husbands, and also by brothers-in-law. Where women are honored, the gods rejoice; where they are not honored, all religious rites are of no avail. Where women grieve, the family perishes; where they do not grieve, it flourishes. Houses which women, because dishonored, curse, perish as if by magic."[57] Women here are honored as potential mothers and it cannot be denied that they are esteemed mainly as obedient wives. Perhaps it is only fair to admit that a wife's chief moral duty is to be obedient to her husband and to regard him as her divinity, as she in turn is a divinity to her children. But all that is necessary to point out

[57] Manu, 3, 55, *seq.; cf.* Mbh. 13, 46, 5, *seq.*

here is that her other moral duties coincide with
those already discussed and are those of her husband.
Baudhâyana asserts that warriors and men of the
middle classes (farmers, traders) "are not particular
about their wives"; but this has regard only to their
caste, not to their morals. Much of the matter connected with women in the law books has to do with
the enormity of ignoring caste-regulations and the
graded sins (of those who belong to lower or higher
castes) resulting from "caste-confusion," social
lapses which in a caste-community attain to the
dignity of sins, quite apart from their ethical content.

The laws in regard to adultery are stringent, but
especially severe in the case of violation of caste.
If a slave commits adultery with an Aryan woman,
he is to be executed; but if an Aryan commits adultery with an slave-woman, he is to be banished. If a
woman commits adultery with a man of low caste,
she is to be devoured by dogs in a public place and
he is to be burned alive, etc. But if of the same caste,
women are not even divorced for adultery, though
"it is no sin to separate" from a faithless wife, and
the epic even goes so far as to say that when a woman
commits adultery, it is all the man's fault. In Manu,
death is the penalty for adultery in the case of any
man except a priest.[58]

[58] Manu, 8, 359; Mbh. 12, 34, 30, "Separation in the case of an
adulterous wife is not a faulty procèdure." *Ibid.* 267, 38 (only
the man sins): *evam strî nâ 'parâdhnoti, nara evâ 'parâdhyati.* A
son is here commanded by his father to slay his mother, suspected
of adultery. His sin in not obeying his father is annulled by the

LAW AND ETHICS

The widow in India always had a hard fate and her deplorable condition, of which the codes take note and which is described quite pathetically in one of the Buddhist Jâtakas,[59] undoubtedly led her to prefer death to so wretched a life and was the chief reason why the practice of Suttee, that is, the voluntary death of the widow (usually on the funeral pyre of her husband), showing that she was a "good wife" (Satî), gradually became an illegal but common custom. The early code-makers, far from recognizing such a practice, show by their elaborate rules regarding the way a widow should live, as well as by the ancient levirate law, which they endorse, that they recognized no such usage. First about 600 A.D., in Vishnu (probably in later added statutes), is Suttee legally countenanced. It is recognized as a royal custom in the later epic poetry and probably began with kings, whose chief wives had the painful privilege of dying with their lords. It was then gradually extended to other classes,[60] not ceasing to be a practice followed by good women till about a hundred

fact that his father did wrong in giving the order (*ibid.* 19, *seq.*). This tale gives the reason for 'worshipping' a mother. The worship, *pûjâ*, of parents, mother as well as father, is said to be the most important duty in the Dharma-patha (Mbh. 12, 108, 3). The Jâtakas also recognize that "mother and father were gods of old," J. 546.

[59] Jâtaka, 547, section 508: "the widow is neglected and badly treated; her children are maltreated," etc.

[60] In Mbh. 12, 146-148, a female pigeon commits Suttee (after her 'husband' has sacrificed himself to feed a guest), saying, "What good woman, *satî*, could live deprived of her husband?"

years ago (under British coercion), but it was followed even later than that by the wives of native rulers. Also the practice of female infanticide has been in vogue in certain parts of India till the present time, though not permitted by any Hindu law. In these cases, social and economic conditions have sadly influenced religious and ethical ideas.

The authority for all the later laws is derived from divine commands. In the earlier law, the Vedas[61] and good usage and occasional commands of the Lord of Creation embodying divine law are the authorities for conduct. But already in the Upanishads we see that the great god of later Brahmanism, Brahmâ, tends to take the place of Prajâpati as Lord of Creation and as oracle of laws. Later works identify Brahmâ with Prajâpati and Manu's whole law book is based on his teaching, besides numerous verbal quotations from Prajâpati under his old name. Besides Veda, usage, good custom, and general divine commandments, if one still has no moral guide in a specific instance, one's last recourse when in doubt must be to one's own conscience or inner self and its satisfaction.[62] There was this last element to give exercise in self-reliance, but the ethical system as a

[61] Knowledge of Vedic rules was acquired by studying the codes in which they were laid down. The codes make it a sin for a priest to instruct any except Aryans in the Vedas, but the epic says, "a Brahman should cause (all) the four castes to hear" (the Vedas, from the context), *çrâvayec caturo varnân,* Mbh. 12, 328, 49.

[62] See Manu, 1, 26, 58; 2, 12; "Self-satisfaction" in the sense of spiritual satisfaction.

whole bound a man for his own good at every point, as the ritual system encompassed him from before birth till after death. However, it is said in the epic that "people like a great many rules," and doubtless the morality of the Hindus was in no wise impaired by the minutiae with which it was expounded and illustrated. In actual life, if epic poetry reflects such a thing, a genial freedom from all restraint marked the behavior of the heroes, who gambled, drank, killed "unrighteously" (though not without being reprimanded), ate meat, hunted, had affairs with the fair sex without asking their wives' permission, and behaved generally as if they had never heard the moral laws which the same epic on soberer occasions sets forth at stupefying length. Probably both the behavior of the warriors and the exhortations of the moralists are to be seen as idealizations. No real Hindu history is reflected in the epic tales of savagery and license; no people ever followed out all the moral rules expounded in the same epic. But it was no bad thing for the Hindu to have moral teachers of such severity or to believe that ethical conduct was founded on divine law. He may have revered the priest too much and the priest may often have been less a "god on earth" than the priest thought and taught; but as an ethical teacher the priest filled a gap left by the unscrupulous trader on the one hand and by the arrogant warrior on the other. He confused ethics with religion; but he also did much to make religion ethical.

And we should be far from just if we slurred over the emphasis on inner morality as a trifle, compared with the countless rules as to outer conduct and the insistence upon austerity as a remedy for sin. As well condemn the laws of other nations for the same disproportion. The appeal to the "inner man," the weight laid on purity of spirit as well as on outward observance, exhortations to that "self-restraint" which leads to ethical conduct (for, as Vishnu says, "restraint of mind implies restraint of the senses") are as real and as truly meant as are the injunctions not to commit overt acts of "illegal" nature. "Remember (says Manu) that when thou comest to die, neither father nor mother nor wife nor sons nor relations will accompany thee to the next world to be thy companion there; only thy Virtue will go with thee and be thy companion"; and the judge addressing witnesses says: "Think not that no one will see thee if thou givest false witness; for the gods see thee and thy man within. . . . Ever in thy heart stands the wise seer who sees evil and good."[63]

The Buddhists accused the Brahmans of not distinguishing between true worth and caste-position. Pride of caste did indeed lead the priests to say that the priestly office is not impaired in its sacrosanct character by individual baseness; that a priest re-

[63] Vi. 72, 2; Manu, 4, 239, and 8, 85, *seq.* Confession of sin is required in Brahmanism as the first step, before the proper penance is inflicted. In Buddhism, public confession of sins was required of the friars every fortnight and penances, as in Brahmanism, helped to lighten the offence.

mains a priest capable of conducting sacrifice even if he be a bad man. Something of this sort is known outside of India, but even in India this idea was repudiated by the ethical teachers within the Brahmanic pale. Moral values as compared with ritual observance are emphasized continually. "Truth is better than a thousand horse-sacrifices" is a byword of Brahmanism and the epic merely sums up the thought of the past in saying: "He who is self-restrained (morally pure) and dedicates all his acts to God without heedlessness wins immortality. . . . Now immortality depends on truth; all the worlds rest on truth; let truth be your very self, for he only is a true Brahman who swerves not from the truth. . . . Let one therefore be pure, speak the truth, and ever and always be doing good," with which may be united another dictum of the epic, which may have been affected by Buddhistic teaching but is nevertheless promulgated by Brahman authority, to wit, that any other than a virtuous Brahman is no Brahman at all but a Brâhmanaka, a petty Brahmakin, "no better than a slave." Not caste (says this teacher) but character makes the true priest; it is behavior that has made men into castes; for all are essentially one and "there is no caste-distinction," *na viçesho 'sti varnânâm*. When a priest acts unethically, like a low-caste man, then he is of that low caste.[64]

[64] Mbh. 5, 43, 49, *seq.;* 12, 188, 10, *seq.;* 271, 27. So Yâjña-valkya, 1, 200, says that a worthy priest is one that unites good conduct to knowledge and austerity. Without the first the other two are vain.

Strange as seems this doctrine, it is merely transferring to the ethical side what had always been taught from the side of social observance, that there was no inherent caste-nature, that neglect of religious duties made a priest an outcast or demoted him socially, for, as Manu says, a Brahman who does not live as a Brahman is no better than a slave.[65] Nor is it out of accord with the moral requirements exacted in earlier texts of a "true Brahman." As will have been noticed, one expression is found over and over again in defining a true Brahman; he must be a man of "self-restraint." Now no formal definition of this word occurs in the early texts; its meaning is taken for granted and sometimes a list of virtues containing this word appears rather jejune, if not positively deficient. But every religion has its technique and one cannot estimate the value of a phrase without understanding its connotation and real meaning. Our "Christian charity" does not mean almsgiving and so "self-restraint" implies more than it seems to indicate. The author of the Sanatsujâta episode, for example, gives a list of a dozen good qualities incumbent on a priest, such as right behavior, lack of fault-finding, veracity, patience, generosity, self-restraint, etc., and then, after remarking that veracity is of prime importance, proceeds to give this explanation

[65] Here again it is interesting to see that where Manu says a Brahman must *live* as a Brahman, meaning in occupation, socially, the later ethic gives the same rule ethically; the Brahman must *be* a Brahman, that is, must be morally worthy of his name.

of "self-restraint": "A man loses self-restraint through untruthfulness, backbiting, lust, unreasonable dislikes, ignorance, discontent, hatred, haughtiness, quarrelsomeness, injury to others, reviling, garrulity, brooding over trouble (or, thinking ill of others), want of endurance, lack of courage, lack of piety, any falling into sin, and slaughter of animals."[66] The author mingles "mental, vocal, and bodily" faults in illogical sequence, but his intention is clear, to define the shibboleth "self-restraint" so as to make it include observance of ethical qualities and to insist that without these qualities a Brahman is unworthy of his name.

Such a passage as this is by no means unique. Another gives as the result of *dama*, self-control, the attainment of forgiveness, patience, non-injury, impartiality, truth, sincerity, subjugation of the senses, skill, mildness, modesty, steadiness, lack of avarice or of a miser(able) nature (as in Gautama's rule above, p. 90), freedom from wrath, contentment, kind speech, non-hurtfulness (scarcely to be distinguished from non-injury, above, *ahinsâ* and *avihinsâ*), benevolence, and absence of malice. The self-controlled man, *dânta*, will avoid all forms of maliciousness, gossip (*janavâda*, talk of the populace), greed, pride, arrogance, boasting, envy, and depreciation; "he fears none and none fears him"; he will be thoroughly enlightened, *buddha*, spiritually as well as mentally; avoiding all kinds of *droha*,

[66] Mbh. 5, 43, 20, *seq.*

that is, mental, vocal, or bodily injury, and will prove to be not only truthful, but helpful and generous.[67] A later section includes among the "good qualities" which one should strive to possess, *alaulyam*, absence of restless craving, compassion for all, and *parârthatâ*, regard for others' interests. This passage is late, but it only echoes what law books and epic reiterate in regard to the need of an ethical disposition (as well as good conduct).[68] It is not mere form when one is told to be "pure, *çuci*, in speech, pure in mind, pure in body" and to "practice purity, *çubhâni*, in speech, in intelligence, *buddhi*, and in acts," nor when one is exhorted to "cease from ceremonies and practice morality," *çîlam*.[69] Not less important is the reason why one should be pure: "God (the Absolute) is pure; *therefore be thou pure.*"[70]

[67] Mbh. 12, 160, 7, *seq.*, and 162, 21 (this section inculcates truth-speaking). Similar virtues arranged by *gunas* (inherent qualities) will be found in 12, 212, 15, *seq.*

[68] One of the *sattvagunas* (good qualities) here is *âcâram* (*sic*), "good conduct," a late form, 12, 314, 17, *seq.* (neuter also in the Southern text). The definition of a "true Brahman" in Mbh. 12, 189, 4, is similar. "He who has truthfulness, liberality, non-injury, *adroha*, compassion, modesty, benevolence, and austerity, is called a (true) Brahman." (*ghrinâ* implies warmth of feeling, not formal benevolence.)

[69] Mbh. 12, 215, 3 and 5; and *ibid.* 175, 37. As to speech, see *ibid.* 343, 75, "saying nothing that is vulgar or indecent," *kshudram açlîlam vâ*. Compare in general Mbh. 12, 300, 36: "The gods keep afar off those who are sensualists, *çiçnodare ye niratâs*, even if they have been freed (by penance)."

[70] *Brahma parât param nityam çuci; tasmâc chucir bhava,* Mbh. 12, 319, 102.

CHAPTER VI

BUDDHISTIC ETHICS

TURNING now from the Brahman to the Buddhist we find first that, like the Brahman student, the Buddhist novice had special rules forbidding certain luxuries and indulgences permitted to the laity. The ten precepts for novices combine moral and sumptuary regulations, as follows: Abstinence from taking life, from theft, from impurity, from lying, from intoxicants, from irregular eating, from dancing and singing and music and shows; from garlands, scents, unguents, ornaments, and finery; from high and broad couches; and from accepting gifts of gold and silver. Expulsion from the religious order follows in ten cases: When a novice destroys life, commits theft, is impure, lies, drinks intoxicants, speaks against Buddha, or against the doctrine, or against the religious community, holds false doctrines, or has forbidden intercourse with a nun. It is also an offence to bathe oftener than once a fortnight.[1] The first four precepts above, added to three prohibitions regarding speech that is harsh, malicious, or foolish, and three against mental faults, covetousness, anger, and heresy, comprise, as already explained, the ten commandments of the Buddhists. All in all, the ethi-

[1] Dîgha, 2, 320; Majjhima, 1, 313; Mahâv. 1, 56, *seq*. The first eight of the precepts for novices (above) constitute the "Sabbath vow" of the laity, taken by the very good as a daily vow (J. 489).

cal ideal here is one with that of the Brahmans, except that sumptuary rules are stressed rather more heavily and heresy is extended to false views in regard to the religious order and its founder.

Meditative calm, full of kindly feeling, takes for the early Buddhist the place of prayer. It is a condition which is aimed at by both the Brahman Yogi and the Buddhist adept for the attainment of peaceful, serene aloofness, leading to the highest state. It differs from the aggressive love which inspires the Christian missionary, but it is philanthropic enough to send the Buddhist missionary over the earth to preach the new gospel. Later Buddhism, reflecting on Buddha's own sacrifice of immediate felicity to save the world, made for itself a similar ideal and imitated Buddha in copying his self-sacrificing spirit. But this did not affect the general Buddhist conception of all-embracing "love" (really kindness) as a means of reaching perfection. The Buddhist's all-pervading kindness was in fact, from his own philosophic point of view, a stepping-stone, a *pou sto*, from which he was to reach out farther and stride on to that absolute serenity in which the "love," for which he had previously striven, was implicitly suppressed, as all feeling was happily lost. Through this love or kindness he hoped, primarily, to suppress evil passions in himself and subdue them in others, human and non-human creatures, till he could attain to the better state, that of absolute indifference, an ideal shared by the Yogi. Yet in the preliminary stage, for which the ordinary Buddhist strives, because the higher stage is not accessible to most people till they have endured many more lives, there is, it must be admitted, a pleasing gentle affection for all, which is most attractive and on the whole exhibits the Buddhist in a more sympathetic attitude than that of the Brahman, who tries to attain the perfect state without the intermediate outflow of brotherly sentiment recommended to the Buddhist. The Brahman is not urged to love other people, especially low-caste people, only to be kind to them, to pity them, and to sympathize with them, which, indeed, may be enough. At any rate it does not expose him to the absurdity of employing his "love" as a magical means of preventing wild beasts from hurting him, as does the Buddhist, who, when a roaring lion would attack him, simply stands still and inundates the lion with "love," till the beast retires in confusion. But apart from this fabled magical power, the Buddhist in his practical intercourse with his fellows seems to be full of a really affectionate interest for his brothers, human and non-human. The Brahman could not forget that he was better born than other men and though his formula of good-will, expressed by "not injuring," is sometimes exchanged for the positive injunction which we call the Golden Rule, yet the atmosphere of Brahmanism as a whole seems more remote from hearty human kindness than does that of the Buddhist.[2]

[2] The negative formula (as in China) is usually given as, "You

Apart from formulas, sympathy as well as compassion is often enough lauded in the law books, but the Brahman's pride of caste remained a real obstacle to his theoretical ideal. It is probable, however, that in some expressions of kindly courtesy the original form is Brahmanic rather than Buddhistic. For example, Dh. P., 109, is like Manu, 2, 121, in saying that life, beauty, happiness, and power increase as a reward for being courteous to the aged; but the reward in older form appears in Âpastamba (1, 5, 15) as "heaven and long life."

In both religions, extremes, even of laudable action, were deprecated. Too lavish a person is not better than a generous man, he is simply foolish.[3] Enjoy innocent amusements, said the Brahman; but, he adds, addiction to sport becomes a vice. The Buddhist tabooed all amusements for the friars, but he had to allow some relaxation for the laity. On

should not to another do what is repugnant e'en to you"; it refers most often to hurting or killing sentient beings (Mbh. 5, 39, 72; 13, 113, 8, *pratikûlam;* Yâj. 3, 65, *âtmano 'pathyam; cf.* Dh. P. 129). The positive formula occurs, for example, Mbh. 13, 113, 9 (copied Hit. 1, 2): "Good people do not injure living beings; in joy and sorrow, pleasure and pain, one should act toward others as one would have them act toward oneself" (self-similitude is the norm to go by), or, with a broader statement, Mbh. 12, 260, 22: "Whatever one would wish for oneself, that let one plan for another," *yad yad âtmana iccheta tat parasyâ 'pi cintayet.*

[3] Both religions, while praising generous benefactions, admit that the spirit prompting the gift is more important than its material value: "Even the (gift of the) smallest sum, if righteously earned, bears great fruit hereafter," *kâkinyo 'pi mahâphalâs,* Mbh. 12, 294, 16. But extravagance in religious gifts is praised by both.

the whole, however, the Buddhist as compared with the Brahman was puritanical. He held up the friar (a celibate) as model, whereas the Brahman priest married and (theoretically) took to asceticism only in old age.

In the Brahmanic explanation of ethical authority there is lacking the note of personal devotion until we come to the period of sectarian religions based upon devotion to Râma or Krishna, but from the first this note was dominant in Buddhism. The creed of the Brahman gives Vedic authority for moral behavior and even argues that Right (including right behavior) or Righteousness is an eternal principle independent of the Veda and of all other authority, since it is a form of the divine. Hence to do right is to be at one with divinity.[4] But to the Buddhist every rule and precept was uttered by his sole authority, Buddha, in person.[5] This or that specific precept was given to the Brahman by a "voice divine"[6] (otherwise unidentified) or, more particularly, by the Lord of Creation, or by some lesser deity, Indra or Yama, whereas Buddha gave all the law from general rules to special instances. Hence

[4] Dharma is identified with the Supreme Spirit as a synonym of God under the name of Vishnu: "He is Brahma and supreme Dharma, He is Being and Not-being." Mbh. 12, 261; 281, 26. See also above, p. 64.

[5] Not only in ethical matters. Every hygienic or architectural rule in the monasteries was referred to a "Buddha said" for authority.

[6] In ÇB. 13, 6, 2, 13, for example, a "voice divine" forbids human sacrifice.

the weight on faith and the insistence on the ethical quality of faith. Buddha said "avoid desire and hatred, attain patience, be calm, meditate," and forthwith this became the Buddhist's rule of life, whether he understood it or not. The happiness sought by the Buddhist was also a happiness in heaven till he learned a loftier goal and then the Nirvâna which he attained was like the unconscious bliss of the Brahman's union with the All-soul. To the virtuous, but not philosophic, man were offered in both cases a reward in heaven and high birth again on earth; while to the philosopher was offered also, by Buddhist and by Brahman alike, escape from birth followed by bliss ineffable in the loss of individuality (extinction of self). Ethically, every good act aims at the highest goal for the philosopher, as every good act, as he is capable of understanding and performing it, aims at the passing joy of heaven and "good rebirth" for the man of limited mind and hope. The act brings happiness (passing joy hereafter or bliss eternal) because it is good.[7] However, the basic value of goodness is capable of being measured by the result of the act in terms of emancipation. Buddha saw as pressing realities the miseries of rebirth and the need to escape from them, and argued that escape was pos-

[7] It is not good because it brings happiness. Acts aiming at happiness in this life are not good when they divert the soul (self) from its true aim. Compare Professor Keith's *Buddhist Philosophy in India and Ceylon*, p. 278.

sible only through elimination of desire (thirst), which was inherited by each individual from a precedent birth and appeared in any one birth as a predisposition. Gratification of desire therefore only bound one the more, and the way of escape was to eliminate desire of everything except of the highest goal, which was to be reached eventually by absolute indifference; but the way to it was found in a preliminary elimination of everything tending to postpone the desired state. Now to acquire even the approach to indifference one must subdue certain inherent traits such as longings and aversions and hatreds, which were therefore evil in a varying degree. For example, serenity implies an equable mind fostered by a calm and friendly environment. Hence one must cultivate amity and a wide love for all beings; but when thereby one has attained the state of serenity one must renounce love and advance further to indifference. Kindly feeling and love for all are stages toward perfection. Desire itself, according to the Buddhistic theory, is born of ignorance of true values, so that the Brahmanic and Buddhistic theories of the "root of evil" differ chiefly in appraising the "self" as an immortal soul or as a character-like nucleus of predispositions carried from birth to birth but capable of dissolution when the last predisposition (to yield to desire) is severed, which nucleus was the Buddhistic substitute for soul. Moreover, in Buddhism there was the same fear of hell for misdeeds as in Brahmanism; but there was no God till Buddha himself in the eyes of the ordinary worshipper took God's place, and either as Buddha or as a Bodhisattva (prototype of Buddha) was invoked as a divine being and prayed to for forgiveness of sins.

At this point, however, there enters into later Buddhism a fresh conception of what sin means. The commission of sin grieves the divine spirits and saviors of the world. To be good is to please them, to be sinful is to pain them; it is wrong to do wrong, because it wrongs divinity!

This is an entirely new conception to the Buddhist, though it is not so remote from the Vedic notion that sin makes divine beings angry. The idea, however, in the Buddhist's mind is rather that the Bodhisats are pained because every sin adding to a sinner's demerit increases the debt assumed by the divine Power, who redeems all sin by assuming that sinner's demerit. The argument is that the sinner must suffer for his sin unless another assumes the burden; the Bodhisat assumes it in taking upon himself the vow to "assume the sins of the world" and so redeem sinners. Being divine and having an infinite store of merit, this divine being can easily give the sinner enough merit to counterbalance the demerit incurred by sin, so that his divine suffering is more theoretical than real, even if to the eye of the philosopher the suffering were not actually ideal rather than real. But the net result religiously and ethically is that the human sinner (who is not usually a philosopher) believes that in sinning he causes grief to the divine beings to whom he prays.

The original Buddhist has been called an "egoistic hedonist." The term is harsh, but, at any rate, his whole concern was with his private salvation, which lay in his own hands. To secure that salvation he became moral, serene, kindly disposed. Self-development was really his aim, from a practical point of view. Karma, the working out of the act, was alone responsible for the result of acts, which acts it was in his power to do or avoid. He recognized no supreme divine power interfering with Karma. He could not say with the negligent Brahman jurist "malformations result from faults induced by Fate or by Karma or by maternal faults."[8] To him it was the act alone that decided his fate, the act comprising what is thought, said, and done. But to the later Buddhist the Master had virtually become a divine being who as God ruled the world, and this Buddhist, in the gradual decadence of the primitive belief, invented the most extraordinary excuses for sinning. Originally celibate, the friar now married because "it gave pleasure to another," which in general is what a good friar ought to do. Moreover, sin actually became a virtue, because "it is a joy to the

[8] Yâj. 3, 163. Yâjñavalkya cites too the cult of "planets" as deciding human fate, while the Manes alone "give wealth, knowledge, salvation," etc. (1, 269, 307). "Stars and lucky days" determine one's fate in the epic also, Mbh. 12, 180, 46. On fatalism, see above, p. 81, and Mbh. 12, 226 and 227, 86 (Fate, not acts, determines one's fate).

divinity to forgive sin," and a good friar ought to give joy to the divinity.[9] Such aberrations are found in other sects where ethical decadence has gone hand in hand with devotion and mysticism; but in no other case is there so marked a contrast between the early and late stages of religious evolution. However little religion, in the ordinary sense, inspired the primitive Buddhist, he was yet deeply imbued with ethical belief and was a consistently moral person. But the belief in transfer of merit, which was at first heterodox but finally became as general a belief as it was in Brahmanism, paved the way for the intrusion of the idea of redemption through divine mercy and led to the slow undermining of reliance upon one's own need of ethical behavior, so that in a measure religious devotion destroyed the fine ethical sense of the early Church. It did not entirely destroy it, for the idea that sin pains divine saints and that the only way we can recompense them for their goodness to us is to give them pleasure by being good (and by being good to others) was a very real support of morality; but it loosened ethical moorings and sent the ship of Buddhism abroad on strange waters. Incidentally it brought the Buddhist near to the belief in predestination which crops up in the Rig Veda, "whom I will I make powerful," and in the Upanishads, "whom He chooses, by Him is he obtained," ending on the one hand in the belief in Fate and on the other in the belief in the per-

[9] See Keith, *op. cit.*, p. 296

sonal Savior-god, who grants salvation to the true believer. Hence the prayer to Buddha or Bodhisat as to a merciful divinity in whose power lies man's fate.

In still another particular was the Buddhist like the Brahman. In giving up belief in God and an immortal soul the Buddhist by no means relinquished subordinate beliefs and superstitions. The perfected saint could exercise all sorts of magical powers (like a Brahman Yogi) and the exercise of love itself begot a magical mastery over nature. Descriptions of Bodhisats show that they were regarded as great magicians also, but this is natural, as they were divine beings. The saint on earth, however, was no mere modest moralist but had a terrible magical power, though he exerted it only beneficently. Yet the notion that he had such a power made of him a more than human person and was the starting point for all the later religious extravaganza so deleterious to morality.[10]

In minor details there was more resemblance between Brahmanism and Buddhism than is assumed to be the case by Europeans and by the Buddhists themselves. The objection urged against the Brahmans, for example, in regard to the "true Brahman" is voiced, as we have seen, by the Brahmans also, who from an early date distinguish between

[10] It is not good form to show one's Yogi powers (only a fakir exhibits them). As the epic says: "Practice Yoga but do not exhibit it," Mbh. 12, 215, 21.

exaltedness of caste and excellence of character. But in all probability the Buddhistic diatribe against Brahmans as being gluttonous, selfish, and "full of lust, malice, sloth, pride, self-righteousness, and *doubt*" (Tevijja Sutta) was directed rather against the king's sacrificial priests, who were perhaps as a class very like the temple-priests of today and deserved reproach, though one cannot get rid of a feeling that the bitterest reproach was kept till the end; for to doubt meant to discredit Buddha, and the Buddhist, even Buddha himself, was implacable toward heterodoxy. This may surprise those who rely on the expressions of broad-mindedness attributed to Buddha, such as, "Whoever holds up a torch to man is always honored by me" (Râhula Sutta), and his abhorrence of dogmatism, as voiced in the remark, "A dogmatist is no leader to purity; being prejudiced he says that purity is as he sees it"; or, in epigrammatic brevity, "Nibbana is the place where there are no theological discussions" (Mahâ-viyûha, 16); but, in point of fact, Buddha was essentially a dogmatist himself and the gravest sin in his eyes was to doubt the Buddha. The second of the ten "fetters," which bind one and keep one from salvation, is doubt in respect of the Teacher (Buddha), the Law (given by Buddha), the Order (founded by Buddha), the training (instituted by Buddha), and Karma, which Buddha accepted as a fundamental belief though it was merely an unproved dogma. The very preliminary to becoming a good Buddhist is that one should have "the right view," that is, be "orthodox," which means to deny God and renounce belief in soul. Liberality of thought was permitted only within orthodox bounds; no Buddhist might question the received doctrine. The only discussion was in regard to the interpretation of this received doctrine. Now the Brahman rejected all Buddha's orthodoxy except that he became gradually imbued with belief in Karma, so that the Buddhist is not the most impartial judge of the Brahman. The distinction between ritual purity, *çaucam,* and purity of conduct, *âcâra-sam-çuddhi,* was made by the Brahman himself and is implicit, before it is explicitly stated, as early as the Upanishads, which in part precede Buddha, to judge by the fact that Karma there is as yet scarcely recognized, while in all Buddhism the Karma dogma is accepted as a matter of course.[11] Faults of character were doubtless many in Brahmanism and were the more conspicuous because of the prominence of the caste; but Brahmanic ethics was as high at its best as was that of Buddhism, and Buddhism was not without a sophistic touch in its moral teaching. Thus both religions taught that one ought not to injure creatures; but the Brahman said frankly that when one sacrifices animals one is engaged in a religious

[11] Karma usually implies metempsychosis but not invariably, especially in the early texts; it may mean merely that "the fruit of the act" ripens in heaven or hell. On the other hand, transmigration, 'rebirth,' first appears without moral connotation; but later it implies Karma (rebirth ethically adjusted).

duty higher than the moral duty of "non-injury";
but the Buddhist, who could not eat at a sacrifice
because he never made any, yet wanted to eat fish
and meat, said that, though it was immoral to *kill*
an animal for food, yet one might properly eat
thereof if someone else had killed the animal without the eater's instigation; and though the Buddhist
blamed the Brahman for killing men in battle, yet
when the Buddhists, instead of being tolerated prot-
estants (for the Brahmans, much as they disliked
the Buddhists, never fought against them), got
political power, as they did in Ceylon and Japan,
they fought in war for their prestige with all the
ardor of a political party. Asoka lamented the deaths
he had caused in war, but was not converted till
he was safe from further need of war. Moreover, it
must not be overlooked, to return to primitive Buddhism, that a sect raffed together from the scum of
the earth (barring only outcasts) and mixed indis-
criminately with the better social classes, could much
more lightly assert that birth was of no consequence
than could Brahmanism, an order of hereditary
aristocrats.

Again, as for the Brahmans being greedy, it is
true that they praised inordinately those who gave
gifts to the Brahmans; but the Buddhists praised
as highly those who gave gifts to their friars; and
while the Brahmans never organized into monastic
bodies but dwelt apart each in his own home, living
on private emoluments and daily alms, the Bud-

dhists built enormous establishments which, being supported, as they were built, by state patronage as well as by private benefactors, flooded the country with an idle army of begging friars and even from the beginning became a refuge for lazy incompetents, as later (outside of India) they became hotbeds of immorality and political intrigue. Even in India, they fostered private vices (such as the memoirs of the Order recount), though in competent hands and with ethically-minded friars the monasteries were doubtless schools of discipline and philosophy, morally beyond reproach.

The great advance made by Buddhism from an ethical point of view was in the establishment of the principle of causality, since this led to freeing morality altogether from the religious practices with which it had been indissolubly connected and which had in great part been recognized as substitutes for it. We have seen that the moral sages of the Brahmans also declared that ethics was more important than the ritual, but the priestly and popular belief was that sin could be removed by austerity and sacrifice. Now Buddha did not renounce austerity as a means of ethical training; but he taught that all observances of a religious nature kept man from perceiving the vital necessity of purifying himself through himself alone. He made ethical behavior the first necessity, after one had freed oneself from the delusion of soul and belief in wrong doctrines and ritual observances. He insisted upon a man's getting rid of

149

sensual thoughts and acts and malevolence, in order
that he might lose the desire of any life imbued with
these evils (whether on earth or in the sensuous
heaven believed in by most men), and so gradually
shake off the further fetters of pride and self-righteousness and become illumined with the true wisdom
which is reached by noble aims, noble life, and noble
thought. In this path, without any superstitious beliefs or practices, which contradicted the principle
of causality, one might attain to the eventual release
of oneself from every tie binding one otherwise to
repeated rebirths. But, furthermore, in exercising the
moral virtues and in holding them up as essential,
especially the virtue of kindly affection, the Buddhist, whether in the monastery or as layman in the
world, not only dispensed with all religious superstitions, but he disseminated more widely than could
the Brahman, hedged in by caste-restrictions, the
humanitarian spirit, which led to wider tolerance
and to the growing belief in the brotherhood of man,
recognized indeed by the Brahman as a truth, for
he taught that all men were "children of one Father,"
but not so readily acted upon. In this regard the
isolated home-keeping Brahmans and hermits brooding over "secret wisdom" were no match, as fore-
runners of modern thought, for the teachers in the
crowded monasteries and the wandering Buddhist
missionaries, who traversed all India and invaded
other countries.

How much Buddhism took from the earlier Jain

religion (heresy) it is not possible to know. The Jains made conduct as important as faith and knowledge, and their conception of the goal of existence, though it differed from that of Buddhism in stressing escape from the evils of life rather than from conscious existence and in giving a high place to asceticism, is similar in that it was attained by the same ethical road as that blazed by the Brahmans and followed by the Buddhists; but this road was narrower. The non-injury doctrine was exaggerated till it became a bugbear; one must not even kill obnoxious insects or vermin. Otherwise, to be kind (not to injure), to speak the truth, not to steal, to be pure, and to renounce attachments or delusions, which are the "five vows" of a Jain ascetic, do not take us beyond the moral attitude of other Hindu religions.[12]

Perhaps the latest development of the ethical sense is to be found in the recognition of another man's right to his own religion. Heretics were abhorred in India by the Vedic singers, by the Brahman priests, and by the Buddhist saints. They were freely reviled also, but they were not manhandled; at most they were banished by the Hindu kings who

[12] The non-injury doctrine of the Jains led to the animal hospitals, in which worn-out beasts are kept alive, and to the refusal to kill a suffering and dying animal. These are examples of the usual interpretation of "non-injury" as not killing instead of not hurting, for many of the animals in the hospitals would be better off dead, and a dying horse whose eyes are being picked out by an attentive vulture would suffer less if killed.

followed the advice of the more strenuous lawgivers, but even these were content very often to say that heretics were objectionable and it is doubtful whether any kings ever banished a man for his faith. Intolerant as Buddha was of doubt and heterodoxy, his attitude toward the Brahmans was that of one who would not force but argue them into right views and after his death an unbeliever was merely dropped or perhaps ejected from the monastery. As dated monuments of belief and moral teaching are rare in early India it will be of interest here to quote some of the passages from the edicts of Asoka, the great emperor, who became a Buddhist, in the third century B.C. As emperor he felt himself to be patron of all religious sects, though especially devoted to Buddhism. From his Rock and Pillar Edicts we may gather an idea of the practical ethics taught in his day and of the spirit of toleration inculcated. Most extraordinary is it to find such teachings engraved in durable stone as the most important public utterances of a great king. The Edicts date from 261 B.C., at the time when Rome was engaged in the first Punic War, which may serve as a reminder of the difference between East and West at that period. With omission of unessential matter the following sentences reproduce *verbàtim* extracts from these Edicts:

His Majesty in the ninth year of his reign conquered the Kalingas. One hundred and fifty thousand were carried captive, one hundred and fifty thousand were slain and many times that number perished. . . . His Majesty feels remorse on account of this conquest of the Kalingas. . . . Because of the slaughter caused, death, and taking away captive of the people. . . . He feels sorrow and regret. . . . Though one should do him an injury His Majesty now holds that it must be patiently borne, so far as it can possibly be borne. . . . In former times kings went on pleasure tours, hunting animals; but His Majesty in the eleventh year of his reign went on the road to knowledge, whence originated tours of piety, visiting ascetics and Brahmans and elders and giving largess to them, largess of gold. . . . The royal commissioners and district officers must every five years proclaim the law of piety, to wit, obedience to father and mother is good; liberality to friends, acquaintances, relations, Brahmans, and ascetics is good; not to injure living beings is good; avoidance of extravagance and of violence of language is good. . . . For hundreds of years the slaying of living creatures, cruelty to animate beings, disrespect to relations, to Brahmans, to ascetics have increased. But by reason of His Majesty's practice of piety is heard now the drum of piety instead of the drum of war and the cessation of slaughter, cruelty, and disrespect [is seen] together with obedience to parents and elders. . . . The law of piety consists in kind treatment to slaves and servants, obedience to parents, charity to ascetics and Brahmans and respect for the sanctity of life. . . . Father and mother must be obeyed, respect for life must be enforced, truth must be spoken, the master must be reverenced by the pupil, and proper courtesy must be shown to relations. . . . No animal may be slaughtered here [in the capital] *for sacrifice. Formerly in His Majesty's kitchen thousands of living creatures were slain every day to make curries. At present only two peacocks and one deer are killed daily and the deer not invariably. But in future even these three creatures shall not be slaughtered.*[13]

His Majesty does reverence to men of all sects . . . by donations and by other modes of reverence. . . . A man should not do reverence to his own sect by disparaging that of another man for trivial reasons. . . . The sects of other people deserve reverence. By respecting another's sect one exalts one's own sect . . . by acting contrariwise one hurts one's own sect. . . . He who does reverence to his own while disparaging all other sects . . . in reality inflicts severe injury on his own sect.

A man beholds his good deed and says "this good have I done"; he sees not his evil deed and says not "this evil have I done." . . . But let a man know this, that rage, cruelty, anger, pride, and jealousy are in the nature of sin and say "let me not by reason of such things bring about my fall." Let a man

[13] This (first Rock Edict) is surely the most remarkable edict ever chiselled on stone in a king's honor. The citations above are from Edicts thirteen, eight, three, four, and eleven, and the second Minor Rock Edict. The first quotation below is from the twelfth Rock Edict and the next from the third Pillar Edict.

keep the [straight] *course, which will be of avail for the world to come* [not the sinful course leading to worldly advantage].

There are more of these Sermons in Stones; but one in particular must be mentioned, because it brings out a point not hitherto emphasized among moral qualities. In the seventh Rock Edict, Asoka proclaims: *"If one is too poor to be lavish in gifts, he can* [at least] *exhibit these virtues: self-command, purity of heart, gratitude, and fidelity; they are always meritorious."*

The time was soon to come when the epigram was to be coined among the Brahmans: "There is expiation for every sin except ingratitude; but for him who returns evil for good no expiation is known." In the early law books, however, such a far-from-legal sin is not recognized till Manu declares that the food of an ingrate is impure and links him with the slanderer and liar and slayer of children and women. In one passage Manu says that a man should not dwell with "slayers of children, ingrates, slayers of suppliants, or slayers of women, even if they have been properly purified."[14]

But the field in which were planted the seeds of

[14] M. 4, 214; 8, 89; 11, 191. Compare Yâj. 3, 299; Mbh. 12,172, 25: "For one who returns evil for good no expiation is known." The same statement occurs several times in the epic; but the "no expiation" rule is there extended: "There is no expiation for one who injures a friend, or is ungrateful, or kills a woman, or kills a spiritual teacher," Mbh. 12, 108, 32. There is also "no expiation" for one who kills a refugee, *ibid.* 149, 19.

ethical finesse, the more delicate flowers of civilization, which books on formal rules of right and duty
are apt to ignore, was the Buddhistic fable-litera-
ture, in which the Former Births of Buddha as man
or animal were told in connection with some moral
lesson. The tales in many cases were originally related without reference to Buddha; they were simply
beast-stories which inculcated such virtues as generosity, gratitude, steadfastness, loyalty, being true to
one's salt, self-sacrifice; or warned against vices
such as gluttony, pride, deceit, lying, etc. Probably,
back of these moral tales lay still others in which
cleverness and shrewdness rather than ethical qualities came to the fore, tales similar to those of our
Indians and Negroes. In the moral collection of the
Buddhist Jâtakas (Birth-tales) there are several
which are really without any ethical bearing; but
they illustrate the advantage of being clever. A middle sort, which treats stupidity as wrong, forms as
it were a bridge from one class to another. Such, for
example, is the Buddhist equivalent of the Greek
proverb $\mu\eta\delta\grave{\epsilon}\nu$ $\mathring{\alpha}\gamma\alpha\nu$, which (it occurs in different
forms) recommends moderation in all things. It is
not religious advice, to shun license on the one hand
and asceticism on the other, but a more general practical caution couched in the garb of the tale of a boy
who drums too long or blows too long, or, not content with digging out a well, "over-digs" and comes
to grief. In the first instances the tales end with
"blow but do not over over-blow," *dhame nâti-*

dhame; but in the last the story concludes: "And so I say, do not over-dig, for it is a *sin* to over-dig."[15] One version is wholly practical; the other gives an ethical touch.

But, in Buddhistic hands, tales of this sort were as a rule directed toward moral edification and the teacher of the moral is always Buddha (in a previous birth) as the chief actor in the scene, which is sometimes a little awkward if, instead of being the moral hero, the chief actor is intrinsically immoral. For example, in one tale the former Buddha (Bodhisat) appears as a deceiver, in another as amatory, and in a third as the chief of a band of robbers;[16] but the text explains that this was not because the Bodhisat was not incarnate perfection but because a "fault of the horoscope" caused such a character to represent him, which is rather vague but tends to relieve the reader's shocked surprise at finding Buddha in the rôle of a cheat or robber. In one tale it is said that the Bodhisat was born ugly because of his sins; in another, he even tells a lie.[17]

To historians of literature these tales will always be interesting, because it is from them that Aesop and La Fontaine and Chaucer and Shakespeare have drawn (at second or third hand) material for their studies of life; but to the Buddhist they were more important. They taught the "noble way" by precept

[15] J. 59, 60, and 256, *atikhâtam hi pâpakam.*
[16] J. 80, 95, 279.
[17] J. 531, 547.

157

and example and if some or most of them are incredibly naïve, suitable to impress children rather than adults, it must be remembered that they were composed of (or transposed from) material long familiar and always attractive to the mass of Hindus. Talking animals revert to the earliest age and animals that are incarnate gods go back to great antiquity, while such edifying allegories as the "quarrel between mind and the senses" existed before Buddha was born. All the elements of these sermons for the simple were thus already at hand and to a sect deprived of most amusements they must have been as attractive as Pilgrim's Progress on a Puritan Sabbath. A thrilling tale explains the folly of over-digging and this, interpreted as a sin, prepares one for a further tale of wickedness exhibited in excess of grief at some misfortune; which leads on to the story of the folly of grieving for what cannot be helped, with its sharp persistent moral, "do not weep for the dead," based on the fundamental Buddhist axiom, "all is impermanent," and filled out with a note from the old religious fear of wailing for the dead, as liable to bring grief to the one bewailed.[18]

The virtues extolled, though chiefly spiritual, are by no means devoid of worldly motives, such as

[18] J. 317, 352, 354, 372. For a purely practical tale, compare J. 283, "in unity is strength." Compare also with the (Brahmanic) verbal dispute of mind and senses the Jâtaka story of Right arguing with Wrong (457). The 'sin' of overboldness is emphasized by making it also a defiance of good advice, disobedience of elders (427), etc.

would appeal to a commercial people. In what seems like a reminiscence of Asoka's edicts we are told that there was once a king who used to "declare the law to his people" at fixed intervals and this was embodied in the commands: "Give alms; practice virtue; righteously follow your business; educate yourselves in youth; gain wealth; do not act like a village cheat or a dog; be not harsh; be not cruel; care for your parents; show respect to elders." These are the ten commands (points) of wisdom, embodying ethical and practical advice (weight is laid on education while one is still young). Similarly, one is advised not to be overgentle as well as not oversevere, and the reasons given are purely practical: in one case one gets contempt; in the other, hatred.[19] Merit or spiritual virtue may always be transferred to another, according to the Jâtakas, which are imbued with this popular heresy; but luck is not transferable. It rests not in gem or wonder-stick but in one's own energy and deeds in this life and in preceding lives; it is, in fact, the outward expression of stored-up merit.[20] Thus covertly is impressed the force of the truth that a man's whole fate is in his own hands. Success in this life forms in not a few instances the sole apparent motive of a tale, which may even suggest a non-Buddhistic moral, as when the Bodhisat replies to a question in regard to success in life: "First acquire skill, then add virtue and patience,

[19] Jâtakas, 468 and 472.
[20] J. 284.

and so you will be able to do good to friend and ill to foe"; although many tales are given to expound the real Buddhistic doctrine that "love is the best physician" and that to be patient and forgiving to one's enemies is the highest virtue.[21] A more moral tale explains that the "six doors of gain" are wealth, virtue, obedience to elders, study of scripture, truth, and freedom from desire; and, as to the last item, innumerable are the stories which point out that "desire is the root of ill."[22] The punishment for vices and sins is generally hell; thus, the liar and denier of an act done goes to hell; a king of old days who told a lie sank into earth (as in the epic tale, above), but kept on sinking till he reached hell, or rather one of the hells, for in Buddhism there are sixteen minor hells besides eight great hells.[23]

These tales show that meat-eating was common enough, but that killing of any animal was deemed a grievous sin, though eating flesh when already killed was of less importance and was looked upon as a venial or even excusable lapse from the stricter diet of vegetables, fruit, and cereals. Thus roast pig

[21] J. 238, 282, 303. Compare 346, "Love is the best sauce," and 371, "Not hate but love makes hate to end and reconcileth friend to friend."

[22] J. 228, *tanhâ vipattimûlam*. Compare Dh. P. 216 and Mbh. 12, 174, 18, *trishnârtiprabhavam duskham*.

[23] J. 142, 228, and 530 give the number of hells; the minor hells are sometimes reckoned as 128 in number. For the king, see 422; for the liar, and denier, see J. 285 and Dh. P. 306. Punishment may come in this life and then be followed by hell (J. 354, 516). Hells are described in J. 544 (compare the *Kokâliya Sutta*).

is regarded as a natural dish for a wedding-party, and Buddha, who according to canonical tradition died of eating pork, in a previous birth was the inventor of a process of drying meat and taught the world how to do it; yet the received view seems to be that only the wicked kill but the wise (*i.e.*, the prudent) may eat meat without sin.[24]

The teachings of the Jâtakas do not go far below the surface. They are chiefly to inculcate obvious lower truths or to press upon the hearer by fable and allegory the folly of gossip, the power of slander, the ill effects of greed, the fate of the hypocrite, the enormity of doing evil in return for good, the fact that evil communications (generally of women) corrupt the good; to warn him who would do evil in secret that spirits and saints are watching him; to inform him who would give gifts that gifts should be given only to the worthy; to teach, hopefully, that merit may lead to "royal rebirth" and, reprovingly, that cruelty will lead to hell. Occasionally occurs a list of virtues, such as that recounted by the gods: "Avoidance of stealing and of lying, of pride, of fraud, of lust; manly resolution, faithfulness, absence of gluttony, avoidance of calumny, keeping

[24] J. 241, dried meat; 246, the wise eat without sin, *sappañño na pâpena upalippati;* the fatted pig for a wedding (286) is mentioned without reproof. On the maxim "the learned may do ill," see J. 377. It is rather surprising to find truth-telling so emphasized that, in the tale of the ascetic who could not tell a lie (J. 431), it is said: "In certain cases a Bodhisat may kill, steal, commit adultery, and drink intoxicants; but he may not tell a lie."

one's promises."[25] The most interesting list of this sort is the one given in the tale of the Kuru-dhamma, which incidentally teaches that the weal of a realm depends upon the virtue of the king, who is the rain-maker,[26] and that unintentional sin, or sin only thought of, is of little importance. But the Kuru is the type of Brahmanism and it is instructive to see that the plate engraved with "perfect righteousness" is referred to such a source and that the Kuru-rules, which being followed bring blessings, are: "Do not kill; do not steal; do not be lustful; do not lie; do not drink intoxicants."[27]

In regard to women, Buddhism held a peculiar position. Innumerable are the formal passages in which women are reviled as being "torches that light the way to hell," and even the popular teaching of the Jâtakas is full of diatribes against them, not only

[25] J. 326; these add up to ten and remind one of the Ten Commandments of Manu and the Ten Great Crimes, *aparâdhas*, of the criminal codes. For the other points mentioned above, see, in their order, J. 322, 349, 375, and 395; 384, 208, 320, 333; 348 and 435; 305 and 302; 415 and 358. Ten royal virtues are listed in J. 385, alms, justice, mildness, mercy, etc.

[26] That the weal or woe (famine) of the realm depends on the king is taught also in J. 194, 334, 528, etc. This is recognized Brahmanic doctrine.

[27] J. 276. According to J. 183, "aristocrats do not get drunk." The well-born in Brahmanic circles were advised not to drink intoxicants, but drinking, barring excess, was permitted to all except priests. Later centuries have practically prohibited meat and intoxicants in the case of the well-born; though the prohibition has not always been effective. That a Brahman never used intoxicants is incidentally recognized in J. 537, where also a Buddhist is taught not to lie, even to save his life.

wicked women, but, as is expressly said, "all women." The Bodhisat himself calls a great congregation together, and he and other saints recount all the stories against women that they can remember, proving that womenkind in general are a debauched and worthless set of beings, some of these stories being heightened by deliberate falsification of traditional material. The burden of these exhortations is that "all women go wrong if given opportunity." Nârada, a great saint, says that oceans, kings, Brahmans, and women are the four insatiates.[28] At the same time, duty to parents is imperative and the "mother is the way to heaven"; she must always be tenderly cared for. Moreover, nuns were soon admitted into the Buddhistic Order, and though they were not allowed to be autonomous they were highly respected. The diatribes seem to be intended for monkish recluses, to guard them in the main against losing their accumulated merit by unholy imaginings; but it is very perplexing to find these popular discourses almost as misogynistical as monkish maxims.

Buddhist ethics does not really agree with the pessimistic point of view, as that view is usually interpreted. The view that all life is misery is counterbalanced by the cultivation of a spirit not only resigned and serene, but very joyous: "Cultivate that

[28] Kunâla Jâtaka (536). It is interesting to see that the Brahman is insatiate not because he is greedy of wealth but because he never gets enough of studying; he learns all the Vedas and still yearns for more to learn!

part of the higher wisdom called Search after Truth; cultivate that part called Energy; cultivate that part of the higher wisdom called Joy."[29] Pessimistic in regard to life on earth, in his outlook on the future the Buddhist was a cheerful soul, partly because he was exhorted to be so in his progress toward serenity, partly because the ethical training given him from childhood stimulated kindliness, joy, and peace of mind. He believed that the practice of these virtues directed him toward salvation and the certainty of finally getting what he wanted tended also to make him optimistic.

Incidentally, it may be worth remarking that not a few Buddhistic formulas, as well as tales, have been taken up by the great epic and as endorsed by this work may be considered quasi-Brahmanic. Such, for instance, is the apparently pessimistic refrain *sukhâd bahutaram duskham, jîvite,* "there is more sorrow than joy, in life."[30] The virtuous Brahman is praised in the Buddhist scriptures provided he does not scorn these scriptures, for "fools scorn the

[29] Sabbâsava Sutta.

[30] Mbh. 12, 331, 16. It follows a number of other Buddhistic *clichés:* "No eye like that of wisdom, no austerity like truth, no sorrow like passion, no happiness like renunciation," *nâ 'sti vidyâ-samam cakshus,* etc., 330, 6 (compare Dh. P. 202, 251); but the origin may be a general phrase-collection. The next verse at any rate is as much Brahmanic as it is Buddhistic: "To turn away from evil deeds, to follow always good conduct, to act in accordance with virtuous conduct, this brings the highest bliss" (330, 7). Conversely, to renounce good and evil (the fruit of merit and demerit) is also Buddhistic, Dh. P. 39, 412.

Buddhist religion" and are destroyed, but even here there is the constant insinuation that the Brahman does not "purify himself by self" but by external means only (Dh. P. 164). The epic in turn seems to refer to the Buddhists when it speaks of "fools who deny soul, disputatious, who wander over earth."[31]

It has been remarked above that meditation usually takes the place of prayer in the case of primitive Buddhists; but the Jâtakas show that the human need of divine assistance is not wanting in Buddhism. One prays to Sakka, the Buddhist shade of Çakra or Indra, even for spiritual blessings, such as freedom from hatred and malice, though it is admitted that Sakka cannot grant such a boon (the man himself must free his self of vices); but for other gifts the Bodhisat is openly entreated like a god, as, for example, when a childless king and queen join their prayers to the Bodhisat to grant them a son.[32] Prayers made to and granted by spirits, such as dryads, are of common occurrence in Buddhist tales.

The crowning glory of Buddhism is not the doctrine of non-injury, which early Brahmanism also

[31] Mbh. 12, 19, 23, *seq.* The (virtuous) Brahman is defined in Dh. P. 383, *seq.,* but what is meant is that any virtuous man is a true Brahman. It is like defining a gentleman in terms of character rather than of birth. The Brahmans often said the same thing, but it was not a popular doctrine!

[32] J. 263.

teaches,[33] but the inculcation of that devotion to man which leads to self-sacrifice. The typical example is that of king Sivi, who gives his eyes to a blind beggar, a tale admired so much that in various forms it has become Brahmanized and is presented under the guise of king Sibi (the Sanskrit form) offering his life to save that of a refugee. Possibly, with unexpected instinct, the Brahman narrator recognized that the first historical case of self-sacrifice would have been in defence of just such a suppliant; for to defend a refugee is Aryan usage and old Brahmanic law. However that may be, in accordance with the principle of self-sacrifice, to give even one's life for another is eventually a common act in Jâtaka stories and is equally praised in late Brahmanic tales. It is first found in negative form, incorporated in fact with the rule of gratitude, in the denunciation of those who "kill a refugee"; then is developed in the tales of those who die in defence of a refugee, as an act of surpassing virtue, and finally reaches its culmination in the idea of a god sacrificing himself to save suppliant sinners.[34] The model, as ethi-

[33] G. 2, 17, and 9, 68, seq.: "Let the householder be always a speaker of truth, act like an Aryan, be ever free from injuring, mild, firm, controlled, generous," nityam ahinsro mridus, etc.; ibid. 23, 27; and Ch. Up. 3, 17, 4, where ahinsâ may refer only to human beings.

[34] Manu, 11, 191 (live not with the ungrateful, nor with those who kill refugees); Jâtaka, 499: "Self-sacrifice is the noblest thing" (Sivi's tale is sculptured on a Gandhâra fragment). The same theme is repeated in the epic, which also tells of Pratardana's gift of his two eyes to a priest, which made him famous, Mbh. 12,

cal authority for the later Buddhist, is thus found in the person as well as in the teachings of the Buddha himself. In regard to the primitive Buddhist, apart from the Master's teachings, which were of course authoritative, his highest sanction for his beliefs was given, as Buddha himself insisted, by enlightened reason, not by emotion, however well disciplined.

235, 20. The *motif* in all these tales is self-sacrifice for another. That life itself is one long sacrifice, if lived religiously, is, as we have seen, taught as early as the Brâhmanas.

CHAPTER VII

RELIGIOUS DEVOTION BASED ON MORALITY

W E have just seen that, despite the attempt of
early Buddhism to erect an ethical edifice on an
atheistic basis, the natural tendency to seek super-
natural aid converted Buddha himself into a divine
being and that all moral laws were referred to him
as the one sufficient basis of authority. He had by
unquestioned right laid down the law of ethics; to
break one of the moral rules he had established was
to flout his word, and to doubt his omniscience was
to sin. As a Buddha-to-be or Bodhisat he had in previous existences on earth both by precept and example shown the way of moral behavior and had gradually revealed to man that the better way was one
of self-sacrifice for the good of others. He became
an object of devotion to whom prayers were said,
who forgave sins, who was to all except the philosophers the very God whom as man he had denied. The
philosophers indeed raised up a phantom Absolute
of which the Bodhisat was a heavenly expression,
as the man Buddha was an earthly expression or in-
carnation of the same Absolute Power or Form
(Dhamma). But with philosophers we are not here
concerned. The ordinary Buddhist of the first centuries after (and perhaps before) the Christian era
looked back at the earthly Buddha as a divine being
on earth and up to the Bodhisats as divine beings in

heaven, to one of whom, as many thought, the perfected Buddhist would go after death to be received
into paradise. And as Buddha in demolishing God
had not troubled himself to attack the belief in the
countless little gods and spirits, in whom everyone
as a matter of course believed, all these spiritual
beings, as well the evil as the good, continued to hold
their place in the religious consciousness of the Buddhist, who was thus as much of a spiritualist as was
the Brahman.[1] In his religious and ethical struggles
the Buddhist was always surrounded by a great host
of angelic and demoniac beings, who helped or hin-
dered his efforts to do right, who applauded or were
dismayed at his conquest over self and sin. In a
word, within a few centuries of Buddha's death his
followers had practically become almost as religious
in their outlook on ethics as were their Brahmanized
countrymen, who held that ethics was a divine institution, that moral laws had been directly inspired,
and that the gods still watched men to see whether
their behavior was straight or crooked.

That both religions had virtually the same community of moral interests is well demonstrated by
the Edicts of Asoka. He was no king of Buddhists
alone. In fact, in most of his edicts it is clear that
he regarded himself as protector and patron of all
the religious bodies in his realm. His ethical rules
were engraved for the whole community and, with

[1] Thus divine spirits and saints see the unconscious sinner, and
demons torture him "in Yama's world," *e.g.*, in J. 527, 530. Dryads
or Nâgas play, too, a frequent part in Buddhist stories.

the exception of ritual slaughter of animals, were such as to appeal to all as legal and acceptable definitions, authorized by royal authority, of good conduct. Alms to the needy, hospitality, reverence for parents and elders, beneficent deeds, such as showing kindness and building public works for the general good, avoidance of all the long-recognized errors of conduct, such as murder, adultery, theft, drunkenness, the cultivation of gentle virtues, non-injury, gratitude, faithfulness, and, in general, the practice of self-restraint (avoidance of anger, greed, lust, jealousy, gluttony, etc.), and amiability, these were, we may assume, naturalized and universally lauded virtues among the Hindus generally, whether belonging to this or that religious sect, in the first centuries B.C.

It was at this somewhat indefinite period (but it is impossible to be more precise as to the time)[2] that the worship of One God, which had long existed as more or less of a philosophical abstraction, began to take a deeper hold on the Hindus, who for centuries had been, when not Buddhists, inclined to this or that sectarian cult, that is, to the worship of some special god as of supreme importance. But the "god who had been a man" was of all others best fitted to enter the lists in a struggle for supremacy with the idealized Buddha, now worshipped over all India as a

[2] Mr. H. Raychaudhuri has recently shown (JAS. Bengal, 1922) that the epic formula "self-control, renunciation, careful regard (for others)" occurs on the Besnagar inscription of Heliodorus in the second century B.C.

divine being. This god was Krishna, who was identified with the One God of the early philosophers and with the One God adored by certain Brahman saints in the north of India. How this identification was effected is here immaterial; the result was that Krishna was accepted at first by few and then by increasing numbers as God on earth, who at a time of great unrest declared himself and laid down the principles of his religion.

We have now to explain in what regards the ethics of Krishnaism consummates and yet differs from the ethics of precedent Brahmanism and of Buddhism. Strictly Brahmanic, Krishnaism was not; it was not evolved within the fold of the old orthodoxy, which clung to Vedic rites and Vedic gods. But it was not heterodox in the sense that it rejected Brahmanic authority, flung away the Vedas, and ignored the institution of caste, as did the Buddhists. But as to this last point, it is well to remember not only that castes were not then the rigid barriers that they now are, but also that there are meeting places between those who did and those who did not accept the social prestige of caste. One of these, often overlooked, is the suppression of caste-aristocracy in the theory of rebirth. This one earthly life appears a trifle to Brahman and Buddhist alike; each looks forward to thousands of rebirths. Now earthly caste is lost at death; it is but a step to the next birth and to a better caste, if one is good enough to get it. Caste is but a temporary garment. In a few years the social order now existing will be totally upset; the good, but now depressed, will be the aristocracy; the high, but vicious, aristocracy will be slaves or monkeys or asses. The patient uncomplaining servant, now ill-treated, will soon perhaps be the master; his wicked lord will be his humble servant. All this mitigates the sense of injustice in human relations and induces a complacency like that with which the wronged and downtrodden Christian views his own and his injurer's fate hereafter. The second meeting place is in the growing conviction that caste is less important than character. Already in the Upanishads sounds the note that breaks the taut strings of the caste system and the legal authorities of the Brahmans insist that upper-caste men who do not do their duty shall be degraded and become as low-caste men. Then comes the Buddhist with his insistent jingles:

> It is not right
> To call men white
> Who virtue lack;
> For it is sin
> And not the skin
> That makes men black.[3]
> Not by the cut of his hair,
> Not by his clan or birth,
> May a Brahman claim the Brahman's name,
> But only by moral worth.[4]

[3] Jâtaka, 440.
[4] Dhamma Pada, 393, etc. The arrangement of the hair indicated

But the religion taught by Krishna starts from the assumption that caste exists as a divinely appointed institution and that man's first duty is to do his caste-work. If a priest, let him meditate and sacrifice; if a warrior, let him fight righteously and die gloriously; if a trader or agriculturist or farmer (the third estate), let him trade honestly or farm it soberly; and if, owing to former sins, one finds oneself a slave, let one be an uncomplaining, honest fellow. In doing his own work let each realize that he is thereby doing not only his social but his religious duty. By doing it he becomes dear to God, who is the model as he is the ruler of the universe. But dearer still becomes that man who without ceasing to do his duty does it without hope of reward; who toils for God not for himself; who sets his heart on one thing only, that is, likeness to God, and desires only to be united with God. Such a man is most dear to God and he may die knowing that God will receive him, whatever his caste, and he will enter into eternal blessedness.

But there is no thought here that man can by ecstasy rise above his duty or above his ethical obligations. To be pure is really to be purified of lust, greed, anger, and other sins of the flesh. It is only through such moral training that man becomes capable of entering into union with God, which presup-

family and social status; a low-caste man, for example, wore his hair in five braids. To mark degradation the same coiffure was imposed by force (J. 546).

poses that God himself is free from all moral defects. Happiness, in the sense of earthly joys, is not a man's goal. As is said elsewhere in the epic (the religion of Krishna is unfolded in the epic), the stupidest and the wisest men are the only ones who are really "happy" on earth.[5] One of these is grossly happy because he knows no goal beyond pleasures of sense and can easily attain it; the other is happy because he knows that pleasures of sense are a delusion (the miser is really miserable) and finds his happiness in lasting bliss. The middle-minded are all seeking happiness either in this world or the next, but because their hearts are bent on this lower form of happiness (heaven is no lasting home), they are anxious and troubled and have not the blissful serenity of those who seek only God. The way to God is on certain "paths," which are enumerated in the epic discourse on the "knowledge of Brahma." These "paths" to Brahma (the abstract God) are: Benevolence, patience, peace, non-injury, truth, uprightness, freedom from insulting behavior and from pride, modesty, endurance, and tranquillity. Another epic passage, after the writer explains that, despite the diversity of codes, one can be sure that the rule of right is simple, expounds this rule as follows: "Turn from evil and do good; associate with the good; be gentle to all; be upright; speak kindly; give up egoism; be heedful; be temperate; avoid both over-

[5] Mbh. 12, 25, 28.

indulgence and total abstinence."[6] Usually this is part of the discipline of the Yogi, but a neighboring passage in the epic says that even the lowest people may apply themselves to Yoga discipline: "Even a low-caste man and a woman who desires righteousness may by this path attain to the highest state."[7] Now this ideal of ethical preparedness for supreme bliss is identical with that inculcated in the religion of Krishna. Let us compare, for example, the words of Krishna: "Virtues that are a means to emancipation (salvation) are: calmness,[8] purity of heart, perseverance in the practice of (spiritual) knowledge, generosity, self-restraint, sacrifice, study, fervor, uprightness, non-injury, veracity, freedom from anger, renunciation, peacefulness, freedom from

[6] 12, 174, 33; 271, 38, seq. (288, 24, atiyogam ayogam ca). The epic writer remarks that one should rest content with the thought that "the good man gets good" and thank the gods that one can be good, for "no one becomes virtuous unless permitted by the gods" (ibid. 272, 49). There is an old theory that the gods fear men, devânâm mânushâd bhayam, and normally put obstacles in the way of their intellectual and spiritual growth, lest men become as gods (ibid. 48, seq.). Buddhism is full of this superstition and so is Brahmanism, though it is not in harmony with the later theory that "the gods love virtue and favor it." So it is softened down to the view that virtue is obtainable, but only through the special grace of the gods, for which men should be thankful; a view opposed to the Karma doctrine and to Buddhism, but in accord with the old teaching as to special grace and predestination (above, p. 83).

[7] Mbh. 12, 241, 34. Even the slave may become a religious adept; if virtuous, he is a form of Vishnu, ibid. 297, 28.

[8] Literally, "fearlessness." This is not "valor," but lack of apprehension as to the future state of one's soul, serene confidence.

176

back-biting, . . . freedom from avarice, freedom
from the desire to harm, compassion to all, gentleness, modesty, patience, humility," etc. The disciple
of the Lord must, to become dear to him, be "un-
selfish, forgiving, contented, friendly to all, compassionate."[9] All these qualities make part of the
"knowledge" which in this later teaching lead to
salvation. It is not confined to the utterances of
Krishna himself, but is found elsewhere in the epic
in the teaching influenced by Krishnaism, for there
was an unconscious amalgamation of religious ideas
within the general Brahmanic and Brahmanized fold
as there was between Brahmanism and Buddhism. A
few extracts taken from the Brahmanized epic will
make this point clearer. They embody universally
accepted principles of right living and right thinking:

"A friend is one who acts as a friend when services are asked of him (even if calling for self-sacrifice). There is no expiation for the sin of ingratitude. . . . Who are the real aristocrats? Those born
in great families. But what families are great? Great
families are those in which piety, self-control, and
learning abound; in which great deeds are done;
those that practice right and add to the glory of their
race by avoiding all wrong-doing; these are the great
families, not those that are rich in horses and cattle
and grain and deficient in good conduct."[10] "So long

[9] BG. 16, 1, *seq.;* and *ibid.* 12, 13.
[10] Mbh. 5, 36, 24, *seq.;* and *ibid.* 37.

as a man's good fame is extolled on earth, so long is he glorified in heaven. . . . A good man practices sacrifice, generosity, study, asceticism, self-control, truth, uprightness, non-injury. The eightfold path of right consists in sacrifice, study, liberality, asceticism, truth, forbearance, benevolence, contentment; of these eight the first four may be practiced for deceit, but the last four are found only among those of great soul."[11]

Such general admonitions belong to epic ethics as taught by others than Krishna. We may compare from the same section the following words: "Cheerfulness, uprightness, purity, contentment, kindly speech (*priyavâditâ*), self-control, truthfulness, and steadfastness are lacking in those of evil soul; not among the low will be found knowledge of soul, steadfastness, patience, perseverance in doing right,[12] guarded speech, and liberality." The passive qualities are more in number than the active; yet endurance and steadfastness are not negative virtues and the injunction not to do wrong is often coupled with the injunction to do right: "Do no evil, for evil fame and evil fate hereafter will be the fruit of doing evil here on earth. Evil, the more it is practiced, destroys the intelligence; when intelligence is destroyed, one obtains only evil. Let one so act by day that one may sleep happily at night; so act during the eight

[11] Mbh. 5, 35, 4 and 55; copied in Hit. 1, 8, where "benevolence" (warmth of feeling) is replaced by "self-control" and "contentment" by "lack of greed."

[12] *Dharmanityatâ, ibid.* 5, 34, 72-73.

months (of active outdoor life) that one may pass the (four months of) rains happily; so act in youth that one may pass a happy old age; and *so act all through life that one may dwell happily after death.*"[13]

The reproach has often been cast against the Hindus that their ethics was all negative, so that it is worth while to notice the frequent admonitions to exert oneself, to overcome evil, to engage in active good works, to do, and not simply to be. The constant command to have patience is also enlarged to embrace the (Christian) doctrine of non-resistance: "Do not reproach when reproached; do not insult another; the very gods are eager for fellowship with him who when struck does not return the blow, who does not seek to injure even the evil man who injures him."[14] The later epic repeats these rules and adds to the virtue of patience under abuse the demand that one should show sympathy with others: "Compassion, non-injury, heedfulness, sharing with others, offerings to the Manes, hospitality, truthfulness, absence of anger, marital fidelity, purity, cheerfulness, knowledge of soul, and patience, these are rules for all. . . . Neither with eye, nor with

[13] Mbh. 5, 35, 67, *seq.: yâvaj jîvena tat kuryâd yena pretya sukham vaset.* This is an improvement (perhaps meant as such) on the irreligious non-ethical system of Brihaspati (the Cârvâka), *yâvaj jîvet sukham jîvet,* "let one live happily (for pleasure) as long as one lives."

[14] *Ibid.* 36, 5, *seq.,* and 12. Compare Dh. P. 223, "overcome anger with kindness; overcome evil with good."

mind, nor with voice should one injure another; one should not disparage another, nor speak ill of another; one should not hurt any living thing; but one should be always of sun-like (kindly) conduct. Even when one is angered one should speak pleasantly and when insulted answer with a blessing. . . . He indeed is exalted in heaven who looks on all other beings with an eye of affection, who comforts them in affliction, gives them (food), and speaks kindly to them, becoming one (with them) in their grief and joy."[15]

Now in this really notable collection of moral rules, two things are remarkable, first that, as indicated by the phraseology (given in the note) these final ethical injunctions of the epic are practically a mere continuation of those in the discourse of Lord Krishna. They are perhaps a little more inclined to stress the passive resistance of the ascetic, but the fact that the expression "one in grief and joy" is identical with that in the Gîtâ indicates the origin of the sermon as a whole, though the turn of the phrase here converts its meaning from indifference to sympathy. But this is not all. The qualities here extolled are suggestive of Buddhistic origin and they may certainly have been affected by that heresy; but it is quite as important to observe, what has not hitherto been noticed, that the rule "when insulted

15 Another reading (*anu* for *anna*) omits "food." The injunctions, all of the same character, are not isolated, but come from three sections of the epic, 12, 279, 4-6; 297, 23, *seq.;* 298, 36 (*samaduskhasukhas; cf.* BG. 12, 13); repeated in 330, 18.

answer with a blessing" (which is the gist of this later ethics) is here drawn directly from Manu's precepts for the ascetic: "Let the ascetic endure abuse, despise no one, be at enmity with no one, be not angry with an angry man, but when abused answer with a blessing."[16] It is for this reason that the epic composers of these sections refer their teachings to no less an authority than the old Lord of Creation, Prajâpati, from whom the law of Manu was received and with whom he was sometimes identified. But the difference between the two sets of laws is palpable. What the ancient Manu laid down as a rule of forbearance for the ascetic is now made the moral law for good men in general. So the "one in grief and joy" rule (literally, "like in woe and weal") has been ethically converted from an ascetic principle, meaning that one should feel alike toward grievous and joyful things (be indifferent), to a social principle of sympathy (comfort the afflicted, be liberal toward their needs, speak kindly to them, be one with them in woe and weal), a meaning which is really an extension of the Brahmanic principle of sympathy expressed in the other epic (the Râmâyana) by the half of this word, *samaduskha*, "one (with others) in woe," that is, sympathetic or full of sympathetic pity.

The epic Lord of Creation appears in person as an ethical instructor, possibly invented here by those who were not yet ready to accept the Lord Krishna,

[16] Manu, 6, 48, *âkrushtas kuçalam vadet.*

and in a terrestrial form in another section speaks as follows: "Truth, self-control, patience, and wisdom are practiced by the wise. Aryans declare patience, truth, uprightness, and non-injury to be the paramount virtues. When insulted, I do not reply; when beaten, I am patient (or, forgive); . . . when struck, I strike not in return, nor even wish the striker ill. . . . The gods delight in the virtuous and in the wise. . . . Every man becomes what he wishes to be and like those with whom he wishes to associate. The secret doctrine of the Vedas is truth, but to attain to truth one must first attain to self-restraint (all the moral virtues, as explained above, implicit in self-restraint), which is the door to immortality. . . . The secret wisdom (of the gods) is that there is nothing nobler than humanity."[17]

This means that man is himself divine and can by his own exertions, mental and moral, compass the highest. Again, here as elsewhere, the ethical note is emphasized, as in the same book it is said, *satyena çîlena sukham,* "happiness (is acquired only) by (the attainment of) truth and by ethical behavior."[18] Knowledge without morality is as futile as morality without knowledge. Both are to be gained by human effort. Nor are we left without instruction as to how

[17] This *brahma guhyam* may imply a reference to AV. 11, 8, 32: "All divinities reside in man; the sage regards man as Brahma." The epic passage is in 12, 300, 1, *seq.*, and vss. 13, 20, 32, *seq.*

[18] Mbh. 12, 292, 23. The mental state is emphasized, *ibid.* 193, 31: "Let one practice good, *çivam âcaret,* in his mind; the wise say that virtue is mental," *mânasam dharmam âhus.*

ethical behavior works to effect the purity which brings to man oneness with God as the all-pure: "The attributes of a moral person are generosity, truthfulness, modesty, uprightness, patience, ritual purity and purity of conduct, control of the senses (in general), meditation, and study. Through these a man's spiritual energy is increased and this removes sin."[19] Sin is thus the expression of a lack of spiritual power. The old teachers acquired such power, as do savages, by mortification of the flesh. But, in these more advanced views, fasting, the common means of mortifying the flesh, is often omitted and one of the epic writers even says that fasting is only a means of injuring oneself and does no good.[20] But, according to the view just explained, the soul itself is a form of energy, as God is described by the term "the Super-energy": "When one is blinded by the darkness of lust and ignorance, one fails to perceive the soul residing in the heart as part of the Supreme Energy."[21] Now this energy is conceived as radiant force or forceful light and hence it is that, in contrast, lust and ignorance are forms of darkness. A man who is once filled with this divine radiant power has no place in his soul for the darkness of sin and ignorance. The fully enlightened man cannot but be moral. God is, as the sacred tradition

[19] Mbh. 12, 241, 11.

[20] *Ibid.* 221, 4. Buddhism, on the other hand, not only holds to fasting but makes the "suffering of a fast" mitigate the (future) punishment for evildoing (see J. 511).

[21] *Ibid.* 254, 12, *atitejo'nça.*

says, "the Light of all lights, beyond all darkness," a Supreme Power "devoid of all senses,"[22] that is, unsullied by any evil of the senses.

Despite its later phraseology, this takes us virtually back to the early philosophical point of view, namely, that God is the all-pure, devoid of sense-soilure, and that, to become one with God, ethical purity is essential; further, that knowledge of the relation between God and the soul is also essential. But, again, this is what is taught by Krishna as the very essence of wisdom, namely, that saving knowledge implies morality: "Salvation is the fruit of knowledge. Now knowledge is humility, simplicity, non-injury, forgiveness, uprightness, reverence for the teacher, purity, steadfastness, self-restraint, freedom from passion and from egotism, appreciation of human ills . . . loving devotion to the Lord . . . and understanding of the relation between soul and the Supreme Soul."[23]

There is then a special meaning in the sayings: "Truth is Brahma; untruth is darkness; truth is right; right is light; light is felicity" and "in truth is immortality."[24] God is revealed in the heart of the Yogi as a brilliant light, like fire, like sunlight, like a

[22] BG. 13, 14 (and 17), taken from Çvet. Up. 3, 17. The moralists explain the future in similar terms: "Now heaven is light, *prakâça*, which is truth, and hell is darkness, which is a form of untruth." Mbh. 12, 190, 3.

[23] BG. 13, 7-11, *etaj jñânam*, a noteworthy phrase; not that knowledge comes from, or leads to, but *is* morality, etc.

[24] Mbh. 12, 175, 28, and 190, 1, *seq.*

flash of lightning.[25] But apart from this gnosis, which is the true apocalyptic knowledge of the mystic, even the "knowledge" of the ordinary worshipper is no ordinary knowledge or wisdom, but is a combination of ethical, devotional, and intellectual factors. It is not a question between ethical conduct and religious belief as forming the foundation of this moral appreciation of the divine. Intellectual conviction and ethical mentality are blended into one and this union of belief and moral nature is indissoluble. Morality is necessarily religious; religion is necessarily moral. Righteousness is a form of God. Further, it must be remembered that to the Hindu the Vedas, on which Dharma is based, are themselves eternal and divine.

There can be in such a system no further need of authority for what is right; it is given in the terms of the definition. Right is right because it is divine. Divine then is the injunction to uphold all that right implies in Right Order, maintenance of the divinely appointed castes and of the duties to be performed by each of those castes, adherence to the ethical law of the same Right Order.

Buddhism, in converting the Law and the Church into expressions of Buddha himself, followed much the same course, since in that religion the Law, Dhamma, became also an external manifestation of the Buddha. Hence not only in philosophical discussions but also in the naïve teachings of the simple Jâtaka tales, stress is laid on the fact that wisdom,

[25] Mbh. 12, 307, 20.

or the essence of knowledge, precedes morality and piety, because it comes first and involves the others in its train. It is more important because without it the others do not appear; but it is not of greater worth because it does not come into existence without the others. Knowledge (wisdom), morality, and piety thus form a threefold unity which alone eventuates in perfect happiness.[26]

The ethic of Lord Krishna has been regarded by some modern scholars as unsatisfactory because of the "uncritical attitude to Dharma" which is held in the Gîtâ. But it is demanding too much of these ancient thinkers to ask that, after they establish the moral imperative as divine, they should then discuss the validity of divinity. The teaching of Krishna recognized that spiritual growth could be attained by the "difficult" way of the old Yoga discipline; but it not only condemned the Yoga system of "works" (for the Yoga still maintained the essential character of works as means to a higher end, whereas the work a man does is not the main thing but his attitude toward works), but it insisted that to do one's work in the station to which man has been called is man's first duty and that this is better than (Jñâna) Yoga exercises. To this then is added the principle of devotion to the Lord Krishna, which again results in ethical advance, for the devotee of Krishna becomes righteous through his devotion. The very

26 J. 522.

devotion itself is a proof that he is of "good intent" and his devotion causes him to "become virtuous," *bhavati dharmâtmâ.*[27] When "the Lord is seated in the heart" of a man, his own changed nature will force him to do what is right. Then he will perform the duties of his order, but without regard to whether he is to be rewarded for doing so; and in that sense he may be said to "abandon his duties." When that point is reached, he is prepared morally and religiously for the Lord's final utterance: "Come to me as your refuge; I will release you from all sins."[28] Both the devotee and the Yogi are implicitly and explicitly required as a first step toward emancipation to become ethically pure. The moral quality of the soul is not lost in its higher flight. Sin is stain and morality is a process of cleansing. Sin is darkness and the soul has left darkness for light. The soul which reaches emancipation is not again soiled or eclipsed by sin. The soul is thoroughly cleansed of its stains, which are, objectively, the vices it has forever renounced, before it can reach its goal. The root of Krishna's practical teaching is that all work must be in accordance with righteousness.

But the ethics of Krishna cannot be fully apprehended without a deeper look into the world as

[27] BG. 9, 31.

[28] *Ibid.* 18, 66. Similarly the meditative devotion of the Yogi is also a preparation for perfection which cleanses his soul of sin; he becomes "purified from moral stains," *samçuddhakilbishas* (BG. 6, 45).

understood by this teacher.[29] The knowledge or wisdom which is at once ethical and emancipative (leading to salvation) is the "wisdom that is from above, first pure, then gentle, full of good fruits," as another authority describes it in another land. Man's nature shares the threefold state of all animals. It is dark and brutal, light and divine, and thirdly, between the two, demoniac and appetitive, which last strain leads to selfishness, ambition, greed, etc. The man who yields to the appetitive strain will be without self-control. But he who subdues it will rejoice in the serene peace of spiritual interests; he will be kind, charitable, full of mercy. The intellectual view of the world will accord with these strains, conceiving life as dark and dull, in the brutal stage; figuring, in the appetitive stage, a material world with material rewards for its restless energy; but, if the man subdues this strain, he realizes, in the divine stage, a world of law and order in harmony with spiritual things. Appetitive natures worship greedy and passionate gods; divine natures worship deities of peaceful light; men of brutal nature worship devils. As a man feels and thinks, so is he. His nature is colored by his understanding, as his understanding is colored by the dominant strain in his nature. If appetitive, he becomes individualistic, selfish, apt for hate, blind to the spiritual world, incapable of emancipation from the fetters of self till he has emerged

[29] For an excellent exposition, here summarized, see the introduction to Mr. Charles Johnston's *Bhagavad Gita,* N. Y., 1908.

into a serener atmosphere, mentally and emotionally. But, if a man seeks divinity, he will renounce lower aims, he will liberate himself, not by withdrawing from the world or merely doing work, either worldly or heavenly (performing sacrifice), as a preliminary training for spiritual liberation, but by doing work in a spirit of disinterestedness, not for a heavenly reward any more than for earthly gain, but for duty's sake, because the work a man is born to is the work he ought to do, because there is a moral necessity to do it as a service to divinity, and because, if done without hope of reward, it leaves the man free from the bondage of work (such bondage as is implicit in "making sacrifices for reward"), free from anxiety as to the "fruit" of work. The man is free because renunciation leaves his spirit untrammelled by desire. The ascetic gives up all work. But that is not the way to cultivate the spirit; for even the Supreme Spirit works, toiling toward the perfection of the world, and by giving up all work the ascetic renounces not the world but his duty toward the world. The ritualist performs work, yet not with the spirit of renunciation but rather in the hope of a reward, a reward which, however, will only intensify his feeling of separateness and egotism. But he who, without fostering selfishness, has done his work and done no unrighteous work, becomes illumined with the divine light of disinterested serenity. He works for God alone and God is his reward. In dedi-

cating all his work to God,[30] all the stains of selfishness are erased; the dark, brutal side of his nature
and the restless, craving side have been eliminated.
He has passed out of these two states into the highest, where, freed from every bond and from all darkness, working for God alone he is at one with God.
The keynote of this religion is devotion to God expressed not only by devotion to him in words but by
"self-restraint, renunciation, and carefulness" (in
moral and social duties), which are the "three steeds
of Brahma," that is, the three means of travelling to
the highest in the metaphorical chariot, the rein with
which the steeds are managed being *çîla,* "moral conduct."[31]

To the Buddhist, active life is misery and he seeks
to escape it by overcoming desire. Why add fuel to
the flame of life? The ideal man, even the ideal king,
is one who renounces not only lusts but family affections; who can say to the weeping wife begging him
not to desert his family and proper work in life, "I

---

[30] BG. 12, 10, *madartham api karmâni kurvan.*

[31] This moral conduct is exemplified in doing harm to none
and in having compassion for all, Mbh. 11, 7, 23-28. In a passage preceding this, those who have passed out of the worlds of
dullness and appetitiveness are the *sattve sthitâs, i.e.,* "those abiding in the highest plane," or those who have got rid of the inferior
strains (worlds). These reach the highest through wisdom, virtue,
and love of doing good; they must be *hitaishinas,* "seeking what
is beneficial to others," as well as wise and virtuous. It is added
that "greed, wrath, and fear" deprive the soul of understanding,
ibid. 3, 20, and 4, 12, and this is undoubtedly the general interpretation of the relation between sin and ignorance.

care no whit for thee," and desert her and all his social duties to live alone by himself in a cave or with other devotees of self-culture.[32] To the worshipper of Krishna, life is not evil in itself; love of parents and of wife is estimable, as it is natural, and the work for which one is born by caste is to be performed as a religious duty, not shirked for the sake of one's salvation. But to both, as to the Brahmanic ideal, which largely underlies the later Krishna-religion, self-restraint, with the full list of inhibitions, mental and bodily, which it implies, and a spirit of kindly sympathy with others, leading to helpful effort in behalf of others, is the necessary foundation of a truly religious life.

The "devotion" of the worshipper of Krishna leads into unexpected paths, as will be shown presently. But for the present, estimating the ethical religion of Krishna by the first exposition of it in the Bhagavad Gîtâ, we may draw two conclusions. In the ordinary philosophy of religion based on the axioms of Karma all deeds bear fruit. Good ac-

---

[32] J. 525: "I go without one care for thee." The Buddhist recognizes caste-duties, such as those of a king, as incumbent on those who know no better than to accept them. "The virtue of a king is to do what a king has to do"; he must have courage, for the god Sakka (Indra) "watches courage in man and counts it a virtue"; he must "do right zealously, without anger, earnest in effort to do good" (*ibid.* 521; for a less flattering picture of "warrior doctrine," see J. 528 and 537). But this is only the worthy ignorant king; he is not to be compared in excellence with the exalted king, who deserts family and royal activities for salvation by self-culture.

tions as well as evil actions have a result in future births. Hence the pressing need to escape the result of all activity, if one would escape rebirth. Objective goodness, consisting in kindly acts, for example, must in this view be suppressed, or their performer will be "rewarded" in the next life by a "good birth," whereas his aim is to avoid all rebirth. But the man who follows Krishna as his master follows also the Lord's rule, *matkarma-paramo bhava*, "do all thy work for me" and (if the work is done) "abandon all fruit of work in devotion to me." It is by renunciation of reward, it is by doing all for the Lord, that one escapes the "fruit of action" and can be "fearless" as regards the future. Thus the ascetic fear of doing any act (work) is lost; one's acts done for the Lord are not done for oneself. A reasonable ground is given for the practice of those ethical actions which the bare theory of Karma tends to exclude from the religious life as dangerous to the soul's salvation. Renunciation of earthly and heavenly reward is indeed knit together with the practice of self-restraint, serenity, etc., in the Vedânta philosophy, which recognizes no real Lord; but there is no certainty that such a formal act of renunciation can be accomplished, or, so to speak, can be legalized; it may be *ultra vires* of the individual to "renounce the fruit." In Krishnaism, however, the fruit is nullified for the individual by the acceptance of his Master, who takes upon himself the responsi-

bility and proclaims the disciple's release from rebirth in devotion.

The ethics of the Vedânta philosophy lacks inspiration to "call out and strengthen the manly
qualities required for the practical side of life," to
quote the words of Max Müller, but the ideal of this
philosophy was made for philosophers and not for
the ignorant and it must not be overlooked that even
the Vedânta has its pragmatic philosophy with a
world as real as are those who cultivate the "manly
virtues." Still, for the man on the street, the Gîtâ
undoubtedly has a stronger appeal in that it duly
recognizes and urges the practice of all virtues and
puts the stamp of unqualified approval upon the best
activities of social life as being intrinsically real (not
the product of illusion).

The second conclusion which we may draw from
the merging of religion and ethics in Krishnaism of
the Gîtâ type is that, in the "devotion" recommended, there is not the least taint of mystic eroticism. The word devotion, usually translated "loving
devotion," is *bhakti,* which in this first form of the
religion is devout and fond meditation on God, ex-
cluding, however, all emotional love. "Through
bhakti one learns to know me. . . . Taking refuge
in me, through my grace, he who has *bhakti* ('loving
devotion') finds the eternal place . . . men devoted
to me worship me with *bhakti,*" etc. Such expressions are not erotic, though they do imply rather
more than the devout meditation, *upâsana,* which

takes its place in philosophy. *Bhakti* connotes chaste fondness as well as devout faith. A certain warmth of affection is expressed toward divinity from the earliest times. We saw in the first chapter that the personal god was greeted with this same warm but pure affection in the Vedic hymns and that even there it was expressed with almost loving zeal. In the sobriety and even aridity of the Brâhmanas we yet find *preman*, a word signifying strong affection, used to convey the same attitude. Bhaktas may be those devoted to any divinity, as Krishna says in what are perhaps the most illuminating passages of the Gîtâ: "Even those who are devoted with faith to other gods are in reality worshipping me. . . . If one who is pure of heart with faithful devotion, *bhakti*, gives me even a leaf, a flower, a fruit, or water, I accept it as offered with *bhakti*. Whatsoever thou doest, whatsoever thou eatest, whatsoever thou offerest, whatsoever thou givest, whatsoever penances thou performest, make all that thy offering to me. . . . Those who are devoted to me with faithful devotion, they are in me and I in them."[33]

In all these discussions of the ethical character of the later Hindu religions it must be remembered that there was an inevitable development in the real meaning of the salvation aimed at. As in the Christian Church the first idea of salvation was sometimes interpreted as salvation from death and sometimes as salvation from sin, so in the Hindu religious con-

---

[33] BG. 9, 23 and 26, *seq.*, with *ibid.* 13 and 18, 55.

sciousness the word "release" (salvation) signified different forms of freedom from bondage. The release was at first release from the bonds of passion, of the senses, and ethical conduct was the outward manifestation of the first loosening of the bonds. But in the hands of the later philosophers, who taught that man was under the bondage of illusion as to the reality of the world, release became synonymous with clarity of understanding; only he who saw through the illusion of seeming reality was really "released." Morality here also underlies clear vision; good works are a means to an end. The effect of morality is to sustain that spiritual serenity without which insight and illumination are not forthcoming, so that even in the school of the idealists ethics has a real content, as real as the world in which it operates. But in the religion of Krishna salvation is both a release from sin and a release from ignorance, from misunderstanding of the proper relation between the deed and the doer, from that attachment which binds. And, according to his own exposition, this misunderstanding can be done away with, salvation can be obtained, only by those who are morally pure. The ethical value of the Karma doctrine in popular as well as in philosophical religion is very great. It teaches that there is no such thing as a cruel Fate or an unjust God, that it is foolish to rail at misfortune as if it were undeserved, or to expect a better fate hereafter if one is not morally prepared for it. Karma takes, as it were, the place of a just, logical, irresistible, divine Power. It rewards virtue and punishes vice (mental and bodily) with the unerring "fruit of the deed." It is apparently a blind mechanical force, yet it is intrinsically ethical. All its rewards are for the good, all its punishments are for the wicked. It represents a cosmic power of righteousness forever working through encouragement of virtue toward a high ethical goal.[34] Logically, suffering is caused by sin and sin is caused by ignorance, as the Nyâya philosophy says, and that wisdom which brings salvation entails the elimination of sin as well as of suffering.

Hindu philosophy conceives of the personal God as endowed with truth, mercy, loving-kindness, and, in so far as it utilizes this conception of God to influence human activities, it fashions the godlike man after the same model, and requires of him that he be truthful, merciful, full of loving-kindness. Thus the school of Vedânta, which is not "purely idealistic,"[35] grants reality to God and to the human soul. It conceives of God as omniscient, merciful, compassionate, and of the soul as finding salvation in an approach to this ideal, which is, in reality, man's own "inner controller." The souls of *men who*

[34] This view of Karma was first set forth by the author in his *Origin and Evolution of Religion*, p. 268. It is repeated here (almost in the same words) because of its ethical importance.

[35] That is, the partially idealistic school of Râmânuja, as contrasted with the pure idealism of Çankara, whose "God" is not a being but Being and everything else is illusion, including God as a personal being, existing illusively in an illusive world.

have been pure can come to God, no others. Here, too, ethics is fundamentally part of religion.

The ancient philosophical doctrine that salvation depends upon the will explicitly states that will determines the moral nature and therefore makes moral evil as important as ignorance in the failure to attain salvation. Even the extremest idealistic philosophers did not relax in their demands for a moral life. As a great scholar said long ago: "They have shown . . . that goodness and virtue, faith and works, are necessary as a preparation, nay as a *sine quâ non,* for the attainment of that highest knowledge which brings the soul back to its source and to its home, and restores it to its true nature, to its true Selfhood in Brahman."[36]

[36] Max Müller, *The Six Systems of Indian Philosophy,* p. 240.

CHAPTER VIII

ETHICAL ABERRATIONS

THE tendency in India to give a free hand to emotionalism is apparent from the earliest days of the "mad ascetic," to the period inaugurated by the death of Buddha, when earth and heaven yielded to ecstatic demonstrations of woe. But the temper of Buddhism did much to prevent this tendency from becoming dangerous and it is chiefly in the musings of later Buddhist saints that an unhealthy emotion is manifested. Early Buddhism was against a too sentimental attitude toward the divine founder; one revered rather than loved Buddha. There was no opening for eroticism till Buddhism was changed into mysticism. But the doctrine that Krishna's worshipper was "dear" to him and the sliding scale of values represented by the worshipper's attitude of "loving devotion" to the Lord answered to a chord in the human heart which was easily attuned to a sensuous note. As already explained, the doctrine taught by Krishna is ethically pure; it has not, as we read the Gîtâ today, the slightest taint of emotional excess. The Lord Krishna represented in the Gîtâ (c. 300 B.C.) is an austere and rather terrifying form of the Supreme Being, whose teaching is severe, though modified by affectionate solicitude for the well-being of man. This incarnate Krishna is neither a child nor a cowherd in bodily form, but a warrior.

Another Krishna was later (*c.* 200 A.D.?) merged with this figure, a Krishna who mythologically represented the god as a youth before the warrior-period, when, his divinity still hidden, he lived among the common people, the favorite of the female cowherds, whose lover he became. The *bhakti* taught in the older cult, debased by this vulgarian, became erotic. Devotion to God became an amorous sensation, as 'God' became a village lover. There was further added a third presentation of Krishna as a child, whose cult was expressed by tender devotion, which was little more than religious sentimentality. This degradation of Krishnaism has a pale parallel in the divagations of Christian mystics. It is historically possible that the late cult of the infant Krishna in the arms of the Madonna was borrowed from Christianity; and it has also been suggested that the cowherd Krishna may have been an intrusion upon the Krishna-cult from some half-christianized tribe of cowherds who did not distinguish between the two names Krishto (Christ) and Krishna. Yet this ingenious explanation of the rise of Hindu eroticism from Christian religious love is not thoroughly convincing, despite the great authority of its author in matters affecting the history of Hindu religious belief.[1]

But we need not discuss these speculations at present. It is enough to deal with the established

[1] The suggestion is made by Sir R. G. Bhandarkar, *Vaishnavism and Çaivism,* etc., p. 38.

ethical facts of later Krishnaism. It is clear that in any folk eroticism is liable to lead to religious and moral excess. From the African savage to the Christian saint, love has been too often rudely interpreted for any doubt to remain as to what would happen when sensuous emotion is exploited as the correct religious attitude of the worshipper. In India, the probable failure of such a theory to preserve itself from contamination is greatly increased, owing to various factors, such as climate, susceptibility to emotional strain, interest in religion, and belief that the guidance of teachers is inspired. The result justifies expectation. The practical effect was that some of the poems composed to describe the devout feelings inspired by the worshipper's love to Krishna and the religious rites dedicated to Râdhâ, as mistress of the same divinity, are far from furthering morality.

But there are other ways in which ethics is lost in the mystic rapture and there are other cults than those of Krishna in which this loss occurs. The worship of God, whose forms on earth appear as Krishna and as Râma, and who is also called Çiva (not incarnate in human form) by other sectarian believers, resolves itself into a yearning devotion to the object of adoration manifested by absolute surrender of the worshipper's mind and body in an endeavor to show his love. This quickly becomes a form of mysticism which, however, may remain ethically pure; in the great majority of cases it is so. In the early hymns, which preceded the formal presentation of his philosophical religion by Râmânuja, and in the rapt utterances of the saints after his day, there is simply the ecstatic joy of the mystic desirous of union with God in a spiritual sense. But in some cases this led to the antinomian theory that the perfect devotee should be willing to sin, if by so doing he might serve God or please him, or give joy to God's representative on earth, the spiritual teacher. This spiritual teacher, Guru, however, though esteemed divine, was often an ignorant and even debauched man, inflated with his own spiritual greatness and morally unfit to be the leader of any religious body. His type still exists and is one of the greatest stumbling-blocks in the path of ethical advance. Given such a man as priest and such an abject devotee as spiritual slave of such a leader, given the idea that by pandering to the viciousness of this little pope the worshipper is pleasing God in the person of his earthly representative, and the shift from religious rapture to moral default is inevitable. Cases illustrative of this evil tendency and of its effect upon the pious but misguided mystic are at hand. But these are individual cases and exceptional. The mass of such devout mystics are ethically impeccable. Their mentality may be impugned, but morally they are without reproach. The Vishnuite Râmânuja school in general cultivated both Krishna and Râma, but did not fall under the influence of the cowherd cult with its amorous apotheosis of the cowherd's favorite mistress. It substituted Sîtâ (model wife of virtuous Râma) for Râdhâ.[2] It began and has remained a sect or sects (there are sundry later forms) devoted to the ideal offered by the figure of Râma and his faithful wife Sîtâ and has not been degraded into the cult of sexual relations which followed from taking Krishna, the vulgar cowherd lover, and his female devotee, Râdhâ, as presentations of a spiritual union between God and the human soul. Sects founded by adherents of this latter religious mania had a great vogue and have had a vicious effect. They were not content with erotic descriptions of the relation between God and soul but put into practice the amorous situation as a religious rite. The leaders were regarded as incarnations of God. Old authorities gave place to the words of such leaders. The scriptures of the sects were no longer the treasures of ethical teaching of the past but the writings of the fanatic leaders. Sensual desires represented their love for divinity and lascivious dalliance became their religious rite. Even literature of high poetic merit, such as the Song of the Cowherd, by Jayadeva, is perfectly frank in its presentation of licentiousness as devotion. As Barth has said of this poem, it "recalls certain productions of Sufism and the sensual delirium defies translation. We do not know which is more astounding, the lewdness of imagination or the devout frenzy which have

[2] The formal cult of Râma did not begin till the eleventh century; that of Sîtâ was introduced by Râmânanda, born c. 1300 A.D.

inspired these burning stanzas." The sects founded by Caitanya and Vallabha, in which love-feasts and erotic literature are prominent features, have shown that such a disregard of common sexual morality as has been practiced by them cannot be without a demoralizing effect on the general moral standard. Some of the male devotees worship particularly the favorite mistress of Krishna and adopt female garb and occupations in sign of this devotion. They have a "left-hand" cult which brings them into line with those worshippers of Çiva whose left-hand cult is a licentious orgy. At the same time it is to be observed that among even these sects are many who interpret the relation between God and soul not in a gross but in a pure, austere, mystic manner. But these spiritually-minded worshippers are in reality sub-sectarians, who have broken loose from the degraded parent sects and their infamous practices; for the parent sects were mere degradations of original Krishnaism.

The decadence of the idea of *bhakti* leads to its becoming the sole element in religious exercises. First it is most important, its complement being the grace of God; then it ousts all other religious conceptions. A profession of faith expressed by the mere mention of the name of God at death is sufficient to efface all sins[3] and a devotee before death may become indifferent to morality; for he is saved by

[3] Barth, *Religions of India,* p. 228. The parallel idea in Christianity is expressed by death-bed absolution.

grace and he who has once received the grace of God cannot sin. But, besides this, *bhakti* leads in India to the declaration of the pure-minded Sittar that "God is love" and, on the other hand, to the reverse, to the statement favored by the licentious, that "Love is divine," a declaration which might as well read "Lust is our god."

The same demoralizing standard is reached also by those worshippers of Çiva who in reality worship the "female potency" as divinity. These are the so-called Çâktas (*çakti* is potency, a feminine noun), who have elaborated a ritual of debauchery. Intoxication and sexual excess are its main features. The Mother-spirit of the world is in its loftiest expression the object of this cult, which has its respectable and its disreputable side, like that of the worshippers of Krishna's mistress, but there is here a new feature. The old morality sought in every way to inculcate the need of self-restraint. It is only by mastering the senses that one can become free of bondage to them. Restraint, moderation, self-control, are essential. But the worshippers of the "female potency" say that all such attempts to restrain the senses are futile. The only way to escape from the dominion of the senses is to gratify them, drug them with excess; satiate lust and it will trouble one no more. They cultivate the serenity induced by exhausted passion.

The most pernicious result of this singular theory is not the gross orgies to which it practically leads, in which lust and drunkenness are glorified, for these can affect only the vulgar-minded who joy in a motive for debauchery, but the philosophic and literary dress in which it is presented. The so-called scriptures of this school are not so old as they pretend to be, but they revert to the first centuries of our era and are filled with discourses aping a moral tone, mystic, cabalistic,[4] devout, religious, and ostensibly ethical. They present an ancient theory of living under a new guise. The old Cârvâka or materialist of the sixth century B.C. said bluntly: "Be as licentious as you please; live for pleasure; there is no punishment hereafter. Indulge your appetites; this is your only chance to do so. God and soul are myths; the priest is a hypocrite; the body dies and then you end. Be happy while you live; to be virtuous is to be a fool." But no philosophers accepted this doctrine and the Cârvâka became a synonym for antinomian laxity of mind as well as of morals. The Çâktas, however, built their house of license more subtly, laying the foundation stones carefully on ethical and religious ground and appealing to good people to assent to their doctrine on the basis of its higher insight into moral and religious truths. Some intelligent and apparently moral persons belong to the Çâkta school, but its chief followers are ignorant and debauched.

[4] The Tantras (not always, Çâkta) recommending gross indulgence in meat, intoxicants, and sexual excess are full of mystical spells, senseless ejaculations, and absurd posturing, intended to dignify the cult of the Great Mother, *i.e.*, the female power. The classical parallel is obvious.

Buddhism also was caught in the net of this seductive animalism and its decadence is marked by as singular a disregard of its original ethical rightness as is the moral decadence of Krishnaism in the later Vishnuite sects. It would be unfair to attribute the substitution of sensuality for ethical ideals to any one of these religious bodies exclusively. The sensual element represents the recrudescence of the savage, lascivious, magical religion of native wild tribes, which, with the fatal catholicity of India, had always been accepted and adapted by the higher cults as a lower expression of their own religious ideas. The worship of the life-power symbolized by the phallus remains as an innocent usage in the higher cults, but in these lower sects it reverts to the primitive sexual expression which used to be thought potent in revivifying nature and is now explained as symbolizing divine love. With the weakening of Brahmanism by Buddhism and with the change in Buddhism itself from ethical training to self-sacrificing love as its religious motive, the way was opened for the long-submerged cult of obscenity (reprobated as early as the Rig Veda, but not banished from the Brâhmanas and always an open sore in the popular sects) to spread over the whole religious body, infecting Vishnuism in its Krishna-Râdhâ manifestation and even in less degree in its Râma-cult, sweeping through Çivaism, which had always been affiliated with it, and completely destroying Buddhism in the new extension of that faith toward the North, so that

Buddhism there becomes devil-worship infected by the passion of savages dressed up in shreds of Buddhistic trappings. The worship of Kâlî, associated with Çiva and really a form of the Mother-goddess native to the savage tribes, led to religious assassination and to murder under the guise of sanctity. Çiva himself was declared to be the "lord of thieves" and lust became a religious motive sanctioned by sect after sect. Ethics survived by tolerance, but in all these sects the really ethical person remained on the defensive.

One cause for the weakening of ethical restraint was undoubtedly the acrimonious attitude adopted toward each other by the religious bodies. The Buddhists were never weary of inveighing against the Brahmans and ridiculing their belief in God (as a Supreme Ruler). Not Brihaspati himself, the reputed founder of the materialistic Cârvâkas, has spoken more bitterly than the popular preacher of Buddhism against the idea that there is a Supreme Being who cares for man, and that sacrifice to the gods is of any avail; while the Brahman priest was constantly sneered at as a hypocrite. One of the Jâtakas takes up this theme (introduced by Buddha himself) and explains at length in quite Cârvâka language what a fool a man is who worships God. Another has a special hell dedicated to Brahman heretics.[5] The gist of this malevolent discourse against the Brahmans is:

[5] J. 541 and 543.

ETHICAL ABERRATIONS

These greedy liars propagate deceit
And fools believe the fables they repeat.

What causes this animosity is the ethical error manifested in the statement of the Brahmans that sin is
offset by sacrifice. A protest of some sort was well
deserved, for, as we have seen, such was the doctrine
actually taught even by the moral code-makers,
though the Brahman moralists themselves saw its
weakness and struggled to avert its consequences.
On the other hand, the Brahmans ignored Buddhism
as much as possible, but condemned "heretics" in
general in unmeasured terms, even inoculating the
king with the idea that heretics should be banished.
But they did not specifically mention the Buddhists
till the late philosophers discussed their theories.
Whether this silence was because of courtesy or was
a mark of political sagacity (some of the codes were
written under Buddhistic dominance) does not matter; it concealed an intense repugnance against the
sect which had made sacrifice in the imperial city
impossible (as in Asoka's Edicts) and reduced the
Brahmans themselves to a position of inferiority.
But that these two great religious bodies, each teaching ethics as a part of religious discipline, should so
fall foul of each other and stigmatize each other
as liars and deceivers of the people, could not fail
to have a lamentable effect upon the whole body
of serious-minded people, leaving them in doubt

whether any of the teaching was worth hearing.[6]
This attitude is reflected in the epic, where it is
openly debated whether any religious teaching is
valid.

For there is no mitigation of the scorn with which
"heretics" are treated. The Buddhist never says
that the ethical rules (such as have been cited in
previous chapters) of the Brahmans are excellent,
though vitiated by a fundamental defect; he scoffs
at everything Brahmanic, caste, sacrifice, religious
belief, and implies that the priest has usually[7] no
ethical standard at all. Nor is there any recognition
on the part of the Brahman that the Buddhist,
though rejecting the Vedas and Vedic gods, is
morally an excellent citizen; he wants the heretic
out of the way, bag and baggage. That there was no
actual warfare between bodies so hostile is not remarkable. The Brahmans were in the minority for
centuries and they, or their warrior partners in Brahmanism, were the fighters; the Buddhists of India
abhorred all fighting and were naturally (or by conviction) a peaceable flock. But as the Buddhists
began to disintegrate and, owing to their new form

[6] The mutual hostility of Christian sects has a similar effect
upon the objects of missionary zeal.

[7] The scoffing is sometimes condescending and humorous and in
later Buddhistic literature allusions are not infrequent to Brahman ascetics as being worthy companions of the Samanas; apparently any honest ascetic was valued for his moral worth. But the
Brahman priest (not ascetic) is represented always as an ignorant,
greedy hypocrite.

of faith, became less markedly different from the sectarian bodies, and as these in turn grew powerful but represented only a quasi-Brahmanism, for the orthodox Brahman is still not a sectarian believer, there was a general amalgamation of religious beliefs, so that religious bigotry expressed itself rather in the antagonism of sect against sect than in hostility of Brahman to Buddhist.

But it was precisely these sects, chiefly devotees of Vishnu or of Çiva, that permitted devotion to be substituted for that ethical foundation which Brahman and Buddhist had built for their respective religions. Beginning with the Bhâgavata cult, as represented in the Besnagar inscription and in the Gîtâ, two to three centuries B.C., in which the old standard expressed by *dama* and *tyâga* (self-control and renunciation) was still in force but was confronted by the equal claims on religious attention of *bhakti*, the 'devotion' motive came more and more to be the important element, until salvation might be attained by it alone, or, in other words, ethics became far less important than loving faith, as the grace of God far surpassed the grace of a moral nature. This belief might be comparatively harmless and even beautiful, when the ecstatic visionary cast all his sins before the Lord and lived in hopeful rapture at his feet— such a saint, and India was full of them, really sinned only in imagination and was of ascetic severity—but when it was allowed to express itself in carnal imitation of divine love, only a miracle could make it impervious to sensual excess. Such traits were supplied by Vishnuism (which finally included Krishnaism), the worship of a kindly and gentle deity not averse from the love-making element, and by Çivaism, which had always been more or less allied with the cult of the phallus and of its natural coadjutor, extreme austerity.[8]

We are now in a position to judge of the reasons why, in the later developments of certain Hindu sects, ethics was practically lowered, however much it was theoretically exalted. It is not because devotion to God is in itself inimical to morality, but because it was forgotten that God himself is the highest ideal of ethical humanity. The old Vedic saying, "Do not lie, for one law the gods observe, to speak the truth," contains an implication of divine morality which first was expressed only negatively, to the effect that Brahma is pure, and then dwindled to the negation of all attributes in the Absolute. But in revolt against a God without attributes rose the conception of a God who was at least friendly and kindly and had a personal interest in man. Such a God was Vishnu, whose predominance was effected

[8] Both cults were originally means of magical control of natural processes. The early ascetic was intent on power, not on virtue; but he soon discovered that one depended on the other. Even as late as the Jâtakas a loss of chastity destroys one's magical power, J. 507. Hindu ascetics, both Brahmanic and Buddhistic, have always been credited with magical powers. It is only in later literature that the Yogi showed any disinclination to perform wonders (fearing an exhibition of self-conceit); he has never disavowed the power to do so.

through these pleasant characteristics, in which the ethical was popularly subordinated to the attractive qualities. Çiva too, though not of attractive and sympathetic nature, at least represented power and its attainment; but in his cult asceticism and terrible austerities displaced ethical practices, or rather these practices were made unimportant and even harmful to the attainment of the end. The ascetic could not weaken his rigid purpose by the exercise of humanitarian benevolence.

It remained for the author of the Gîtâ and Râmânuja, nominally a Vishnuite, with his followers, to create and then recreate (after Çankara) an ethical divinity combining love and mercy with moral excellence. These teachers have done an immense service by reinstating God as a real being[9] and as an omnipotent ethical being and by making it incumbent upon the worshipper to be moral as well as pious. Râmânuja's God is not an illusion (like that of Çankara and the Buddhists of the idealistic school), but a real Supreme Being, whose nature is intrinsically moral. The worshippers of this school are devout, sometimes mystically so, but they uphold firmly the standard of ethical purity. Not among them does one find the crude and coarse exaltation of human passion, nor does their mysticism often neglect the moral principles which have been taught by the ancient sages, though even in this band an

[9] The Gîtâ and Râmânuja both reject the idea of an "illusive" personal God.

213

occasional mystic will put *bhakti* before ethics. Yet there is this to be said. When this is done, it is done without pretense that immoral conduct is a spiritual manifestation. The religious hysteria does not manifest itself in imagining that evil conduct is moral but in consciously sinning in the belief that the sin committed is to the glory of God, a delusion less unethical if deplorable. The general attitude of the long line of sects which culminate in Kabîr is that sin divides the soul from God. Only the soul morally pure, free from spiritual soilure, can be blessed with the saving grace of God. And what is here said of the philosophical Râmânuja school can be said also of those Vishnuites who, following the cult advocated by certain leaders of low caste but of high spirituality, have disdained to copy the erotic school and have laid stress on conduct equally with faith.

Practical social activity is lacking in these ethical-religious developments. The holy men of India seldom labor to convert the world. They rest content with trying to purify their own souls without harming others. They are saints, or try to be, rather than reformers of society. Their ideal is that of the best of the old Christian saints, with whom also they share some of the defects. But the founders of sects were by no means deficient in the missionary spirit; they preached the gospel without ceasing, the gospel of loving faith and ethical purity. For social guidance they follow the rule laid down by Tulasîdâs, "from sweet words results good on all sides; this is a spell that overcomes everything; avoid all harsh words"; or by Nâmdev, who inculcated "purity of heart, humility, surrender of self, forgiveness, and the love of God."[10]

To close this topic, in reprehending religious debauchery it must never be forgotten that aberrations such as this are not characteristic but are actually deviations from the normal. Most of the sensual sects are the product of city life and overcrowded population. The life of the Hindu in the villages, where the typical life is to be found, is singularly simple and moral, and even the city's lowest classes are not so depraved as are those of the great cities of Europe. So said Elphinstone long ago, and adds: "The Hindus are a mild and gentle people. Their freedom from gross debauchery is the point in which they appear to most advantage."[11] With this judgment most of the observers of native life agree.

But there is another sort of ethical aberration which, instead of filling the modern Western mind with disgust, inspires wonder and pity. It is the result of a want of controlling common sense, for despite the constant advice to be self-restrained, the Hindus seem deficient in respect of control of the imaginative faculty. This lack impairs the beauty of both their literature and their art. In describing a rural scene it is not enough for the epic poet to men-

[10] Sir R. G. Bhandarkar, *Vaishnavism, Çivaism,* etc., p. 91.
[11] Elphinstone, *History of India,* cited by Max Müller in his essay on *The Truthful Character of the Hindus,* p. 48.

tion a few trees and flowers, but he stuffs his verse
with a botanical catalogue of plants. In glorifying
the gods, the artist sculptures them with a grotesque
superfluity of arms, legs, and heads, which make the
deities ridiculous instead of awe-inspiring. In religious ethics, the same unbridled imagination leads
to constant violation of that happy mean which
Buddha tried to inculcate. To give generously passes
into extravagance of giving; to be self-restrained
leads to a certain ferocity of asceticism, which makes
a monster of a would-be saint. The intent is laudable;
it is to remain true to one's ideals at whatever cost.
It is thus a kind of loyalty, such loyalty as in other
forms appears at every phase of Hindu life. In law,
for example, the horrible penalty inflicted on a
woman for adultery committed with one of a low
caste is really inflicted not so much because the of-
fender has been impure as because she has been disloyal to her class, which she has degraded. In usage,
the intense feeling of loyalty of the old Hindus
centered less about the king than about the clan, and
this clan-feeling was so strong that it upheld clan-
tradition even in the face of state-law. Not without
reason does an epic writer, speaking for clan-rights,
say boldly: "No matter what internal dissensions
may rend the clan, if anyone outside the clan (family) insult a member of the clan they all resent it;
the law of the clan and its maintenance is the most
important thing. That anyone outside the family
should make demands on the clan is something that

good people cannot endure."[12] To the clan, goodness is first of all loyalty. Loyalty to the salt is also almost a proverbial expression.[13]

Now it is just this spirit of loyalty, to an idea, which has produced these strange and repellant ideals personified in the perfect king and the perfect saint. Such characters are not usual, everyday citizens, and this fact must, of course, be taken into consideration. What they do is not the norm for everyone, but their attitude and their acts are nevertheless portrayed as super-excellent. The king shows what to us is revolting virtue; the ascetic, immoral righteousness. When poor little Sîtâ, the most devoted ideal wife, is brought back to her virtuous husband, king Râma, after she has been carried off by a demon and been forced to live in the demon's palace, one would expect Râma to express some pity for her and clasp her to his heart with a cry of joy. Not a bit of it. "Is she quite good enough for me?" he asks; "Has she returned as pure as when she was carried off?" "I have been true to you, my dear Lord," says Sîtâ, weeping. "Well, perhaps so," replies Râma, "but how am I going to know?" "I will go through the fire ordeal to prove it," answers Sîtâ bravely. "An excellent idea; let her walk through the flames." So the virtuous Râma is at last con-

[12] The outsider is here expressly *jñâtînâm bâhyas,* "outside of the clan-relations," or *kula,* Mbh. 3, 243, 3.

[13] The one who, being supported by him, "steals his lord's food" (is disloyal), takes on himself the king's sins and "loses this world and the next." Mbh. 5, 146, 17 (*bhartripindâ'pahârin*).

vinced of Sîtâ's innocence, but only when she has had the test applied (the Fire-god sees to it that she is not harmed). Then at last is Râma willing to say, "Welcome back home." Now this scene is as unethical as can be imagined. It is full of base suspicion and incredible brutality; yet it represents to the Hindu the loftiest flight of virtuous honor. Or let us take the final story in the Jâtakas. The Buddha in a preceding birth was born a prince of such unbelievable generosity that he began giving things away as soon as he was born and by the time he reached early manhood he had given everything he had and began to give away things that did not belong to him, notably a white elephant, which caused rain to fall whenever desired and which some priests from another kingdom asked for. In their country there was a famine and the regular rain-maker, the king, had been unable to produce rain, so hearing of the elephant he sent the priests to get it if possible. It was only too possible, for the prince happened to be riding the elephant just as the priests came to town, and with his usual liberality he at once gave it to them. Then the citizens, who held that the elephant was not his to give and that its loss would inconvenience them when they themselves happened to have a famine, went to the king and demanded that the prince be banished. So he was sent away with his wife and children and lived in a mountain hermitage. Here begins the moral. A priest, who is poor and needs a couple of servants, thinks to himself, "Why not go and ask this fool for his children? He 'gives when asked,' that is his rule, and his children would make good slaves." So he goes to the wilderness and says with no pretence of politeness that he wants the children. The children, very much frightened, run away, but are brought back by their father (the mother is gathering fruit for his dinner in the forest), who says to them, "Now be good and go with this man, so that you may help me to ferry myself beyond the worlds of birth," that is, to win salvation. The children are led off bound and whipped by the priest, and crying out: "Father, father, have you a heart of stone? He is beating us; he is cruel to us." But, after a single spasm of emotion, cold and immovable as the mountain walls around him sits the Great Being, and when the distracted mother returns in the evening and begs him to tell her where the children are, he refuses to answer. He feels pained, but at once says to himself remonstratingly, "This pain comes from affection; I must stifle it and be calm or I shall not win my reward as a great saint." Then, having ignored the frantic shrieks of his children and having let them go beaten and weeping into captivity, in order that he may win the reward of having given the "greatest gift imaginable," when another petitioner asks him for his wife, he gives her away also. Thus the stony-hearted one wins the reward of his generosity and of his knowledge that serenity leads to salvation:

Not hateful is my faithful wife, nor yet my children are;
But perfect knowledge to my mind is something better far.

His wife, being better educated than the children, is, it must be admitted, quite ready to be sacrificed: "Let him give, or let him kill; my husband is my husband still" (and I his slave). The tale is well told. The shrieks and appeals of the children, their piteous laments, as the rascally priest twice drags them off (the poor things escape once and run back in vain to their heartless father) are very realistic. The writer wants the reader to appreciate the grandeur of the scene, the heart of stone which only for a moment weakens and then resumes its holy calm.

Now decency is a part of morality and the only decent thing for the saint to do was to kick the priest out of his hermitage to begin with, or to knock him down, if he had been weak enough to give the children up, the moment he saw them being maltreated. Yet this did not seem to occur to him; he honestly thought he was doing the right thing in rather an impressive manner. But it is hard for us to acknowledge that this was a great and glorious act of abnegation, especially as the only reason for it was the father's selfish desire to win his own salvation by means of his brutal "generosity."

It is not likely that either of these scenes had a model in real life; but they show to what extremes the Hindus can go in being loyal to their ideals. The perfect king must have a perfect mate; Caesar's wife must be above suspicion. The ideal Buddhist saint must renounce family and home without faltering in exercising his virtue. Well and good. The theory up to a reasonable point is Christian also: "There is no man that hath left house or parents or brethren or wife or children for the kingdom of God's sake, who shall not receive manifold more in this present time and in the world to come life everlasting." And he who deserts his family has a divine model: "Who is my mother or my brethren?" Only, in the Buddhist application, the renunciation is not only made most callously but it is made for a purely selfish purpose. It must be confessed that even the ideal of the usual Hindu ascetic (not Buddhistic) is also ethically wrong for the same reason; the motive is self-salvation. But in many of these ascetic cases the soul of the Yogi is saved (to speak in Western form) because it is not mere selfishness which prompts him, but an intense desire for a pure spiritual life; and it is ticklish business trying to dismember the ardent soul and see which of two motives is stronger. The souls of a good many Christians, if thus inspected, would show a double strain, one of undoubted spirituality and another of hopes quite personal and selfish.

Perhaps a parable taken from the Jâtakas will, however, illustrate the old Buddhistic position more clearly. The Buddha in a previous birth went out of the city and saw a mango tree broken and despoiled by those who had climbed it to gather its luscious fruit, which had all been taken from it. He went on and saw another tree which was barren; having no fruit it had been left intact. And he said: "Behold the barren tree! In that it possessed naught and cherished naught, it has been saved. But on account of its rich burden of fruit the other tree has been robbed and ruined. When Mithilâ was burning, well said its king, 'Burn, O Mithilâ, naught of mine is burning'; wise was he, for it is ill with him who loses all through having much." And there and then the Master made the mighty resolution, *to be a barren tree*.[14]

The moral here intended is similar to that of "the young man having great possessions"; but though that moral peeps out in the reference to the king of Mithilâ, whose grandiloquent utterance is famous in Brahman circles also,[15] it is almost lost to modern eyes in the stupendous egoism of the speaker. That the mango tree having fruits useful to the world might be a better tree than the one that was barren, did not even occur to the maker of the parable. It was this which made the new Buddhism of the Mahâyâna school (now most prominent in Japan) so ethically potent, for in substituting Buddha's wish

[14] J. 539.
[15] It amounts to saying, "All my wealth is destroyed, but nothing really vital to me has perished; the soul stands alone and has no possessions except itself."

to save others for the determination to save himself (at one birth) it really introduced a new ethics.[16]

[16] Yet, as was said above, p. 166, although self-sacrifice is the great thought which inspires the Mahâyâna, the same note is heard in popular tales. But the Mahâyâna gave this principle the highest religious sanction and made it divine.

CHAPTER IX

PRO AND CONTRA

IT may occur to some reader that it might be worth
while to conclude the subject of Hindu ethics with
a comparison between the ethics of India and that
of America. But, besides being invidious, it would
really serve no useful purpose to prove that India's
ethical systems of more than two thousand years ago
were not erected on modern ideas of social service
and philanthropic institutions. Then, too, in contrast
with life today, the conditions under which the ethics
of India was formulated must be considered. When
a Hindu law book declares that there can be no
proper Veda-study in a city and another warns the
priest to "avoid going often into cities,"[1] this means
that the rules of life laid down in the early Brahmanic codes were composed for villagers, where
lay the real life of most of the people for whom the
priests made their rules. It is clear also that Buddhistic rules are intended primarily for the monastic
life or for the life of a hermit rather than for the
world at large. For, though provision is made for the
laity by providing them with general rules of good
behavior and teaching them elementary truths, the
heart of Buddha's doctrine is for the recluse. Social
activities can play but little part in such a scheme.

Again, we in America, reaping the fruit of cen-

[1] G. 16, 45; Âp. 1, 11, 32, 21, *nagarapraveçanâni.*

tury-long effort, have swept into the rubbish heap
many of the restrictions under which the ethics of
India has progressed upon its sorely beset but upward way. Polytheism and idolatry, as practiced in
many of the sects, tend to place beside ethics other
objects of serious consideration as of profound importance. One must not only have a clean heart, but
one must keep the idol clean; "for in it dwells God."
One must go on pilgrimages as well as give in charity. One's food must be ritually pure as one's soul
must also be pure. One must have five great virtues, truthfulness, uprightness, compassion, charity,
non-destruction of life, but, equally, one must perform five great ceremonies. Loving devotion to God
implies observance of ritual as well as observance of
morality. Such, for example, in the religion of Râmânuja are some of the difficulties under which ethics
is, as it were, weighed down. Love of God and good
conduct are not enough; they make only part of a
heavy load attached to morality as essential to it and
increasing the burden of righteousness. They are not
enough in the minds of many Christians, who think
that one should go on a pilgrimage once a week and
attend to many ritualistic observances. But on the
whole we are freer, because we have fewer of these
rival obligations; though it must not be forgotten
that many Hindu sects also have renounced idolatry
and ritualism of all kinds in favor of faith and clean
living.

But on the whole, what with all these inhibitions

exercised upon morality, of the age, of the environment, and of the rubbish heap, piled high with caste, ritual, Karma, and austerity, it is not probable that it will occur to anybody to desire to exchange our own ethical inheritance for that of India. So that there can be no harm in standing off at a safe distance and calling closer attention to any object of virtue that is to be admired there, even if we decide not to import it for our own use.

There is in India a doctrine called non-injury, which in some regards transcends any ethical teaching to be found in Christianity as known in America. It is the gentle doctrine of harmlessness, which more than covers the precept of the catechism "to hurt nobody by word nor deed," for it means that it is a sin, and a sin far worse than lying or stealing, needlessly to maim or kill any living creature. This is not a teaching of Christianity, though it has been engrafted upon it and finds expression in a small degree in the Society for the Prevention of Cruelty to Animals, the very existence of this society being, however, an indictment of ordinary practice. This ancient rule of Hindu ethics embodies toward all animal life a sympathetic attitude which repels the robust West and is excluded from its "manly virtues." To kill for sport is a commendable amusement practiced by clergy and laity alike; to be a Christian gentleman one does not have to be gentle.

Moreover, there is the irresistible argument that it is natural to maim and kill. Brutes are cruel, so why should not men be brutal? Then again, this doctrine of harmlessness is ridiculous when carried to extremes. One must not kill vermin, what? And the belief that vegetable matter is alive leads even to the inculcation of sympathy for trees: "You should not break the bough of the tree that has sheltered you."[2]

In respect of this last point, it may be said that the sacredness of life in a tree depends, of course, on the idea one has of a tree. The Buddhist did not imagine the tree itself to be alive but to be inhabited by a dryad or Nâga, whose very existence depended on the life of the tree; it was a hamadryad which one slew in slaying the tree. The Brahman, on the other hand, held that the tree itself was alive; it was a living being, with senses to feel, hear, taste, smell, and see, and it shrank from hurt. There is a chapter in the great epic which explains this at length.[3] To cut down a tree was like killing a bird; one should repent, tell of the evil deed, and fast for three days.[4] Trees are cursed for their actions as if they were moral creatures, though elsewhere it is said that morality is confined to human beings. But the tales of virtuous beasts and kind trees ("the tree does not refuse shelter even to the man who comes to cut it

[2] J. 545, and elsewhere. It is an act of treachery to do so. Compare, "Woodman, spare that tree, touch not a single bough. In youth it sheltered me and I'll protect it now," regarded by us as a delightful absurdity.

[3] Mbh. 12, 184.

[4] Ibid. 35, 34.

down") show that trees were regarded as having a moral nature and indeed they even inherit a sin cast upon them by a god, and, just like men, they expect to go to heaven when they die.[5] Some modern scholars argue that plants think as well as feel, but perhaps it is enough to maintain that they have feelings.

So much for trees. But exaggerations of this sort may be compared to speaking the truth with such scrupulosity as to endanger one's life by so doing, or to the exquisite Buddhistic sin of "stealing the perfume of a flower." It does not impair the value of the general precept. And there is something valuable and beautiful in the doctrine that one should feel such sympathy for other living beings that one refuses to hurt them, that one will not unnecessarily injure an insect, that one will not needlessly maim and kill animals, that one will refuse to follow "warrior ethics" and not even kill in war.

This more than humane doctrine was carried out consistently by the Buddhists of India (in Ceylon and Japan the fighting spirit prevailed against it)[6] and it is still practiced by the Jains, in what we

[5] Trees cursed, Mbh. 12, 343, 59; recipients of Indra's sin, 283, 36 (an old tale); on trees going to heaven, see *ibid*. 269, 24.

[6] The Ceylon Buddhists of today are such a gentle, placid band that it is hard to remember that they originally "fought for glory to the doctrine" (of Buddhism, not of non-injury). In the Mahâvansa a king is comforted for killing millions on the ground that they were "unbelievers and sinful" (Mahâvansa, 25, 2, *seq.*, and *ibid*. 108). In Japan, the monasteries in the Middle Ages became armed forts of fighting friars.

regard as its risible form, while among the Brahmans it held good as a moral precept except where the higher law of sacrifice and "righteous war" made it impossible to follow it. The priests would have lost their livelihood in one case and the warriors in the other, if they had given up sacrifice and war; but we need not impugn the motives of those who honestly thought that offering meat to gods and Manes or that "fighting righteously" was a religious duty. As it was, the worshippers of Vishnu gave up even sacrificial slaughter and contented themselves with making offerings of cakes and flowers and paste images. But the general principle of "harmlessness" is surely one that must commend itself to the enlightened moral sense of the West. It would do away, not as a matter of sentiment, as it is now, but as a matter of duty, with cruelty and war, and that is enough in its favor. It might eventually lead to the suppression of needless slaughter and killing for fun;[7] yet we must remember how far behind India in this regard we are ethically and not frighten our manly virtues into revolt against all attempts to elevate them. But the world has been changed before

[7] Hunting wild animals for food was always recognized in India as a "warrior-custom," to be condoned as a regrettable necessity. The authority for this was the Saint Agastya, M. 5, 22; Mbh. 13, 116, 15, seq. Hence the combined rule, "animals may be slain for sacrifice and to support dependents." Vas. 14, 15, cites the same authority. One great cruelty which the present author would like to see abolished is practiced in every zoo. To keep tigers and lions for life in close confinement is a moral offence not justified by the "educational value" of the pitiable exhibition.

this and a new renascence is always possible. The
Brahman soon rose above the old savage notion that
"the eater will hereafter be eaten by the eaten," as
a reason for not killing animals. He began to see life
as a whole and, years before the thought that all life
is one had dawned on the West, he declared that "to
take oneself as the norm" in ethics was the inevitable
corollary of "every soul is part of the All-soul" in
philosophy. Love thy neighbor as thyself, in a new
interpretation, became his rule. Moralizing his law
of retribution he turned it for himself into a law of
mercy. As I suffer (said he), so suffers the one whom
I hurt; and the animal pleading for life suffers as
well as the man injured and dying. To injure this
other life, which in reality is one with my life, as
both our lives are one with divine life, what could be
more sinful? "He who injures another life, goes to
hell," was the Buddhist's religious attempt to check
the abuse of cruelty. We may pass lightly over the
fear of hell, but not when it is of our own making;
the hell of war and the hell of cruelty are real enough
and the only way to escape from them is to follow
the moral rule of the Hindu, which thus aims at a
social service of unprecedented value.

Eventually (perhaps) the world will come to believe that this one doctrine, which, however, has a
host of implications, such as not injuring by speech
or by malicious thought, is of more importance even
than the costliest philanthropic institutions, though
it would be absurd to maintain that public service in

the Western sense was unknown to the ancient Hindus. Works of public charity were frequently erected by those able to pay for them (including women) and the planting of trees and constructing of bathing pools, besides the giving of private wealth in charity, were not unusual, as might be guessed from the casual reference in the epic to the proper procedure when one has proved oneself a public benefactor: "Let no man through desire (of praise) continue to live where he has given away his wealth."[8]

The ethics of non-injury may be extended to include self-sacrifice, to prevent injury to another, as it is often thus extended in Buddhistic writings, and to the thought of self-surrender, which is prominent in the later religion of Buddha and of Râmânuja; or the process may be inverted and the moral value of self-sacrifice and of self-surrender to God may precede all analysis and spring into being as a natural expression of love, as in Christianity, so that West and East may meet by different ways on a common ground. Much is done today in the West toward the saving of life and amelioration of living beings and the idea has been expanded into an active pursuit of the salvation of others, which on the human side goes farther than mere cessation from doing harm. Yet it is in its whole scope that the Hindu ethics surpasses ours; in the inclusion of the beasts and birds and even of the trees and flowers in its all-embracing tenderness and kindly sympathy.

[8] Mbh. 5, 45, 13.

And we, who are only beginning to hear that trees and flowers have life and feeling comparable in weak degree to our own, and condone, if we do not inflict, so much of the misery suffered by dumb animals, may properly, as we learn to be less cruel, turn back with some humility to the time long before the Christian era, when so good and perfect a doctrine was not only preached as an ethical ideal but was accepted by millions of people as the normal rule of life for every good man, and confess that, however excellent our ethics may be, India has taught us something better than we knew.

It has been cynically said that the more statutes there are against a vice the more probable is it that the statutes are needed. Thus, because the Hindus were forever inculcating the virtue of speaking truthfully, the inference should be that they were naturally consummate liars, not that they were lovers of truth. By the same rule, the Hindus must have been monsters of cruelty. But both conclusions would be faulty, though the injunctions against these vices undoubtedly reflect the fact that in India, as in any country five hundred years before the Christian era, or even a thousand years after it, there were a host of people who were really only half-civilized and not very deeply affected by any moral precepts. Thinking India, the India we know from literature and history, was actually a small group within an endless environment of barbarous tribes, which were not extirpated, like our Indians, but assimilated, as well as such hordes could be assimilated, that is, slowly and not thoroughly, so that the environment affected the civilized group as well as the group affected the rude mass with which it was struggling. Now, while some savages are truthful, very few are humane, and many of these barbarians were the rawest recruits from the hill-tribes. We must imagine the vast rural population as largely composed of this admixture of a few high and many lower people, believing for the most part in every crude superstition, practicing every sort of religious-magical rite, and ill-trained ethically. It implies therefore no real condemnation of Hindu ethics, as taught by members of the civilized community, that their teachers felt obliged to insist strongly on what they regarded as the chief moral rules to be popularly inculcated, speaking the truth and reverence for life. The Hindus as a people were perhaps not over truthful (what people is?), though the British judge who put down thuggery in the last century has left on record the statement that he had heard hundreds of cases among the rural population "in which the property and the life of the speaker depended on a lie and he refused to tell it," and, like all people of low intelligence, the half-civilized tribesmen were careless of suffering in others. So much more to the credit of the better classes is it that they so persistently hammered into their countrymen the divine precept of the sacredness of life that, long before the Christian era, not to injure or kill had become an axiom of decent behavior.

Yet the object of this recapitulation is not to criticise adversely any system of ethics, but rather to spread out before the reader the pro and contra that can be urged in regard to India's morality, that is, to show the outstanding features of India's ethical life in the old days. As we have seen, in India, as in other lands, ethics was hampered as well as helped by religion. To perform sacrifices was for many centuries more important than to be moral, or rather, it was more immoral not to serve the gods than to serve men, for that was what it came to. But finally the point was reached when men no longer asked, "Is it not better to sin against men than against the gods?" Instead, they said that to be moral was better service than to be ritualistic, for they had come unaided to the discovery that it was more religious to cleanse the soul than to mutter prayers. The Pharisee's brother was not unknown in India and his scrupulous care of the outer observance led him to maintain, long after the opposing view had been promulgated, that the sins of the soul could be washed away by the stream of religious ritual, which is still flowing on beside the Ganges. But his view was virtually superseded ages ago: "If a man be intemperate and lustful, of what use his penance, of what use his sacrifice?"[9] India evolved for herself the idea

[9] Mbh. 12, 270, 29, *kim tasya tapasâ kâryam, kim yajñena.* Here *tapas* may imply fasting.

of a merciful God, of a soul that must be pure, of a life that must be harmless and helpful, even the idea that, as his highest duty, man must seek to do that which is beneficial to all men, *sarvaprajâ-hitam,* as it is expressed in the *Râmâyana.* Despite the handicap of an overstressed religious ritual, which nearly blinded her to the greater light of ethics, India emerged with the belief that religion is a matter not of form but of mind and will,[10] and that a good character is more essential than a good ritual. Her priests thought that they were gods on earth; her kings were taught that they were themselves vice-gerents of the gods and embodied divinity; and her philosophers maintained that everybody was essentially divine; but all this made no difference in the theory of what a good citizen, be he priest, king, philosopher, or common man, should be and do. Even the gods, if they would be reborn in the highest state hereafter,—for the gods were subject to decay and rebirth,—were warned that they "must avoid all evil acts, all evil words, all evil thoughts, and do much and boundless good."[11]

The rewards of virtuous conduct are, as has been

[10] A Vedic text, VS. 34, 3, says: "Moved by right resolve be my mind, mind which is wisdom, intellect, firmness, and the eternal Light within; it dwells within my heart, like a skilful charioteer governing horses." The later doctrine of character and future happiness being dependent on will has already been explained.

[11] Such impiety as may be charged to the speaker must be laid to the Buddhists (Itivuttaka, 31, 83). But the Brahmans also are not slow to preach morality to the gods, who, in the later belief, were only spirits inferior to men; for to attain felicity a god be-

shown, interpreted variously. In the earlier period, when the gods were like men and good men joined the gods in the sky, sensual pleasures for the virtuous after death were merely enlarged and intensified; for there was no lack of virtue in sensuality. With increasing moral and bodily restraint, heaven was resolved into a state of peace and joy devoid of sense-gratification. The body now could not be resurrected; even the *jîva,* or vital animal spirit, passed, as something material, with the body, and pure soul alone remained to enjoy its own immaterial bliss. But in whatever form presented, the idea of a place free from sin (as sin was conceived from time to time) remained. There were of course contending interpretations of the future life. The old belief that good Aryans "shone like constellations, being forms of light in the sky," persisted.[12] And side by side with this was the notion (also antique) that the "other world" lay not in the sky but in the extreme north, "on the northern flank of the Himâlayas, where in a pure and happy land good men are reborn";[13] but the usual idea was that heaven is in the sky, where the clouds are,[14] and this heaven is described as a

comes human and, as we have seen, above, p. 182, "there is nothing nobler than humanity."

[12] Mbh. 12, 271, 24, *jyotirbhûtâs.* Resurrection is impossible without the intervention of a great god like Çiva, who raises a dead boy to life, *ibid.* 153, 13.

[13] *Ibid.* 192, 8 and 21 (*paro lokas*).

[14] A rain cloud ("a heavenly giver of good") is revered as being "a creature living nigh the gods," *ibid,* 272, 9, *seq.*

place in which "there is neither hunger nor thirst nor weariness nor old age nor sin."[15] Finally there is Nirvâna or Brahma as goal of the weary philosophic soul, peace or existence as part of pure, intelligent, blissful being. In all these forms of happiness hereafter sin will be no more, only bliss, which is incompatible with sin. Nay, but there is one more possible existence hereafter, later imagined but now more universally the object of religious faith, life with God, who in his own person is both Absolute Being, Brahma, and Virtue incorporate, or perfect Righteousness, *Sa Brahma paramo Dharmas.*[16]

But now, to conclude this long description of ancient ethical ideals, a few passages will be cited which may be helpful as illustrating those principles of right and wrong which the Hindus, before they were affected by foreign modern ideas, were wont to set before the rising generation as the best guides to lead one through a good and happy life to a good and happy hereafter. Though themselves foreign to us, they will not be found altogether alien to our own

[15] Mbh. 12, 190, 13; in 193, 27, the gods living in this heaven (as in Vedic times) "see every sin a man commits though men may see it not." The note of bodily and mental purity as conditioning admittance to heaven comes before this. Âpastamba says almost in epic language, "By avoiding with mind, speech, and body (the last literally, nose, eye, ear) sensual gratification, one gains immortality" (2, 2, 5, 19). The epic is never tired of repeating this: "If a man's nature is not pure, *yadi bhâvo na nirmalas,* signs of religion (ablutions, vows, etc.) and observances are all in vain." Mbh. 3, 200, 97.

[16] Mbh. 12, 281, 26.

thought, for they are not the precepts laid down for saints and philosophers, but for ordinary citizens like ourselves, and good men think much alike all the world over. But, though some of these may not be novel, they have this new attraction, that they were thought out and enunciated many centuries ago and they reflect life not as it might be imagined in some Utopia but as it was actually lived in the little towns and villages of India, when the worthy citizens listened with reverence to the wise sayings of their venerable teachers and the harmless friars of the Buddhist faith filled the land with their joyful hymns and pious admonitions. Though the Buddhist scriptures are intended chiefly for hermits and friars, yet we must not think of these friars as in any sense monks vowed to perpetual celibacy and to a religious life apart from the world. They entered the Order of Buddhists simply as converts to the faith and were free at any time to give up the monastic life and return to the world. The mass of nominal Buddhists were not friars at all but laics, people employed in their ordinary occupations. Rules for them were far less strict than for the friars. The Brahmans, too, were only one class in a community consisting of people of all trades and occupations, whom the Brahmans taught religion and ethics, not living in seminaries or monasteries but in their own homes as simple teachers. Except for the few who were officially employed as court chaplains, their sacerdotal functions were only occasionally exercised, for conducting a sacrifice or attending to some domestic rite, which they were especially invited by a king or a householder to perform. Their main function was that of a private tutor. In this way, both the Brahmanic and Buddhistic spiritual heads lived much more simply at one with the people than is the custom where priests or friars live apart by themselves. The feeling that the Brahman was in a class apart spiritually was indeed strong and was steadily fostered by the priest himself. He felt superior to the crowd and so he was, by birth, by learning, by his sacred office, and, if he was really "a true Brahman," by his rigid morality. But socially the village priest was no recluse. The stringent and foolish caste-rules of today as to eating and marrying were unknown. Caste-privileges were known and were strictly enforced, and there were certain rules as to caste-precedence and pure food. But in a small village the Brahman was the teacher and guide of the community and was friendly with all, looked up to by all. He might even take a slave girl as one of his wives, though it is improbable that he often did so. But his position was not much more aloof from the little world he lived in than that of an English squire, or rector. It was not always he, however, who in the centuries preceding the Christian era, taught the masses. For there were teachers of allied but non-conformist faiths who in those days wandered about the country or settled down with large followings and gave instruction in religion and ethics, as well as in philosophy, which did not always coincide with that given by the orthodox priests. Thus, as has already been shown, we find a teacher expressing the view that fasting, of all rites most dear to the orthodox priest, is a useless performance; another (and him not a Buddhist) saying that even to kill for a sacrifice is wrong; and a third declaring that even a slave might be instructed in the Vedas and become a religious mendicant. It is these more liberal views that are so largely represented in the great epic, which is only partly brahmanized and represents the more popular views of the great half-brahmanized population, which still stood apart from Buddhism in the early centuries before our era.[17]

Let us imagine[18] one of these teachers addressing his pupils, for the most part sons of noblemen and wealthy merchants or, in a village, the sons of the Aryan soldiers and farmers domiciled about him, with here and there a priest's son, destined in turn to be educated for the office of teacher. He has finished the formal lessons for the term of teaching, during which, to be consecrate to his office, he has

[17] The date of the epic *terminus ad quem,* which the author twenty-odd years ago set at about the fourth century A.D., must now be put much earlier (probably as early as the first or second century B.C.), as stated in 1915 in his *Epic Mythology.* Later intrusions here and there are of course to be admitted. The recently published *Southern Recension* shows that the process of adding to the text was never discontinued.

[18] Only the scene is imagined, not the precepts given below, references for which, unless provided here or occurring *passim* in the codes, will be found in the preceding chapters.

241

neither eaten meat nor had his hair cut. Of lighter
hue than most of his pupils, emaciated by religious
austerities, high-born, proud, yet kindly, he gives
them their final instructions:

You, who are now going out into the world, should
bear in mind not only the words of the sacred texts
which I have taught you, but also the precepts of the
old teachers whose wisdom was divinely given. Go to
your homes, revere your parents, marry, raise up
children. A life lies before you of your own making,
to be good or ill, as you shall choose. Choose the
better part; do not let the world blind you to the life
beyond the world. As you control your will, so will
your desires be, and your fate after life will be in
accordance with what in this life you think, and say,
and do. Think no evil; think kindly of others; be
pitiful and sympathetic; think of high things, not
of low things; think of your soul as more important
than your body. Speak gently, not roughly nor maliciously; avoid gossip, slander, and harsh language;
avoid irreverence and obscenity. Do well, not ill; do
the work you were born to do, contentedly, joyfully;
do not harm or kill living beings, for when harmed
they suffer as you would suffer. And for you who are
to lead the active life of merchant and of soldier,
remember in particular the rules of your profession.
Be energetic, do not procrastinate; death is ever
likely to come. Remember the wise word of old, "Do

today what must be done tomorrow."[19] You sons of
honest merchants, be yourselves honest; do not use
false weights or measures; amass wealth, but use it
righteously. Give to the poor; for it is said that "the
Creator permits men to grow rich in order that with
the wealth they do not need they may endow those
who have naught." Do unto others as you would
have others do unto you.[20] You farmers' sons, be
kind to your slaves and cattle, as says the old rule:
"Stint yourself, if you must, and your wife and son,
but do not stint the slave who works for you," and
also: "Let a student and a draught-ox eat as much
as they like."[21] And be hospitable; it is said that a
guest who is disappointed in his host takes with him
as he goes his host's merit and leaves behind his own
evil, even as a king who fails to do justice takes upon
himself the criminal's sin. If you have nothing else
to give your guest, give him at least "water and a
welcome," as the saying is.[22] You who are to be
soldiers, remember that "Aryans do not boast"; they
neither praise nor blame themselves; and in fighting
remember the old rule, "Do not strike below the
belt,"[23] which rule take as a guide for other cases,

[19] *Çvas kâryam adya kurvîta,* Mbh. 12, 277, 13 (the text con-
tinues, "and do in the morning what must be done in the after-
noon").

[20] The last two precepts are found *ibid.* 260, 22, *seq.;* for the
care of cattle, see 263, 37, *seq.,* and 12, 15, 51.

[21] Âp. 2, 4, 9, 11, *seq.*

[22] Vas. 13, 61; Âp. 2, 2, 4, 14; Mbh. 12, 191, 12, etc.

[23] Mbh. 8, 35, 45, and 9, 60, 6, *adho nâbhyâ na hantavyam*
(literally, "below the navel").

such as not using in fight or war unfair weapons, poison, or any deceitful means; unless indeed deceit be used against you, when you may without sin use deceit or spells or any other means to frighten, *vibhîshikâ*, previously used by an opponent.[24] Yet this is a delicate matter and not to be resolved offhand; only this is clear, that deceit is sinful in all ordinary circumstances, and for the rest you will later be instructed by the War-teacher.[25] In this life it is true that, as the adage has it, "Unto the strong all things are pure," that is, it is right for them to do what they choose to do; but do not believe that power determines right, for there is a law above the strong.[26] And this I would have all of you remember, that morality is the basis of religion. To sum up: Speak the truth, keep control of your passions, be generous, sympathetic, follow the old rules of good conduct, for these are more essential than family or clan, in the making of a man.[27] So teach the Buddhists and many of our own people say the same thing. But it is only our own teacher who says, speaking of God as "the great, pure, wise, eternal

[24] Mbh. 6, 65, 16. Another passage says expressly that "killing by deceit one who deceives is not called a sin," *ibid*. 3, 52, 22; but a moral doubt lingers with the hearer. See 12, 100, 5.

[25] Special rules were given to the warriors in the art of war, *dhanurveda*.

[26] *Ibid*. 15, 30, 24, *sarvam balavatâm çuci* (also *pathyam* and *dharmas*, "to the strong all is proper and right," and *svakam*, "all belongs to the strong").

[27] *Ibid*. 3, 180, 33, to 181, 43 (SI. has *yoga* and *jñâna* for *dâna* and *dharma!*). This passage may be Buddhistic in origin.

Spirit," that "he who everywhere follows Him and always goes according to His way,[28] will rejoice in heaven."

But there is an evil teaching which even the Buddhists avoid, that Fate is more powerful than man and Karma is vain. For why, they ask in mockery, do we see a rich woman who is ugly? For if it was her previous evil life which caused her to be born ugly, then why is she rich; and if her riches are her reward for good conduct in a previous life, then why is she born ugly? But they speak folly, for in that she did good is she rewarded and in that she did ill is she punished, and all men do both good and ill.[29] Regard not 'Fate' and its "precepts of cowards," as they are properly called, but believe that every man makes his own fate by what he thinks and says and does, birth after birth. I spoke of truthfulness. Now it is a form of ingratitude to break a promise, which is untruthfulness, and you know that ingratitude is a sin without expiation.[30] I spoke of generosity. But do not confuse this with paying your debts. For all men are born in debt; that is, they owe something to the gods, as they owe something to men, even to

[28] Âp. 1, 8, 22, 8: *tam yo 'nutishthet sarvatra prâdhvam câ'sya sadâ 'caret.*

[29] Mbh. 12, 224, 34, on Fate (as *bhavitavyam*, "what is to be," and *Kâla,* Time personified). The adjustment of future retribution, according to whether one "does more evil than good or more good than evil," is made in the law texts.

[30] This thesis is developed in Mbh. 5, 107, 10, *seq.* In J. 516, an ungrateful person becomes a leper in this life and goes to hell after death.

their servants. To pay these born debts is not generosity. Give to the gods; but do not call it generosity. Give to guests; it is what you owe to men; it is not being generous. Give to the dead. And how, you ask, shall I give to the dead Fathers? Give them what you owe to them, remembrance, food at the funeral feast, and something more, for you owe it to your fathers to study what they have handed down to you. Hence the saw: "Man pays his debt to his ancestors by studying what they have said." You owe to your servants care and sympathy, as it is prescribed, "Do not eat dainties by yourself but share them with your servants," a little point, but it will show you what is meant. But (leaving debts) as to gifts, the sages say that it is not the value of the offering but the spirit with which it is given that counts.[31] Do in each case what you know you ought to do; if in doubt, ask the wise, or ask your own soul (conscience), and it will tell you; for it is the voice divine within you. To do what one ought makes both oneself and others happy, and it is said also that "the gods rejoice when mortals are happy."[32] But one rule especially for the priest is still to be mentioned, since he alone must receive alms as well as be himself a giver. That rule is given by Vasishtha: "Those are true Brahmans who, well-taught, have subdued their passions, injure no living beings, and close their fingers when gifts are offered

[31] For debts and spirit of offering, see Mbh. 12, 293, 5, *seq.*
[32] *Ibid.* 294, 13.

to them," which means that you should not be greedy.[33] And the same teacher has told us that a Brahman by birth is no real Brahman but a slave, if he is ignorant or lives not as a Brahman should, as trader, actor, thief, leech, or slave's slave,[34] while many of our teachers have taught us that a Brahman to be a real Brahman must not only eschew low forms of livelihood but also live a moral and noble life.

And so farewell. I give you my blessing and do not forget to give me, as you leave, my little "teacher's fee."

Therewith let us imagine that the group of boys leaves the Brahman teacher and in going on is arrested by hearing a voice tell this tale: "Once the Buddha said: I was born on earth of old as a wise teacher called Vidhura and these were the precepts I gave: Let the householder live with one wife in conjugal amity and mutual faithfulness. Let him not eat dainties alone, nor talk foolishly, but be virtuous, faithful to all his duties, not careless, quick to discern, humble-minded; not hard-hearted, compassionate, affectionate, gentle, skilful in winning friends, ready to distribute alms, prudent according to the seasons, and give food and drink to both Buddhists and to Brahmans. Let him long for righteousness and be a pillar of the sacred texts, ever ready

[33] Vas. 6, 25, *sankucitâgrahastâs.*
[34] *Ibid.* 3, 3.

to learn, ever reverent to those deserving reverence for virtue and learning. So shall he, being ever a speaker of the truth, prosper and find favor in this world and escape suffering in the next."[35]

For monastic consumption the Buddhists had little manuals of sayings of the Buddha, which sometimes, as in the Itivuttaka, extol boundless love (or kindness) toward mankind, but more commonly praise the simple meditative life and its ethical conduct, such as the well-known collection called the Dhammapada, a few excerpts from which will illustrate this point: The bane (stain) of women is ill-conduct (usually given as "curiosity" in Brahman texts); a bane are all false doctrines; ignorance is the worst bane (242, seq.). The wise are restrained in body, speech, and mind (or, in hand, foot, and speech, 231, 362); "all round restrained" are the wise (234). Possessions kill the fool who thirsts for them (355). Self is the lord of self (380). Put yourself in another's place and remember that life is dear to all; do as you would be done by and kill not nor cause to kill (129, seq.). He alone is an Aryan who does not injure other beings (270); he who harms the harmless is born in hell (140). Five sorts of men

[35] This little sermon is given thus *verbatim*, J. 545. Vidura (Vidhura in Pâli) is a famous expositor of moral truths in the epic, though his mother was a slave. The future reward is here rather vague, as it is in many Buddhistic passages. Sometimes, as in Dh. P. 220, the reward of the good man is expressed merely in a poetic figure: "His good deeds welcome him to heaven, as kinsmen welcome one home."

dig up their own roots, a slayer, a liar, a thief, an adulterer, and a drunkard (246). All that we are is the result of what we have thought. If a man speaks or acts with a corrupt mind, pain follows him as the wheel follows the beast of burden (1). Attend not to others, as to whether their ways be perverse or not; regard not others, as to whether they do their duty or not; but regard thy own deeds, whether they are done well or not (50). Meekness, non-resistance, restraint under the Confessional, temperance in eating, secluded residence, and devotion to high thought, this is the religion of the Buddhas (185).

Except for the allusion to the Confessional, at which the Buddhists were expected to stand up before the congregation once a fortnight and tell in public what sins they had committed since the last meeting, these precepts might have been taken from a Brahmanic manual. The moral training was similar, although to the Buddhist the misery of human life was more real. He had no illusions as to illusion. He could not escape the recurrence of misery in the next life (and for millions of future lives) except by the strictest ethical training, which built up character and with it mental clarity. All feeling was unhappiness to him; his Nirvâna was happiness because in it no feeling remained; while the Brahman, freeing himself from unreal misery, entered upon a future existence of which bliss was an essential element. However, both of these worthy men believed thoroughly in almost the same moral training, given (as the reader will have noticed) in almost the same words, though the persistent note of "all life is misery" was sounded loud by the Buddhist and muted by the Brahman. But we are not to imagine that this note was offensively dinned into the ears of the young men who entered the Buddhist church too young to understand the graver verities. For them sufficed a training in simple truths, and nothing could be more charming than the tone of some of these early discourses attributed to Buddha himself, such, for example, as that translated by Rhys Davids and contained in the following discourse entitled Tevijja, where Buddha explains how a young friar may be a "man of good conduct":

"A man of good conduct must abstain from destroying life, lay aside the cudgel and the sword, and be full of modesty, pity, compassion, and kindness to all. He will not steal, but passes his life in honesty and purity of heart. Putting away unchastity, he lives a life of chastity and purity. Putting away lying, he abstains from telling lies; he speaks truth;[36] he deceives no man. Putting away slander, he abstains from calumny; he does not repeat tales told to the detriment of another, but he lives as a binder of those divided, an encourager of friends, a peacemaker, a lover of peace. Putting away bitterness of speech, he abstains from harsh language; he speaks words that are pleasant, humane, urbane, reaching to the heart and pleasing the hearer; he

[36] The Buddhist will not tell a lie even to save his life (J. 537).

puts away foolish talk, abstains from vain conversation, speaks seasonably and in accordance with facts, and utters good doctrine in speech wellgrounded and full of wisdom. He refrains from injury of herb or creature;[37] he eats only one meal and not at night; he abstains from dance and song and music and theatrical shows, from garlands, perfumes, unguents, and luxuries; he lies on a small low cot; he accepts no gold or silver; stores up no uncooked grain or raw flesh; has no possessions of women or slaves or sheep or goats or fowls or swine or elephants, cattle, horses, fields or lands; he buys not nor does he sell; he uses no false weights and measures and alloyed metals; he abstains from all bribery, cheating, fraud, and crookedness; he obtains no wealth by maiming, killing, imprisoning, robbing, plundering, or by threats of violence."

Other restrictions follow: the Buddhist must not tell ghost stories or indulge in fortune telling, or in wrangling about doctrine, or in acting as a go-between, or in hypocrisy, divination, sacrifices, spells, auspices, prophesying, astrology, oracle-giving by means of a mirror, spitting fire, etc.;[38] he must not act as a leech or bless fields or impart virility or cite

[37] These rules are to instruct the young friar. The rule of kindness for the laity is not to kill or cause to be killed any living thing and to treat animals kindly: "Put not to labor the aged man, nor the aged horse or ox; give to each the honor still due, for when he was strong he fulfilled his position of trust" (J. 544).

[38] Vasishtha (10, 21) and other legal writers forbid these practices to the Brahman ascetic also.

charms, *mantras*. He must pervade the universe with kindly feeling (or friendliness), far-reaching, grown great and beyond measure, with pity, sympathy, equanimity.

The psalms of the early Buddhists have left a clear record of their clean and simple lives. A few examples will show how strong is the ethical element in the religion of Buddha:[39]

> With sensuous desires, with enmity,
> With sloth of mind and torpor of the flesh
> A Buddhist has no dealings; in his heart
> Turmoil of every kind and doubt are dead.

The hermit in his hut, enjoying the rain without, extols his own peace of soul:

> God rains, as 'twere a melody most sweet,
> Snug is my little hut, sheltered, well-roofed;
> The heart of me is steadfast and at peace;
> Now if it pleases thee to rain, god, rain!

The Buddhist has no fear when once he has overcome the evil desires of this life:

> Whose heart stands like a rock, and swayeth not,
> Void of all lust for things that lust beget,
> And all unshaken in a shifting world?
> To hearts thus trained, whence shall come aught
>   of ill?

[39] From *Psalms of the Early Buddhists*, after the translation by Mrs. Rhys Davids. In the expression "god rains," god means only the spirit of rain. The more scrupulous Jain objected to this phrase and said always "the cloud rains."

The answer follows in another stanza, "Because my heart is thus trained, how shall ill come to me?"

These are, of course, only the musings of the good friar in cell or hermitage, yet they show of what sort were the teachings spread abroad by these disciples of Buddha for centuries before the Christian era. Theirs was a training not in outward observance but in inward spiritual culture. A thousand years later a lay member of this organization of Buddhists, who, however, was so liberal that he also offered prayers to God as Çiva or Vishnu indifferently, left as his legacy to the world little lyrics devoted to the exaltation of ethics, love, and religion. Under the first head he has this typically Hindu stanza: "They that are lacking in wisdom, in fervor, in generosity, in knowledge, in good conduct, in (good) qualities, in righteousness, they in the form of men wander like beasts in the world; they are only a burden on earth." Three or four more of these stanzas will explain his code more fully. "To refrain from killing living beings, to covet no man's wealth, to speak the truth, to give with timely generosity according to one's means, to be mute when there is talk about other men's wives, to quench lustful desires, to be reverent toward spiritual teachers, to be compassionate toward all creatures, this is the path of good men, *this is the law that is in accord with all the codes*, this the universal law." "To be generous and not talk about it, to be quick in hospitality to any wanderer coming to the door, to be silent when one has done a favor and to proclaim it when another has done one a service, not to be proud in prosperity, not to talk depreciatingly of others, this is the sword-edge rule, hard to follow but taught by the good." "Destroy lustful desire, be patient, kill pride, take delight in no evil, speak the truth, follow the path made by the good, cultivate the wise, honor those worthy of honor, make peace with your enemies, proclaim not your own virtues, protect your good name, show compassion to the unfortunate—this is the mark of the good man." "He that has a steadfast nature does not lose that nature in misfortune; you may turn a torch to the ground, but the flame will still ascend."[40]

These verses also, like those of the friars, inculcate as the "universal rule of all the codes" the building up of character. They give, as it were, a *résumé* of what had been zealously expounded "in all codes" up to the seventh century of our era, at which time King Harsha himself proclaimed, as a summing up of virtuous conduct, the following stanza:

By deed, thought, and word, one should do good to
(all) living beings,[41]
This Harsha has declared to be the highest way of
earning religious merit.

[40] Bhartrihari, Nîti, 13, 26, 64, 78, 106 (*jahi madam,* in 78, may be 'destroy illusion').

[41] Cited by Professor Jackson in his edition of *Priyadarçikâ,* p. xliv.

254

This old rule, "by deed, thought, and word," or, as it is given in older texts, "by mind, word, and body," runs all through the ethical literature of India. In Manu alone the phrase occurs three times. It emphasizes mentality and lays weight on the spiritual as well as on the bodily. It seems to rule out as ill-deserved the criticism which declares that Hindu morality is only a matter of form. And the century-long insistence on kindness and doing good shows that Hindu morality is not all negative. Hindu ethics starts with the training of the mind and spirit. Centuries before King Harsha it was said by Yayâti that the way to God begins by "being fearless and causing no fear, by having no evil disposition toward any creature, no evil nature shown by action, mind, or speech." Manu says: "That man obtains supreme happiness hereafter who *seeks to do good to all* creatures," *sarvasya hitaprepsus*. The first code-maker tells us that the man of good conduct is he who "speaks the truth, acts like an Aryan, . . . never hurts any being, is gentle, yet firm, keeps himself under control, and is generous."[42] Kings, private individuals, rich merchants, even women, were renowned for their philanthropic works; but running alongside of this stream of benefactions was always the warning call: "First cleanse thy soul." Charity, forgiveness, and kindness to all were preached by Buddha and by the wisest sages of the Brahmans.

India has indeed preserved for us a most remark-

[42] Mbh. 12, 327, 33; M. 5, 46; G. 8, 23; 9, 68-73.

able record, perhaps the most remarkable record in the history of the human race, of man's never ceasing effort to raise himself above the control of the senses to a moral and spiritual height. We can watch the struggle going on for nearly two thousand years. The naïve belief that the gods in the sky are watching to see whether man worships them correctly and is "straight" in conduct as the gods are straight and true; the feeling that wrongdoing is sinful because it is not in accord with the ways and wish of the gods; the temporary chaos resulting from the conviction that the gods can be overcome by magical means and that the gods after all are only forms of One God, who represents all life and as such has no regard for morality; the recovery therefrom, through the increasing certainty that this One God, while representing all life, represents, above all, spiritual life, and that all besides pure sinless spirit (soul) is of no importance or even is a mere illusion of the senses; the firm conviction that the emancipation of the soul is based on a cleansing process, which frees it from sin; the sudden irruption of materialism, which denies God and yet holds that to free oneself from all ill one must free oneself first from all evil; the gradual weakening of this materialism with the belief that the Great Master is himself a divine exemplar of virtue and that to be like him, to imitate him in ethical conduct and devotion to man, in sympathy and in self-sacrifice, is the only way to reach lasting happiness; the endowment of the All-soul with ethical qualities, after the denial that it has any qualities at all, first by identifying Righteousness with God[43] and then by making ethical conduct a part of the knowledge through which man may become divine; the final effort to free oneself from all sin by casting oneself before God and trusting to his grace to accept the suppliant and forgive what sins still burden him; the ever growing insistence upon gentleness and compassion as marks of the truly virtuous; the belief that religion itself is based upon ethics; the realization that men are all brothers, no matter what their social rank, and that it is better to be a virtuous slave than an immoral master; the perpetual endeavor to find a synthesis of religion and morality, ending in the conviction that morality and sympathetic kindness are essential elements of religion itself—this record of a people's spiritual and ethical development, in its greatness and in its weakness, in its backsliding and in its irresistible advance, is one of extraordinary and poignant interest.

And when we of the West visit India hoping to instil into the Hindus the "higher spirituality" of which we vaunt ourselves the proud possessors, it will be well to remember that, as a goal of living, strict morality and high spirituality will not seem to the Hindus a sudden revelation from abroad, but

[43] Right and its expression in conduct is divine; although special points of right action are often dubious and so make the half-informed fancy that Right itself is a mirage. Mbh. 12, 261, 5-12.

that they have had that goal before them for many centuries.

What India needs is to realize herself, to broaden out her spiritual heritage until it meets the further requirements of this later age, not to rest upon the foundation already nobly erected by her own saints and scholars, but to continue to build along the same inspiring lines. The Hindu epic says "every man is king in his own house," *sarvas sve sve grihe râjâ*, and everyone likes to feel that one is living in a spiritual house of one's own, of which one is hereditary lord. It is well for the Hindu to be able to think: This is our spiritual and ethical heritage; here is the word of our own saint, who says, "bless them that curse you"; of our own sage, who declares that "the Vedas do not purify an immoral man"; here is the injunction, taught us long ago, to define a nobleman as one who is noble of soul; here is the statement that God is a spirit devoid of all evil and that righteousness is divine; here is the commandment to pity the unfortunate and to seek, not condescendingly but sympathetically, to do good to all.

It is upon this basis that the Hindu can best go forward, extending the sympathy taught of old to the more comprehensive needs of today and rearing upon the foundation his fathers builded a still greater edifice of good works, in harmony with their ancient endeavor but commensurable with the wider outlook now demanded.

INDEX

259

INDEX

Children, sale of, 108, *seq.;* sin in, 110.
Çiva, Çivaism, 201, 205, 207, *seq.,* 211, *seq.,* 237.
Clan, 30, 110, 173, 216.
Codes, 88.
Compassion, 11, 90, 117, 190; better than gifts, 93.
Confession, 116, 130, 249.
Confusion. See Ignorance.
Courtesy, 138, 154.
Covetousness, 118.
Creation, lord of. See Prajâ-pati.
Creator, 52.
Credo, 1.
Crooked, as wrong, 3, 30.
Custom. See Usage.

Dancing, 93, 135.
Debts, of man, 32, 57, 245. See Redemption.
Deserters, no expiation for, 106.
Desire, 79, *seq.,* 141, *seq.*
Determinism, 43.
Devas, 1, *seq.; devakâma, de-vayu,* 9.
Devotee, devotion, 187, *seq.,* 190, 193.
Dharma, 64, 70, 85, 90, 92, 108, 139, 238, 257; Dhamma, 169; embodies Buddha, 185; Dhammapada, 248. See Right.
Disease, 9, 26.
Divorce, 126.
Dogmatism, 146.
Doubt, sin of, 146. See Heresy.
Druhas, 23.

Drunkenness, 30, 55, 65, 78, 96, 119, 162.
Dryad, 170, 228.
Duality, 70.

Earnestness, 95.
Earth, 42.
Egoism, 222.
Election, doctrine of, 68, 82, 144.
Elphinstone, 215.
Emotionalism, 199, *seq.*
Energy, 59, 93, *seq.,* 164; spiritual, 183.
Envy, 94.
Eroticism, 9, 193, *seq.,* 200, *seq.,* 203.
Ethics, 170.
Evil, 141; God free from, 72; overcome evil with good, 179.
Evil Eye, 47.
Expiation, 112, *seq.*
Extremes, deprecated, 138.

Faith, 1, 5, *seq.,* 30, 56, 78, 96; give with faith, 73.
Fasting, 56, 183.
Fate, 81, 143, *seq.,* 159, 195, 245.
Father. See Parents.
Father-god, 1, 52, 150.
Faults. See Vices.
Fear, 9, 133; gods fear men, 176.
Fire-god, 5, *seq.,* 9, *seq.,* 12, 15, 29, 31, 36, 43, 46, *seq.;* cult of as immortal, 57; as truth, 58; ordeal by, 218.

INDEX

Flesh-eating, 53, 61, 111, 160, 231, *seq.*

Forgiveness, 13, 18, 30, 32, 34, 39, 41, 56, 160.

Friend, 177.

Gambling, 12, 30, 39, 48, 93, 95, *seq.,* 135.

Generosity (and Gifts), 60, 65, 74, 117, *seq.,* 138, 148, *seq.,* 159, 170, 178, 245; to the poor, 243.

Gnosis, 185. See Mysticism.

God, etymology, 8; One God, 52; Supreme, 59; gods as good, 2, 171, *seq.;* related to man, 12; gods see sin, 22, 170; men as gods, 60; laws of gods, 34, *seq.,* 36, 38; God is one with man, 59; is ethically pure, 59, 64, 174, *seq.;* as energy, 183; in Buddhism, 142; of Râmânuja, 213.

Golden Rule, 137, *seq.*

Good, as fitting, 2; as straight, 3.

Gossip, 133.

Grace, 46, 176, 204. See Election, Predestination.

Greed, 117. See Vices.

Grief, sin of, 158.

Guest, as divinity, 73. See Hospitality.

Guru, 202.

Hair, 173, 242.

Happiness, 175, 178, 182.

Harmony, cosmic and ethical, 2, 38, 44.

Harsha, 254.

Heaven, 56, *seq.,* 60, 140; is temporary joy, 78, 175; Heaven-god, 4, *seq.,* 7, 12, *seq.,* 21, *seq.,* 30, *seq.,* 33, 43, 46, *seq.,* 237.

Heliodorus, inscription of, 171.

Hell, 4, 28, 47, *seq.,* 53, 60, *seq.,* 93, 113, *seq.;* gates of, 107; in Buddhism, 141, 160; for heretics, 208. See Pit.

Henotheism, 36.

Heresy, heterodoxy, 30, 66, 96, *seq.,* 105, 118, 135, 146, 151, *seq.* See Hell.

Hippocrates, 122.

Honesty, 118. See Truth.

Honey, forbidden luxury, 93.

Hospitality, 30, 49, 55, 74, 171, 179, 243.

Hospitals, for animals, 151.

Humanitarianism, humanity, 150, 182, 233, *seq.*

Hunting, 96.

Idols, 226.

Ignorance, root of evil, 80.

Immortality, 56, *seq.*

Impermanence, 158.

Incest, 30, 54.

Indifference, 92, 141.

Indra, 7, 10, 16, 31, 36, *seq.,* 40, 139; sin of, 13; as life-spirit, 68; as Sakka, 165.

Infidelity. See Heresy.

Ingratitude, no expiation for, 155, 177.

Insolence, 38. See Arrogance.

Intemperance, 66. See Extremes, Moderation.

Intercession, 15, *seq.*

INDEX

Intoxicants. See Drunkenness.
Intuition, 78, 83.

Jackson, A. V. W., 254.
Jains, 111, 114, 120, 150, *seq.*,
229, 252.
Japan, 229.
Jâtakas, 156, *seq.*
Jayadeva, 203.
Johnston, C. J., 188.
Joy, bliss, of gods, 58, 72;
ethical, 163, *seq.*

Kabîr, 214.
Kâlî, 208.
Καλός, bright and good, 1.
Karma, 43, 49, 80, *seq.*, 119,
143, 146, *seq.*, 176, 191, 195,
227.
Kautilya, 106.
Killing, 101, *seq.* See Non-injury, War.
Kindness, 95, 136, 177; kind
speech, 178; to animals, 242,
251. See Non-injury.
King, 89; divine, 107; as rain-
maker, 162, 218; ethics of,
103; ideal king, 190, *seq.;*
every man king in his own
house (Mbh. 12, 321, 147),
258.
Knowledge, not sufficient, 182;
implies morality, 184.
Krishna, Krishnaism, 138, 172,
seq., 179, *seq.*, 186, *seq.*, 200,
seq.

Lanman, C. R., 61.
Laws, of gods, 34; ethics of
law-books, 87, *seq.*

Liberality. See Generosity.
Licentiousness, 204.
Lies, lying, 27, 30, 53; venial
untruths, 97, *seq.*, 161, *seq.*
Lévi, S., 62.
Love, 136, *seq.*, 141, 160, 201,
seq.; love-feasts, 204. See
Eroticism, Kindness, Lust.
Loyalty, 122, 216, *seq.*
Luck, 159. See Fate.
Lust, 66, 79, 205, 208. See De-
sire.

McKenzie, J., 44, 115.
Magic, 14, 44, *seq.*, 59, 145.
Mahâvansa, 229.
Mahâyâna, 222.
Maitra, S. K., 81.
Malformations, caused by sin,
114, *seq.*, 143.
Manes (Fathers), 29, 41, 72,
143, 179, 246.
Manu, 77, 81, 109, 118, 181,
255.
Maruts, 9, 12, 29.
Meat. See Flesh-eating.
Mediation, 15, 52, 165.
Mercy, 17, 23, 30.
Merit, 48; transference of, 94,
144, 159.
Metempsychosis, 44. See
Karma.
Might *vs.* Right, 106, 244.
Miser, miserable, 78, 90, *seq.*,
133.
Missionaries, 150, 214.
Mithilâ, proverb, 222.
Moderation, 156, 159, 176.
Modesty, 73, 93.
Monasteries, 149, 229.

262

INDEX

Morality, essential, 64, 174, 244; necessarily religious, 185, 190.
Mother, 124, 163. See Parents.
Mother-goddess, 206, 208.
Müller, Max, 193, 197.
Murder, 30, 60, 66, 114; killing in war no murder, 102.
Mysticism, 49, 54, 144, 185, 201, 204.

Nâg, Kâlidâs, 107.
Nâgas, 170, 228.
Nâmdev, 215.
Nature of man, threefold, 188.
Negative virtues, 179.
Nirvâna (Nibbâna), 140, 146, 238, 249.
Nivritti, school, 83.
Non-injury, 65, 77, 93, 138, 147, 151, 154, 165, *seq.*, 179, *seq.*, 227, *seq.*
Non-resistance, 179.

Outcasts, 121.

Paradise, 170. See Heaven.
Parents, worship of, 55, 72, 153, 163.
Path, of Right, eightfold, 178.
Patience, 90, 179.
Penance, 66, 79, 112, *seq.*
Pensions, 107.
Perjury, 98.
Pessimism, 42, 163.
Phallic worship, 30, 207, 212.
Philanthropy, 171.
Philosophies, 81.
Physician, oath of, 121.
Piety, law of, 153.
Pit, 12, 28, 47. See Hell.

Planets, 143.
Pollution, 46.
Prajâpati, Lord of Creation, 49, *seq.*, 54, 59, 65, 73, 139, 181; ten rules of, 76.
Pravritti, school, 83.
Prayer, 165.
Predestination, 51, 144.
Priest, 60, *seq.*, 103, *seq.*, 121, 146.
Procrastination, 107.
Prostitute, 31.
Purification, by sacrifice, 53; of self, 56.
Purity, 41, 55, 64, 90, 130, 147, 174, 187, 238.

Râdhâ, 201, 203, 207.
Rakshas, 2.
Râma, 201, 203, 207, 217.
Râmânanda, 203.
Râmânuja, 196, 202, 213, 226, 232.
Raychaudhuri, H., 171.
Rebirth. See Birth.
Redemption, 54, 57, 59, 94; in Buddhism, 142, 144.
Refugee, 166.
Religion, necessarily moral, 185.
Renunciation, 76, 189, 192, 220.
Repentance, 33, 116.
Resurrection, 237.
Rewards of action, 84, 236.
Rhys-Davids, 250; Mrs. Rhys-Davids, 252.
Right, Righteousness, 1, *seq.*, 3, 40, 65, 73, 85, 139; Right and Wrong, 3, 74. See Dharma.
Rita, 2, *seq.*, 40, *seq.*, 52.

263

INDEX

INDEX

Vishnu, 37, 47, 107, 139, 176, 211, *seq.*, 230.
Vrata, 34, *seq.*

War, ethics of, 101, *seq.*, 243; opposed by Buddhism, 210.
Wealth *vs.* Virtue, 177.
Will, 75, 79, 81, 197, 236.
Wisdom, spirit of, 3, *seq.*, 182.
Witnesses, 98; of the soul, 47.
Women, 93, 96, 123, *seq.*, 176; not taxed, 105; in Buddhism, 162, *seq.*, 232.
Word, divine, 51.
Work, divine, 189.

Yajata, *yazata*, 1, 42, *seq.*
Yama, 47, 108, 139, 170.
Yoga, Yogi, 76, 136, 145, 176, 184, 186, *seq.*, 212, 221.

Zoroaster, 1, 23.